# The College Game
## How Anyone Can Get a University Education - and Afford It

by

William Kibler

*Cover Art by Nathaniel Kibler

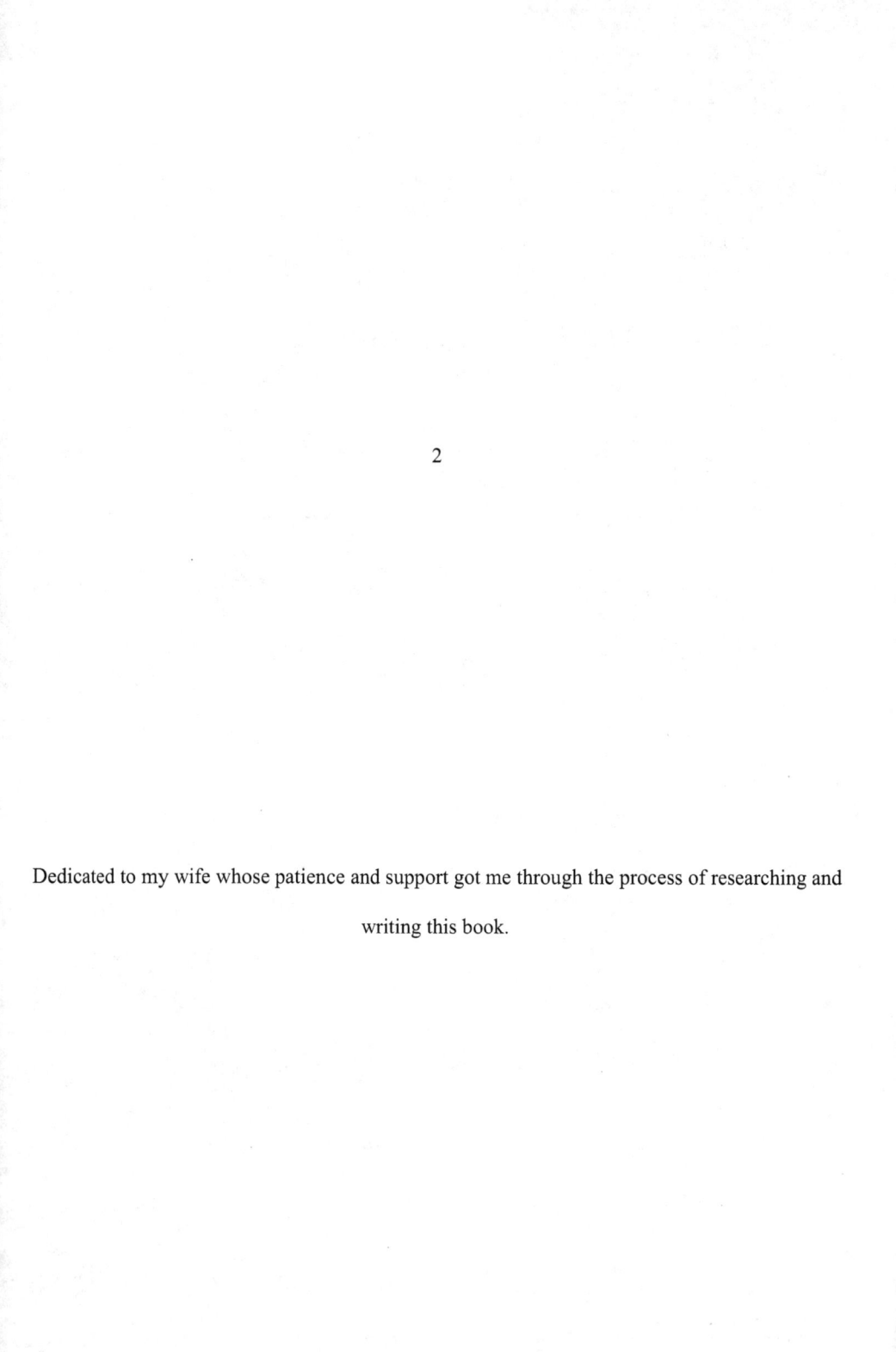

Dedicated to my wife whose patience and support got me through the process of researching and writing this book.

## Table of Contents

Chapter 1: A Journey Begins - Introduction   4

Chapter 2: What Does That Mean - Basic Terminology and Definitions   10

Chapter 3: Learning to Fly - Setting Goals   20

Chapter 4: Doing it by the Numbers - Grades, Class Rank, Scheduling and Testing   28

Chapter 5: Let's Play the University Admission's Game - Community Service & Activities   58

Chapter 6: Touchdown: Sports   77

Chapter 7: Where is the Circus - The College Fair, and Visits   94

Chapter 8: The Advantages of Charm, Wit and Preparation - Interviews and Resumes   116

Chapter 9: My Kingdom for a Horse - Letters of Recommendation, You and Your Counselor   129

Chapter 10: Defining You in 700 Words or Less - Personal Statements   137

Chapter 11: Your Life in Someone Else's Hands - Application Time   147

Chapter 12: Take a Deep Breath and Hope for the Best - Acceptance, Rejection, Waiting   197

Chapter 13: Show me the Money - Financial Aide and Scholarships   212

Chapter 14: Letter to Me: For Your Student   262

Chapter 15: Sage on the Mountain - Further Sources and Information   270

Appendix 1: Year by year plan   274

Appendix 2: List of colleges and universities   278

Appendix 3: Competitive programs, contests and summer school   311

Appendix 4: The College Game   318

## Chapter 1: A Journey Begins

Sandra was in tears. This is how my journey would begin, with tears streaking the black mascara of one of my favorite students. Were this a fairy tale, I would explain that the tears were tears of joy as Sandra shared an acceptance letter from a prestigious university whose name rings with acclamation. Instead I live in reality - a reality rooted in the inner city of Phoenix. Sandra was in tears because it was May of her senior year, and she was going nowhere. The worst part about the situation was that Sandra hadn't done anything wrong. Quite the contrary. Sandra had done everything right. She was graduating number two in her class; her grades were a mark of perfection; she was president of the National Honor Society and the Spanish National Honor Society. She was active in other clubs and had not only participated in community service, but had created community service opportunities for the school community. She showed leadership, initiative, fortitude, brilliance and a willingness to achieve. Sandra by all counts should have had colleges begging for her. Her only option in May of her senior year, though, was community college.

My first response was outrage with the high school counselors. I had been under the impression that the college thing was their job. I had been under the impression that the counselors were taking care of the kids. I had been under the impression that the first priority was helping all the students achieve their dreams and aspirations in the perfect university. I was wrong. It turns out that counselors take lots and lots of classes on psychology and behavioral science, classes on writing and research methods, classes on leading groups, classes in educational pedagogy. Counselors do not, however, take any classes on getting students into colleges. What is more, at least in my school district, counselors are more about paperwork, administration, scheduling and providing additional secretarial services than actually talking to students. Most counselors I know go into the profession with the hope of actually speaking to students and making a difference. Instead, most counselors are buried in paperwork and administrative minutiae.

The more I looked into Sandra's problem, the more I came to three conclusions. First, college admission is a game. Furthermore, it is a game where it is not in the best interests of the colleges and universities to publish the rules. This has the very real effect of stacking the deck in favor of those that do know the rules. Second, the average high school counselor - and there are exceptions - doesn't know anything about the rules or how to play. Some are not even aware we are playing a game. Third, there was nothing that could be done to help Sandra at this point. It was quite simply too late.

I decided that week to learn how to play the game myself. Blaming others is often easy and fun, but pointing of fingers solves nothing in the end. I always had an outlook to seek solutions to problems, to be proactive. This was not an entirely altruistic endeavor. I certainly did want to be able to help my students for I had many more like Sandra. Much closer to home I had two boys that were quickly approaching high school - and college. If I chose not to learn how to play this game, then my own boys - and my own bank account - might pay the price.

All that follows is based on reading everything I could find on the college admissions process, speaking with scores of university admissions and financial aid officers, visits to colleges and universities on every vacation and break over the past ten years, fourteen years of trial and error with my students, and my efforts to get both of my own sons into the right school for my boys. An astute reader will note that much of what I say goes against the current. I encourage anyone beginning the college admissions process to read multiple sources and weigh the value of each. In college admissions, there is no sure thing. I can make no promises. I play the odds. I can tell a student what should and shouldn't happen or what his or her chances really are. Every year I have surprises. Every year there are students that should not be able to get into "X" and do or will surely get into "Y" and don't. I can not account for the discrepancies other than that every admission's office approaches every student as an individual, and real people make real decisions that have a real impact. Anyone that makes guarantees in the college admission process is a liar.

I have written this book primarily as a guide for parents to help their own son or daughter attend a university at a cost the family can afford. I know from experience that my teenage sons were never as interested in the cost for college as I was - being my checking account and all. Over the last twenty years college and university prices have approached the level of completely unrealistic. I just read an article in the *Arizona Republic* that says, "The cost of attending an Arizona university was about $2,600 a year in 2002-03. This year, it's $11,877 at the University of Arizona (a 457 percent increase), $11,059 at Northern Arizona University (a 425 percent increase) and $10,792 at Arizona State University (a 415 percent increase)." (Http://www.azcentral.com/story/opinion/op-ed/laurieroberts/2017/09/08/brnovich-takes-regents-over-cost-tuition-hallelujah/647748001/; https://trends.collegeboard.org/sites/default/.../college-pricing-2012-source-data_0.xls) Keep in mind, this is not including room, board, books or fees. I only wish that my income had gone up 400% in the same time frame.

When I received my B.A., $12,000 a year was considered expensive. Today that does not even pay for many community colleges where the student lives at home. Increasingly the political rhetoric is one that says "college isn't for everyone," "maybe families should emphasize blue collar jobs more," or "one can find lots of success without college." Yet, the same pundits who smile on camera with these platitudes are sure to send their son or daughter to the country's most prestigious universities. Increasingly there is a movement in politics that college should be reserved for the elite, and so many schools agree with this. I had one experience with a small liberal arts school in California. One of my students was admitted, but the price was unrealistic. I personally called the school and asked if there was anything the student could do. The response I received was, "We at _____ only take a certain type of girl." Being a bit stubborn and not understanding the code, I persisted. The school told me that financial aid was computed by subtracting her parents' income from a minimum wage and multiplying by 18. The school wanted everything else.

    I have personally heard financial aid officers ask families if the family is willing to refinance their home in order to pay tuition or ask someone to liquidate the retirement account. I have heard other financial aid officers ask a family to take a second or third job just to pay tuition. Many financial aid offices will (almost gleefully) tell parents that $100,000 in college debt is normal. Too often I have myself asked financial aid officers if the price being offered was one he or she would pay for his or her own daughter. Most often, the financial aid officer admits that he or she would send the promising academic to another institution instead. Far too many times that I have worked with students, I have seen colleges and universities try to drain every penny from a family for an education.

    If you read no further or simply decide you are looking for a different type of book, understand that college admission is a game and everything is negotiable. Few families I know would pay the first offer price on a used car. Why pay the first offer price on a college?

Let me put my cards on the table. If your income is such that you can pay full price without blinking, if you can simply write a check for $320,000 and not have heart palpations, then you don't really need this book. I would urge those families to look beyond the "Ivy League" and Stanford or MIT, but with enough money anything is possible.

If you are completely broke, making minimum wage or just above, I have written this book to help you understand how to get your son or daughter into a college or university that will launch a career and a life in a direction far exceeding what society too often expects of low income families. I put a real emphasis on small liberal arts schools.

If you are middle class, you really need help. If not this book, then please seek help somewhere. The game is stacked against middle class families. Just as the government asks middle class families to bear the brunt of taxes, so too colleges ask middle class families to bear the brunt of education costs.

Let me put this in simple terms. If a family makes $24,000 a year, financial aid will cover the vast majority of costs. A good student who has made the right choices and looks competitive on paper will have plenty of choices. Does that mean completely free? Maybe not, but I feel confident that a student in this position will graduate owing less than a used car.

If a family is making $1.2 million a year, how much is $65,000 really? I know it is a lot of money, but at $1.2 million a year, a family can afford that. If a family is making $120,000 a year, though, even $30,000 a year is nearly impossible to save. After the expenses of a home, two cars, the new dining room table that was financed, a vacation every three years, a respectable retirement account and regular monthly bills, there is nothing left for college. Most parents don't want their children taking a $100,000 dollar debt, but there is no way for the family to absorb those costs without it being an undue burden on the family. You don't have to pay this price. You don't deserve to pay this price so that your children can have a better opportunity.

Most books on university admissions really focus on the Ivy League schools. While Harvard and Yale and Princeton and the rest are awesome schools, the schools are simply not for everyone. The odds are that your student will not be able to gain admission to these universities. Some of the most famous schools have acceptance rates of less than 15%. That is a hard nut to crack. Though I will speak of the top tier schools, I am really looking at small liberal arts schools. I do not really emphasize the large public schools. These schools are more and more prohibitively expensive. Quite simply, I am trying to find my students the best possible education at the lowest possible price. If one of my students is accepted at a MIT or a Stanford, hallelujah. Knowing the odds, I really push for different schools. I am a firm believer and have hundreds of students as evidence that small liberal arts schools can offer a tremendous education at a fair price without excluding all but the elite.

Parents resist me as the parents want name recognition. The "Dartmouth" bumper sticker seems like a prerequisite for the aspiring soccer mom's SUV. Students resist me as the students are often far too spoiled and far too fearful to leave the security of home and friends. I ask that both parties try to keep an open mind. In the end I usually counsel that we split the difference. I let Mom pick the bumper sticker school and junior pick the state flagship. All I ask is a decent smattering of small liberal arts schools like I suggest. After all the applications are in and acceptance letters and financial aid packages are received, make an educated decision about what is best. What do you have to lose?

Finally, I want to state my own biases and background clearly. I firmly believe that while college is not for every student, college does offer the best opportunity for most students to have a better future. I personally want all of my students to attend the university. I will mention quite a few colleges and universities. These schools are by far not a comprehensive list. Please research and look for more. I hesitate to endorse a university as the schools are always in flux. A school that was great this year, may not be great the next. A school that was wonderful for Peter may not be perfect for Paul. Don't trust anyone on what school is best for your child. Make your own decision - or rather help your child make his or her own decision.

No matter what choices are made, please be clear that college admission is a game. Far too much money is involved. Your student's future is at stake. One can learn how to play the game or lose.

### Chapter 2: What Does That Mean?

I learned a long time ago as a teacher that any lesson that doesn't begin with basic definitions is set for headaches. My experience as a whole has been with lower income and middle income students. Most of the parents I work with have not finished the university themselves or have attended a local state university. Even for me, the game changed since I was in school. I remember the entire college process being much more streamlined and with fewer pitfalls. As such, I am going to begin with the very basics.

*What is the difference between a college and a university?*

This is a much more complicated question than it appears at the outset. There are three different levels of schools with which I work. The lowest level is community college. Community college is often the cheapest option (at least front loaded) but only allows students to finish the first two years of a college education - what is called an associate's degree. Unfortunately an associate's degree is only marginally more valuable than a high school diploma today. At the end of that degree process, the student will need to transfer to another institution to finish his or her degree. I will return to community college shortly.

The second level are "colleges" like Coe College in Iowa. Colleges offer a four-year degree - a bachelor's of arts (B.A.) or a bachelor's of sciences (B.S.). They do not have advanced degrees. A bachelor's degree seems to be the basic educational plateau for today's youth. Just like in my father's generation where most serious job candidates had a high school diploma and the elite had a bachelor's degree, today's youth have seen a leveling up where a high school diploma affords little today and bachelor's degree is the basic unit of educational attainment. The elites go on for a master's or a doctorate. In fact, some of the most popular courses of study - engineering, law, medicine and increasingly business and education - really require higher degrees.

A university like the University of (name your favorite state) offers a bachelor's degree but also offers advanced degrees - a masters (M.A.) or doctorate (MD or PhD or EdD). Universities typically have a wider assortment of majors available and offer more options both in academics and in extracurricular possibilities.

*What is the difference between an undergraduate and graduate student?*

Most students are undergraduates. This is generally the first four years of a college education. A graduate school is at a university and requires additional course work. A student that hopes to be a lawyer will often (not required) begin with an undergraduate degree in political science or social science - though in theory art history or general business or chemistry could also work. After about four years, that student will need to take the LSAT (the lawyer's version of a SAT) and move onto a graduate school like the University of Notre Dame or University of California - Berkeley.

*Should my son or daughter attend a community college first?*

My very first institution of higher education was community college, Lincoln Land Community College just outside of Springfield, Illinois to be precise. I have attended six separate community colleges at some point including ones that were completely online. In addition, I was an adjunct professor with the Maricopa County Community Colleges for ten years at three different campuses. As such, I have seen the community college system from both sides. That being said, I do not usually recommend community college for high school students.

Most often cited as a positive of community college is the cost. The cost, while indeed cheaper than other colleges or universities, is usually more deceptive than it seems. I will explain that shortly. In my mind, the greatest benefit of community college is to the student who made poor choices in high school regarding his or her grades and performance. Attending a community college can hit the reset button on a flagging academic career. Community college can also benefit a student who lacks the maturity to live on his or her own. In general, a community college is not a residential college and the campus is entirely a commuter campus, that is to say a school where students travel back and forth to school on a daily basis. Finally, community colleges usually have a close alignment with the local state university making the transfer of credits to that particular institution easy.

I strongly feel there are more negatives than positives, though. What you save up front, you will often lose in having a cheaper overall financial aid package for the final two or three years of the bachelor's degree. The short reason is that the university or four-year college wants their cut. A four-year college or university rarely gives the same financial aid or depth of grants to a transfer student as it does to a freshman. What is saved in the first two years at community college is often spent the next two years after a transfer. With a four-year degree, a community college saves little money in the long run, just the short run.

Community colleges often feel emotionally and socially like a continuation of high school. As a teacher and as a parent I understand how hard it is to let your kids go. I look at the young people that surround me and think, "She is so not ready for life," or "He is going to make so many mistakes." What better vehicle to teach independence, motivation and maturity than a university? For the same reason, I often advise against going to the big state university just down the street. One of my biggest goals is for my students to become mature, rational, functioning adults. I want to throw them in the deep end of the pool and make them swim. A college or university at least two hours away offers the student the chance to swim on his or her own while not being completely unsupervised. All colleges and universities today have numerous safety nets built in for students that are struggling. It has been my experience that the girl whose diapers you can still remember changing like it was yesterday will surprise you with the decisions she will make and the direction her life will take. That is not to say that your all-American beef eating boy will not make mistakes; mistakes are part of life. No matter how many times I told my own sons the hard won lessons of my life, there are times that my boys had to learn the hard way. A college or university will allow some leeway without being a completely open field for experimentation. I would rather my own sons experiment with adulthood in a contained and semi-controlled environment at 18 then complete independence without training wheels at 23 where the mistakes can be more costly.

My single biggest complaint is that community colleges, because they are so open to enrollment, do not foster an academically supportive environment the same way that a university does. A shockingly low percentage of students actually matriculate on time to a four-year institution. It is almost as if there is a disembodied voice whispering all through the campus. "Don't finish." "Come back later." "You can do college after you had some fun." Community colleges seem to offer a malaise and disconnected apathy that encourage students to quit and give up. That is not to say that a student can't succeed at a community college. There are plenty of examples of students that have gone onto very successful careers after beginning at a community college. It is simply more difficult.

Finally, though many community colleges have credits and classes that transfer to a university or another college, not all credits or classes transfer to all colleges and universities. I can almost guarantee that a student will lose some credits. It is even possible to lose all the credits. If you know that community college is the best option, then flash forward two years. Figure out where your student wants to be in two years. Call that school - and follow up with an email so that it is in writing - and ask what classes will and won't transfer typically. The school will not usually give a concrete answer until your student actually has a transcript, but the school will have a general idea. Also ask if the school accepts transfers. Not all schools do. Ask if a student can transfer in January or only in August. The answer depends on the school.

*When is community college a good choice?*

There are a few times I recommend a community college. The most common case is the student who did not perform well in high school. If the grades or test scores are so bad that the student can not get admitted to a university - or so bad that the student is admitted but can't get financial aid, then community college can be a good choice. After going to community college, a university will no longer care about high school. The university is now looking at what the student accomplished in college. That can be a double-edged sword. All the negatives - like poor grades - are erased but so are all the positives - like community service and extracurricular involvement. If this is the path you choose, please remember that *everything* starts over in community college. A student's grades may improve, but he or she still needs involvement in activities and clubs, leadership positions, community service and other ways to stand out from his or her peers.

I recommend community college where there are some serious health issues - mental or physical. For example, if a student is struggling with depression or suicidal tendencies, a community college where the student is still living at home and is more closely monitored may be ideal. By the same token, if a student is undergoing treatment for cancer or something equally severe, a community college may be best for the sake of scheduling medical care and providing a support system. If two years later the depression or other mental ailment is still to the point where a student is receiving treatment, please consult with a psychological professional before committing to a university. If a major illness is an obstacle, please consult with your personal physician about treatment options and monitoring before sending your son or daughter to an unfamiliar city.

*What is better, a college or a university?*

The short answer: yes. Both can be great options, and I encourage my students to apply at both. A college is generally a smaller environment which means more opportunities to stand out, more opportunities to get to know your professor, more opportunities for internships. It is easier to begin your own programs or clubs at a smaller school. The larger size of a university means there are more degree choices, a more developed facility, more interactions and extracurricular activities. I can make a strong argument for both and encourage students to apply at both. The one word of warning I give is size. A school with 2,000-5,000 students is my personal ideal. I like this size because the college / university is obviously well developed and has enough of a base to offer quite a lot of degree choices. When we get to mega-universities like Arizona State University or Ohio State University, the school is so massive that the students are at risk of becoming just a number.

In my current teaching assignment I am blessed to have a core of students two to four hours a day over the course of three years. In the process, I really get to know my students well and genuinely like all of my students - as cliché as that sounds. When I send a student to . . . Concordia University - Wisconsin, about 4,000 students at the time of this writing, I know my student will be treated like an individual. I know the professors will generally honor office hours and be available for help. I know that my students have a lot of opportunities to stand out. I know that it would be highly unusual for my student to be in a class of more than 30 and thus impossible to hide. I want my students noticed, so the university professors will get to know how awesome that particular student is. Arizona State University in contrast is huge. A student can expect classes of more than 200 students in the course of four years. Professors are harder to approach and even harder to get to know. It is far too easy to blend into the background and never be anything more than row 17, seat 4. That is not to say that students can not do well at a large state school, but the students might have to work a little harder at standing out and seeking opportunities.

In terms of financial aid, size is also paramount. Just in terms of simple math, the number of students really affects financial aid. For example, imagine I have a hypothetical school A and B at 5,000 and 50,000 students respectively. If school A has an endowment (gifted money) in the amount of $200 million available for financial aid, the amount comes out to $40,000 in aid on average (though to be fair "average" doesn't do this process justice.) If school B has $200 million available for financial aid, each student's share (if divided equally) is $400. In addition, a huge school with tens of thousands of students tends to invest quite a bit into its sports teams, especially the holy trinity of basketball, football and baseball. These three sports take the lion's share of scholarship money one way or the other with all the other students fighting for the scraps. Ironically, many of the smaller schools also have larger endowments freeing up even more money per student at the smaller schools than the big state universities.

There is a caveat to this logic, though. Some students really want the big school experience, the Greek life, the major sporting events. An Illinois Wesleyan just can not compete with the loyal fighting Illini shaking the stadium and painting the town orange. There is something to be said for the social atmosphere at a larger school. Athletes in particular need to weigh advantages of larger schools, but that is a topic for another chapter. Other students have a rather obscure major, like library science or marine biology, which can only be obtained at a larger school.

Because both university and four-year college are largely synonymous, I will use the two interchangeably through much of the remainder of the book. Unless otherwise stated, "college" refers to a four-year college not a community college.

*What are FAFSA (Federal Application for Federal Student Aid) and the CSS Profile (College Scholarship Service)?*

This is something I will bring up later in Chapter 13. As I need to mention these frequently, know for now that both are used by financial aid offices to determine how much need based aid a student is eligible for.

*What is an EFC (Expected Family Contribution)?*

There will be more detail on this later as well, but the short version is that it is a number that the government says a family can afford for college tuition based on the families assets. I can almost guarantee that your family will think this number is unrealistically high and the university of your choice will think this number is unrealistically low. The smaller the EFC, the better for a financial need package.

*What is the difference between a nonprofit and for profit school?*

I have a special disdain for "for profit schools." To be clear, "nonprofit" schools still want to make a profit. Money is part of the game no matter how one plays. The for-profit institutions are much more focused on money, though. Let me give a specific example: Grand Canyon University. When I first moved to Arizona, I had never heard of Grand Canyon University. It was a small Christian liberal arts school with a decent reputation. Some years ago, crushed by debt, the school decided to change to for profit. They were listed on the stock exchange and promised investors a huge profit margin. Where do you think the profits came from? Profits of course were largely generated by students - and student debt. The reputation of the school since that decision is not what it was.

I have spoken with almost a dozen for profit institutions over the years. The schools often promise a lot of financial aid that is actually a loan at a huge interest rate. The for profit schools often make lots of glitzy commercials and hit small niches like art or computers promising alluring careers at Microsoft or on Madison Avenue. When one looks into their numbers more closely, the numbers rarely add up. Many for profit schools like Trump University end up falling foul of federal laws. The response has been to back politicians who promise to remove the restricting laws. Whose interests are being protected here? Other schools have simply filed bankruptcy and walked away. What value does your degree have from a school that no longer exists?

In almost every case I would avoid the for-profit schools and pursue your art or computer science degree at an accredited institution. I have found the small liberal arts schools and large public universities more than capable of filling professional goals more efficiently and more economically.

*What is a liberal arts school?*

Liberal arts schools are some of my favorite schools to use. This does not designate a political bias, though many of the schools do have a decided political or religious bias. The schools tend to be small private schools. The schools as a whole have excellent reputations and do fabulous jobs educating the youth of America. The price tags are really scary, but if a family understands nothing else, understand that almost no one pays full price. To illustrate, I will use a specific example from 2017 and pick a school at random: Boston College – it has a big price tag ($55,464 for tuition and $14,478 for room and board – yes per year). But, 88% of students who needed money last year received financial aid. The average package was $41,768 (a year). In

2016, the average student graduated with a debt of only $20,849. Any time a student of mine who can receive a four-year education at a preeminent college for the price of a car - a cheap car - is a win.

## Chapter 3: Learning to Fly

Living in the United States is a blessing. Few countries have an educational system more developed and open than the United States. America is a country where any child can attend the university. According to the National Center for Education Statistics (http://nces.ed.gov/fastfacts/display.asp?id=372) approximately 2/5 of American students attend a university or college. Keep in mind that this is the number that attends, not the number that finishes. I am mystified why so few of our students attend a university. It seems clear that a university education offers one of the surest paths to a secure financial future. College is not for everyone, but it is certainly for more than 40%. Other countries, many of whom are touted as having a better educational system, tightly control who attends a university. In the United States anyone can attend. I make clear to my students day one that I expect all of my students to attend a university.

*When do I start the process for helping my child go to the university?*

The inception of a university education is long before a student reaches senior year. In fact, if a student does not approach the idea before senior year, there is little that can be done. One of the greatest advantages that the upper stratum of American socioeconomic society has is the insistence that their children will attend a university or college. So many students from lower socioeconomic strata are not encouraged to do so. A university education really begins at home - long before students apply to universities. Make university education expected in the home. Talk about college on a regular basis. When you take a family vacation with your high school student, stop and tour a university. Don't just go to the space center or the art museum in Houston. Also, tour Rice University. Don't just go to the beach in Los Angeles, take an afternoon to visit Chapman or Harvey Mudd or Pepperdine or Pomona or Scripps or the University of the Redlands or a half dozen other schools in the Los Angeles area. Have a dozen conversations a year around the dinner table about colleges, careers and school in general throughout the year. Have your son or daughter meet with and speak to someone in his or her chosen career. If your daughter wants to be a doctor, have her speak to her own physician about the career the next time she goes in for a shot. If your son wants to study business, ask your boss if your son could shadow the boss for a day. In short, set an environment at home where college is a priority; it is an expectation.

This particular book is designed for high school students early in their scholastic journey. I generally begin by working with sophomores. I don't always worry about freshmen as the transition from junior high to high school is daunting enough. Freshman year is often overlooked, discounted completely or at least down played by most colleges. (Please note: the Ivy League and similarly elite universities are the exception to the last statement.) Students often do not have the emotional maturity to tackle the idea of college which at 14 seems so very far in the future. I prefer to begin working with sophomores. Junior year I can still do a lot, especially if I start working with the student early junior year. Senior year is really too late. At that point the student is in a good position - and I need to do little, or the student has dug a hole from which it is impossible to extricate him or her at that point.

*How can I help my child get ready?*

When your child is growing up, encourage - no demand - that he or she read on a daily basis. There is no substitute for reading. There are so many ways that reading develops a student. The biggest impact in terms of this conversation is the test scores. Whether a student takes the ACT or the SAT (which I will discuss in the next chapter), both tests are basically English and math. Not to slight the math portion, it is easier to cram the math. Months before the test a student poor at math can memorize some formulas and run through several hours of worksheet practice to markedly improve the math scores. English is harder. Reading especially is not something that can be crammed and studied at the last minute. When your student takes his or her final standardized test fall of senior year, how much he or she has read will be clearly demonstrated. Additionally, one of the favorite interview questions asked by college admission's officers is, "What is the best book you read this year that was not assigned reading?" I never want my students to answer, "Ummm, I don't read." Reading increases reading speed, reading comprehension, vocabulary, problem solving, and critical thinking. I can not emphasize the impact of reading enough. With almost no exception, the students I have that are "readers" perform better on standardized tests.

Even for students that read, I would recommend intentionally increasing vocabulary. If a student begins early, increasing vocabulary is relatively easy. Reading at or above grade level is the easiest way to improve vocabulary. There are also books designed specifically for high school vocabulary like *Fiske Word Power, Vocabulary Cartoons: SAT Word Power*, or novels focusing on vocabulary like *Tooth and Nail* by Charles H. Elster. There are even SAT and ACT vocabulary flash cards. At a minimum, pick ten good vocabulary words for your student to memorize and use. Students, and people in general, are judged by command of the English language. A strong vocabulary is one of the first clues indicating an individual's education.

Another step to take is being involved in your child's education from day one. As a parent, please do not assume that the school is challenging your child enough. Do not assume that the class schedule your child has will be adequate. If your student is struggling in school, sit down with your child and his or her teachers immediately to understand why. Give your student a place to study or arrange to take him or her to the public library three times a week to study. From freshman year on, sit with your child's school counselor and explain that the ultimate goal is a university education. Speaking from experience, I can tell you that most high schools have two unstated tracks. Track A is for most students. It is a path to simply graduate high school. Track A does not always include everything that a student needs to be competitive in a university. Track B is for the students who want to attend a university. I have known far too many counselors who rush to judgement about what track a student is on. Many students find themselves in a situation senior year where they are graduating high school but are not ready for more than a community college. It is rare that I have met a counselor who intentionally puts a student in that position knowing the student is planning to attend a university. Freshman year sit and talk with your child's counselor. Make it clear that a university education is priority one. Take an active role in asking for - demanding - the best classes possible.

*If I am not pleased with the school choices around me, should I transfer my son or daughter?*

I always hesitate to recommend transferring. In general, most parents find that the student moves from a school with problems to a school with problems. My personal experience is that more is accomplished working with the school and trying to improve the school from the inside. Transferring also has added complications. There is always the risk that the new school will not credit all transfer grades or will have additional graduation requirements. Some years ago a student of mine transferred to California from Arizona. She transferred awfully late and was unable to graduate on time as there were too many other classes needed for graduation. A student loses contacts with teachers for letters or recommendation, clubs and activities, and officer titles. The student must begin from scratch. Some schools will not allow a transfer student to compete with the rest of the class for class rank. Other schools will not allow students to transfer into advanced classes. In general, transferring sets a student back academically. This does not even account for the emotional impact such a move can have. Under almost no circumstances would I recommend a transfer senior year. Too much is at stake to uproot at that time. I have advised students whose families had to move senior year stay with an uncle or a cousin or older sister just to finish senior year of high school without transferring. I have had other students drive 45 minutes to school each morning to avoid transferring. If a transfer is in the cards, it is better to transfer as early as possible.

*If I have to transfer, how do I do it?*

There are times when a transfer is unavoidable. I have had students transfer due to custody issues, job changes, loss of a home, a death in the family or even bullying. The first step is to speak with an administrator or counselor at the new school and verify what classes will transfer and what other classes would be necessary for graduation. Some schools will mandate a loss of credit after a certain date. Make sure your student can get credit for the classes begun. Also, have your student ask favorite teachers at the previous school for letters of recommendation or contact information. In a worst case scenario, if the student can not get a quality letter of recommendation from the new school, I would use a letter from the old school.

*In high school, is a private school, a public school or a charter school better?*

I have had the privilege of teaching at all three. I can tell you unequivocally that it depends on the school. The biggest difference I have noticed in the school is the climate of the school as a whole, the involvement of parents in the school community, and the expectations set by both of the above groups. In the right environment, public can be the best choice, private can be the best choice, and even charter school can be the best choice. One consistency I have found is the kids. It is rare that I have found "bad" kids. Students are about the same no matter where you go. In the same way, the teachers are about the same. Every school boasts a handful of super motivated, goal oriented students (and teachers), and a handful of individuals making really bad choices, and most everyone is somewhere in the middle.

One of the biggest influences on which way this goes is the administration. Administration has quite a lot of power to determine the focus of the school. I have seen administrators who are truly gifted at what they do. I have also seen administrators that could best serve the school by leaving for another profession. The right administrator will set a positive tone, hire forward thinking teachers, set high standards and keep the school student focused.

In the end, I will tell you that the biggest influence on your student's education is your student. If a truly motivated student is put in a bad environment, he will still find a way to make the most of it and rise to the top. If a student who consistently makes poor choices is put in the best school in America, he will never perform at the level of his peers.

In some ways, being in a "bad" school can work to a student's advantage when it comes to college applications. One advantage is in terms of class rank. At a really competitive school, students fight tooth and nail for the top 10%. At a less competitive school, a student who is motivated can really rise to the top and shine in ways that are not as easy elsewhere. A student from such an environment can also use the experiences to demonstrate how hard she had to struggle and the obstacles that she had to overcome.

One of my favorite students began his personal statement with the line, "Superman didn't come to my neighborhood." He then elaborated on some of the very real struggles he had to overcome to carve out the life he wanted despite all the obstacles he was facing - poverty, drugs, racism, police brutality, low expectations. Conversely, at one of the more affluent schools I taught, I had a young woman come to my class terribly distraught one day because her father "forced" her to drive the BMW on the weekend instead of the corvette. She was in tears and sure that her social life was over. Which experience do you think a college admissions officer can relate to better? What does each experience show about character and perseverance? At what point did the BMW become a lesser car?

*Can my student shoot too high?*

I can not always predict what a school will say. I can take an educated guess based on the numbers, but there is no accounting for how a student will affect his or her admission officer. Some years ago I had a young woman who really struggled with her test scores. In truth her scores were dismal. Despite this, she shot high. Several schools rejected her. Haverford was willing to overlook her test scores, though, and admitted her on the strength of her leadership, her compassion for others, her tenacity and her interview. On just test scores, there is no way she could have been admitted.

On the other end of the scale, I worked with another young man who was a star in every sense of the word. He could not have done better and did everything right. In addition to being valedictorian, he had perfect test scores. He was homecoming king and fluent in four languages. He was gifted musically and mathematically. His resume simply oozed with leadership, potential and brilliance. He should have been an easy admit to any school. I made the mistake of telling him this. He applied to only one school (against my advice) - Harvard. He wasn't admitted. When his mother contacted the school to ask why, she was told, "There are too many Koreans this year."

The moral of this story is that college admission is unpredictable. There is no sure thing. I will never discourage a student from applying somewhere. I will tell the student to add other applications including some schools that do not reach quite so high. If all you apply to are the "name" schools, a student runs the risk of being rejected everywhere.

I tell my students to apply at ten schools. I want one dream school - which I call the OMG school. I want one in state public university - because one can never predict the direction life will take. I want the other eight to be a mix of schools. Most books like this would never recommend so many schools. I do this primarily for financial aid. When I attended university, and this will date me a bit, a really expensive school was $12,000 a year. As of this writing, $60,000 a year is not extraordinarily expensive. That is an increase well above the increase in inflation. I wish salaries had risen commensurately. Every school will give you a different financial aid package. To use my own son as an example, his financial aid packages ranged from a full ride to "Are you joking!" The best offer was full tuition. The worst was $1000 off a

$65,000 a year tuition. Yes, this was with the exact same application. About a third of the schools were in a place that I considered affordable. There were another two or three schools with which I might have been able to bargain. The rest were simply nowhere near where I needed them to be. I advise applying at so many schools so a family can weigh the financial aid packages. Of course, if you are in the enviable position where your family can just write a check, you can apply at fewer schools (three or four).

## Chapter 4: Doing it by the Numbers

We live in a world that wants to measure everything qualitatively. Everything can be broken down into numbers; everything can be displayed as raw data. As a teacher I have always believed that there is an art and a science to teaching. The art is woefully hard to measure and quantify. As such school administrators, state legislatures, and the general public overemphasize the "science" of teaching. What grade does the school receive? What do the tests tell us? How many state titles does the basketball team have? Similarly, students can be measured by exacting numbers - grades and test scores - but students should also be measured by data that is more . . . ephemeral. First, the data.

*What is the biggest factor for admissions?*

      I have met so many admissions officers that insist in their meet and greet presentation that their school, "looks at the whole picture." "We at _____ don't see your student as just a number." And when asked if a particular struggling student should go ahead and apply, "Of course! There are a lot of factors that we at _____ take into consideration."

      They lie.

The very first cut - always - is grades and test scores. Many schools make a snap decision based on grades and test scores without reading the rest of the application. Put this in perspective. A highly competitive school will have thousands of applications for a few hundred spots. The admission's office rarely has more than ten people working full time. That means in January, right after everyone returns for the semester, each admission's officer has a veritable tower of applications ready to be read and disseminated. Admissions are still staffed by human beings - though some schools are beginning to use automated computer programs. As such, if the student is clearly above the line, the student is in. Depending on the school, the rest of the application may not even be read at that point. If, however, the student is below a certain line, he or she is rejected. No appeal, no second read. The vast majority of students fall somewhere in the middle. These are the applications that are scoured with a fine-toothed comb. Make no mistake, the first cut is grades and test scores.

*If the first cut is grades and test scores, why did the admission's officer tell my son / daughter to apply despite the fact that his / her scores are low?*

There are two possibilities. The first possibility, I'm wrong. Schools are really much more sympathetic and really don't rely on grades and test scores as much anymore.

The second possibility is cynical. Schools today are ranked. One of the primary ways to rank a school is selectivity. In other words, there is a clear perception that if a school accepts fewer students, the school must be a better school. If that is the case, isn't it better for a school to ask easy rejects to apply? The school gets the application fee, it doesn't waste time or resources reading the application, and the admission's officer doesn't have to be the bad guy explaining that your son or daughter has no chance of getting in.

*How do I know what my student's chances are?*

You may love or hate President Obama, but in terms of colleges he did something that was invaluable. When I first started working with colleges and universities, the game was infinitely more complicated trying to understand what the real numbers for colleges and universities were. Obviously, in a market economy if a college or university has the unique access to information, the college or university has all the advantages. When the Higher Education Act was reauthorized in 2008 by President Bush, the law greatly expanded access to universities for students with disabilities. The rules' committees for HEA which met in 2009 under President Obama made some significant changes in terms of what colleges must publish. Since 2011 colleges must have a "cost calculator" and publish numbers on retention rates, acceptance rates and financial aid. Prior to these changes interpreting such a vast array of data when all the colleges and universities used a different system or simply refused to release their numbers was the purview of a handful of specialty books and web sites. Now everyone has access to these numbers. There are a number of web sites that compile these data. The best is https://www.collegeboard.org/.

If you access the website (and I will refer to this several times), at the top is a box titled "college search." For argument's sake let's type in a school . . . Grinnell College. Go to the tab marked "applying." At the top the reader will note that (as of 2017) Grinnell has an acceptance rate of 29%. Under another tab "SAT and ACT Scores," one can see that (as of 2017) Grinnell's average SAT scores are roughly 640-770 per section and the average ACT scores are 30-34. As a whole these are tough numbers.

Let's look at another school for a comparison . . . Pacific Lutheran University. The acceptance rate at Pacific Lutheran University is 75%. The SAT mean is roughly 520-640 and

ACT is 21-27. A bit more flexible than Grinnell but still more competitive than the average large state universities.

I will use Grinnell College and Pacific Lutheran University and ACT scores for the purpose of this next example. If a young man has a 29 on the ACT - a decent score - he is at the bottom end of what Grinnell is looking for and at the top end for Pacific Lutheran. He may get into Grinnell, but he will have a tough time getting merit based financial aid. He is almost a sure accept at Pacific Lutheran with a good chance of a competitive financial aid package. If the boy's twin sister only scored a 21 on the ACT, Grinnell is a long shot. Pacific Lutheran is a possibility, but financial aid will be more restricted.

A general rule of thumb, the more your student's test scores are higher than the school's average, the better the student's chances of getting in *and* affording the school. If the test scores are below the average, the chances for an admission drop as do the chances for financial aid. If the student is right in the middle of the range, an admit is likely, but financial aid may not be as generous as the parents are hoping for.

This is quick and dirty. There are absolutely more factors that come into play. I am only suggesting that this is the first cut - not the final cut. Obviously exceptions are made for the student with low scores who is also a nationally recognized athlete or musician or . . . By the same token, the student with perfect scores is sometimes rejected because there are too many applicants with perfect scores or because he did nothing to stand out other than test scores.

To be perfectly clear, test scores are not enough by themselves. The test scores are just the first stop. Financial aid, which I will discuss in more depth later, is strongly affected by test scores.

*What classes does my student need to take in high school?*

There is no simple answer to this. The answer really depends on what school he or she is attending. There are three different levels that need to be taken into account: classes needed by the school or the school district for graduation, classes needed by the state for graduation and classes needed by a university for admission. There is considerable overlap, but by making it clear to the high school counselor from day one the ultimate goal is a university, class schedules are easily built to accommodate all three. For example, many states or districts require physical education. No university that I know of requires physical education. You may need the class to graduate with a diploma in the first place. Inversely, many districts only have fine arts as a suggestion or one possible choice for graduation while most universities demand a fine arts credit.

As a whole, I tell my students to take as many honors or weighted classes as possible. These classes have three effects. First, the weighted classes tend to have more rigor. I want students to experience rigor. Most schools have a mix of teachers. Every school I have ever seen has a handful of phenomenal teachers, a handful of awful teachers, and a majority of teachers who are somewhere in the middle. Take the hardest classes. To be clear that does not always mean the teacher is personally difficult. When a student says, "Mr. Kibler is hard," he could mean that I am really difficult to work with, or he could mean that my class is challenging. Strive for the second and avoid the first. A class with more rigor will help the student prepare for the ACT / SAT, will help the student become a better student, and will make it easier for a student to survive the first year at the university. I want my student to smile and think, "After Mr. Kibler, this is easy."

The second reason I like weighted classes is that these classes usually affect class rank. The short version is the higher the rank, the better. When the class rankings come out, the top five or ten students all have excellent grades. The single biggest difference is usually the number of weighted classes. Class rank in the end is just math.

Third, I like weighted classes as the classes show universities that your student was seeking a challenge. The irony, of course, is how these classes are assigned. In a typical public high school, a teacher will have five classes. It is unusual for a teacher to have all honor's classes. Instead most teachers have a mix of honors and on level classes. I would like to tell you that teachers are machines, love the extra work, and have all taken vows for a monastic life to go along with their vows of poverty. This is simply not the case. A lot of teachers (not all) will teach the same lesson to both the on level and honor's classes. The difference between the classes is too often just an "H" in the title.

To answer the initial question, after meeting district, school and state requirements, fill the remainder of the schedule with as many academic classes as possible. Instead of taking photography, take physics. Instead of weight training, take human geography. Instead of drawing and painting, take art history. Be sure to take foreign language. Take at least three years - and preferably four years - of the same language. Do not mix and match languages. Finish with the most advanced math course possible without taking a huge hit on the grades.

As with everything else, don't take my word for it. Investigate a university that you fantasize about your student attending. Pull up . . . Carnegie Mellon University on the Internet and see exactly what classes Carnegie Mellon is looking for or simply call the admissions office. The universities are not shy. The schools will spell out exactly what is wanted. Carnegie

Mellon's website as an example: https://admission.enrollment.cmu.edu/pages/academic-requirements

Please do not hesitate to be an advocate for your child. I had an administrator tell me once that he doesn't care what schedule a student gets. He will assign whatever is most convenient and easiest. He believed that if a parent really cared, the parent would come in and argue for a better schedule. The parents who did not argue simply did not matter. If you know your child needs the second year of Spanish and Spanish is not scheduled, make an appointment with the counselor and ask why not. If the counselor refuses to meet with you or misses the appointment, go over the counselor's head to meet with the vice-principal or principal. *You* are your child's best advocate.

*Which is better for my student: Advanced Placement, Dual Credit, International Bachelorette or Cambridge?*

The short answer is ... yes. All the above programs, and I am sure there are one or two I did not list, are designed to offer more of a challenge. I am a fan of all the programs. All the programs represent an effort to raise the level of expectations and better prepare a student for the university.

Now that I am finished being politically correct, all things being equal I prefer Advanced Placement. Cambridge and International Bachelorette are more designed on the European model. While both programs have much merit, American universities - and American university admissions' officers - are less familiar with the programs. The programs do not mesh as seamlessly with the curriculum in most American high schools.

Dual credit is most often completed in tandem with a local community college. If the student's ultimate goal is only community college or a local big state university, this is an attractive choice. If however, the student dreams of attending a University of Notre Dame or Stanford University or Dartmouth University, dual credit is not often honored. Once again, Advanced Placement is more widely accepted.

My final decision comes down to word of mouth. Having spoken to dozens and dozens of admission's officers and reading hundreds of books and Internet articles, the general consensus is Advanced Placement.

I want students to take as many AP classes as the student can handle. When looking at schools freshman year, I would recommend asking about the AP program. Can my son take AP classes as a freshman? What are the requirements to be in an AP class? How do the school's teachers compare to the national averages in terms of the passing rate for AP tests? Is there a limit to the number of AP classes a student can take at once? How does the school decide who teaches the AP classes?

If a student can take - and pass - several AP tests before senior year (right now the number is approximately four classes), then the student can apply to universities as an "AP Scholar." This title really stands out in universities because so many students are unable to take many AP classes prior to senior year. Being an "AP Scholar" really stands out to colleges. To earn the title the student needs to pass the tests, not just enroll in the class. The quality of the AP teacher can make a difference. If stuck with a poor teacher, some AP classes can be passed with hard work and good study skills. This will require more effort from the student.

*My son's school does not offer advanced classes. What should I do?*

There are a variety of reasons for this. The most benign is that the school is a private school where all the classes are taught at an advanced level and none are labeled as such. In other cases, the school administration simply has not understood the need for such classes. In that case, make an appointment with the administration and inquire about adding some classes to the curriculum. Please keep in mind that these changes take time and staffing. If the administration will not listen to you, then form a parent group and go to the superintendent or the school board with your request for equity and equal access.

*Is it better to get a "B" in an Advanced Placement class or an "A" in an on level class?*

I have asked this question to more than a dozen schools. I have always received the exact same answer - and I am sure each admission's officer thought that he or she was being terribly witty and original. "Get an 'A' in AP." I understand that this is not a real answer. There is no one answer for everyone, though. Obviously an "A" in and AP class, especially when matched with high test scores, removes the need for the conversation. Realistically the rest depends not only on the university but on the admission officer reading the application. An admission's officer who was himself a "C" student tends to be more lenient. An admission's officer that was at the top of her class tends to take a more narrow view. In general, I would tell you that universities will argue for class rigor over grades any day. That being said, I can make an argument for a "B," but less than a "B" in an honor's or AP class will hurt. No matter how you cut it, "C's" begin to hurt. "D's" and "F's" will kill your application.

*What about taking dual credit classes?*

Dual credit is a type of class that is becoming more and more popular in high schools. The dual credit classes have students take a class (i.e., United States history) in high school with his or her regular high school teacher. Upon completion of the course, the student will receive high school and college credit for the course. In theory a student could begin college as a sophomore. While not all bad, I am not a huge fan of dual credit. I am speaking from my own experiences and each state does the process slightly differently, but the basic dynamics are the same.

My first problem with dual credit is that the classes often require a family to pay the college tuition - a tuition that in this case is not offset by scholarships or Pell grant or financial aid. While each class is not terribly expensive, if the goal is to complete an entire year of classes, the price adds up. In addition, the college that is facilitating often asks for the college's own final exam before credit is given. In some scenarios, the high school teacher never sees the test. In other scenarios, the provided college final exam is much more challenging than anything given at the college itself. In most cases, the high school teacher will teach her curriculum in the same manner as she always has with the hope that the school or district curriculum will match the college curriculum. The end result is that receiving credit for the class can become a real challenge and can become rather expensive.

My second issue with dual credit is the credit itself. This is community college credit. The more prestigious a school and the further away the school is located, the greater the risk that any earned credit will not be awarded. The theory is that your little community college credit, which we know was really just your high school class, could never compare with the rigor and intensity of the same class at the University of OMG. Why should Hamilton College or Swarthmore College of Bowdoin College (all truly prestigious) give credit for some local community college class? What incentive does the out of state university or college possess to excuse your student from more classes at the four-year university?

Third, I always worry about setting a bar low. In my experience when a high school is pushing a lot of dual credit classes the motivation is that the high school does not expect your student to excel or go far. Sights are narrow and limited. I would much rather shoot high than low.

*Should my student take a university class while in high school?*

I tend to have a much more positive outlook on actual university classes or even community college classes at local community colleges. Many universities and community colleges will allow high school students to take classes part time. For example in Maricopa County where I work and live, the local community colleges allow any student over the age of sixteen to take college classes in the evening or the summer. The local universities are not quite as flexible, but I know of exceptions.

One positive, and the reason I use this avenue the most, is that the college offerings are more expansive and diverse than the high school offerings. For example I currently have a young woman with whom I am working. She began her freshman year in pre-calculus honors. Sophomore year she took Calculus AP. By junior year the high school she attended had run out of math courses for her to take. The high school counselor ingeniously recommended the girl go backwards and take basic algebra to finish her graduation requirements. Instead I pushed her father to enroll her in a community college math class of appropriate level and then pushed the school district to count the math toward her graduation requirements. The same is true for an advanced student in just about any field. A college or university can offer far more diverse and higher level programs than most high schools.

I have also valued college classes for showing a student interest in a specific field of study. I had a student who really loved astronomy. The high school had no astronomy classes. Absolutely nothing fit. I urged the parents to contact the local university about the possibility of their daughter taking some basic astronomy courses. The same was true of another student that was desperate to study Korean. The high school was limited to Spanish and French. The local university was a different story. Taking advanced classes with a college or university can really demonstrate an academic interest. Any student can say he likes Korean or she wants to study astronomy. Neither interest is very easy to demonstrate on a college resume.

Finally I have used college classes to circumnavigate a particularly bad teacher. One of my students some years ago had a distinct problem with the unique physics teacher in high school but really wanted to study engineering. The problem was a personal issue, but the teacher had a reputation for not being professional enough to put that aside. I urged the student to take high school physics anyway. How bad can the teacher be? Two weeks in I had the parents drop the student from the class. Ok. Next idea. Enroll the student in the local community college. He still received a physics credit for his resume without the trauma of a particularly bad experience.

There are some challenges with taking university or college classes as well. First and foremost, just like with dual credit, is the cost. A family will need to pay for class without any financial aid. In this case we are looking at one or two classes, not six or seven. No matter how many classes taken the price can add up. The price also includes transportation. The student needs to find a way to get to and from college. Classes in the afternoon are challenging especially if the student is involved in anything at the high school like sports or drama.

Another challenge is that your sixteen year old is now in a class full of adults. That can be a sudden jump not only in expectations but also social interactions. As a parent, I would urge other parents to have long conversations about what social interactions are appropriate and how old is too old to date.

Keep in mind, just as with dual credit, there is a strong possibility that whatever university your student attends may not accept the transfer credits. This is not an avenue I am pursuing to eliminate some credits. I am following this course of study to improve the resume. Let's use these classes and this expressed interest to get into the University of Pennsylvania and worry later about if UPenn will honor the credits (probably not in this case). The credits are less important to me than the resume.

A crucial issue is grades. A student that pursues college or university credits MUST get an "A." Most major universities and colleges have a dim view, warranted or not, of community colleges. The thought is that the colleges are not nearly as rigorous as their vaunted institution. Community colleges are lesser options, easier options. A student who receives an "A" has shown that he or she might be ready for college level work. A student that receives less than an "A" has shown that he or she can not even excel at a community college. If the student can't do well at a community college, how can he do well at the University of OMG? Students must make sure that grades for community college classes are perfect. Anything less than perfect is unusable. Be careful, having three great classes can be ruined with one bad class. All the classes show up on the same transcript.

*What class rank should my son or daughter aim for?*

Of course, 1, 2 and 3 are best. Many schools even offer special scholarships for the valedictorian (first in the class). While some elite schools like Harvard and Yale pride themselves on how many valedictorians are rejected every year, most schools will note this as an accomplishment. After the first three spots I look for top 3%, top 10% and top 25% roughly. There are a lot of variables in the percentages. Specifically every school is looking for something different and has a different cut off point. I use 3%, 10% and 25% as very rough markers. Top 3% and the student is solid. Top 10% and there are still a lot of positive markers. Top 25% is pretty much the minimum. After 25% a student's class rank now becomes a liability. A low class rank is telling schools that of all the students in the graduating class, your student can't quite cut it among his or her peers. Because class rank is so dependent upon the rigor of the school and classes, colleges put a great deal of weight on the rank. A student with all "B's" and "C's" who is in the 10$^{th}$ percentile is thought to have come from a relatively easy school. If a student can still be in the top 10% with "C's," then the school must not be terribly challenging. Conversely, if a student only has one "B" (the rest are "A's") but is 6 of 400 in the class, then the school must be more competitive.

This is one way where a mediocre or less challenging school might benefit a student. At a private prep school, a student will have to really fight to be in the top 3%. At a less rigorous school, close to half of the students are not competition to begin with. Many of the less competitive schools will offer a school within a school experience as an honor's student tends to track in the one section of honors history and honors English and honors science and honors math with all of the like-minded peers. It is entirely possible to graduate in a class of 500 and only know 50 students.

If your student is number 12 in a class of 400, have your son or daughter counsel every student who is thinking of dropping out. Every student that drops out lowers the class total and your student may drop from top 3% to top 5% or lower. I will sarcastically tell a student who is number 3 in the class to figure out who is number 1 and 2 and get them dating. Nothing destroys class ranks faster than a new love interest.

*What if my son or daughter has some bad grades on his / her transcript?*

A lot comes into play. First it depends on how bad. Second it depends on the school. A Vanderbilt University in Tennessee will take a dim view of anything below an "A." Even two "B's" can hurt. Ohio State University would be very pleased with a transcript with all "B's." It depends on how selective the school is, and who your student's competition is. If most students are getting excellent grades, then your student also needs to get excellent grades.

Bad grades freshmen year are not necessarily damaging. Many excellent schools like Illinois Wesleyan largely ignore the first year. The school does so with the understanding the transition to high school - both academically and emotionally - can be a bit jarring. The most important year is junior year. Junior year should show a student at his or her maximum potential. Senior grades won't even be posted by the time your student applies, so the senior year grades can not help you much.

Probably the biggest thing that most universities are looking for is growth. If a student begins with a mediocre track record, but gradually increases not only the grades but the rigor of classes, most schools will forgo any negative conclusions. The growth is exactly what a school is looking for. Bad grades are never good, but the grades can be minimized with consistent growth. Remember that this growth includes a growth in the rigor of the class. There are some schools, like Cornell University in New York, that simply expect straight "A's" for four years and anything less will hurt.

The inverse is that a decrease in grades can kill a student. If a student begins with high grades freshman year and then consistently drops, a university will assume that the student does not have the maturity for school or the intellectual ability to cope with classes that increase in difficulty. Just as a strong junior year can help an application, a weak junior year can kill an application. I have worked with students that show consistent growth and students whose grades resemble a roller coaster. If the end GPA (grade point average) is the exact same, the student with consistent growth ALWAYS has a distinct advantage.

*What if my son just isn't good at math?*

This is a problem I run into a lot, and it is usually with math. If a student has strong scores in English and humanities, but weak scores in math, most universities will be willing to give the student some credit for the learning curve. A poor showing in math is often reflected in poor test scores on the ACT or SAT for the math section.

There are schools (i.e., Cornell) that simply expect the students to be good at everything. Most schools are willing to accept that not all students are renaissance men or women. A student that has real gifts for language and literature may just not be gifted at math. The reverse is also true. I would not try to explain it or argue it. If a school is not willing to see the differences, it is probably not the right school. Remember, "D's" and "F's" always hurt. If the grades are lower than a "B" in an on level class, please ask the school for options with tutoring and speak with the math (or English or science or Spanish or history) teacher about why the student is not doing well.

*Once my son is accepted, can he stop worrying about grades?*

Absolutely not! There is a final transcript check at the end of senior year. A small dip might be ignored, but crashing grades are certainly not. Some years ago the vice-principal called me into her office in late June. There were a tearful girl and a distraught mother in the office. The girl was not a student of mine. The girl had been accepted at an out of state university in part on an athletic scholarship. Once she was accepted, she just gave up on her classes. A previously very strong academic record had been completely undone by some poor choices senior year. The university had sent a letter which I need to paraphrase as I did not make a copy. The letter roughly said, "After reviewing your final academic record, we at _____ have decided to withdraw our offer of acceptance for the 2011-2012 school year. Likewise, we will also retract all promised financial aid. If you are still interested in attending _____, please reapply for admission next year for the 2012-2013 academic school year. We wish you luck in your future endeavors." The vice principal wanted to know what options the girl had in late June. My answer was really simple. Community college.

*Is it better to have good grades or good test scores?*

Again, the factitious answer is both. Ask what each says to an admission's counselor. If a student, Angie, has poor test scores but excellent grades, there are a couple possibilities. The nicest conclusion for Angie is that she just does not do well on tests. Other possible conclusions are that the school was too easy, there was no rigor in the classes, or in the worst case that Angie just does not have the intellectual caliber that the school is looking for.

If a student, Brett, has great test scores but poor grades, an admission's counselor jumps to different conclusions. One possibility is that Brett does well testing or simply got lucky. A more likely jump is the idea that Brett actually has a brain, but is extraordinarily lazy with his class work.

In the end what should a university admission's counselor pick? Does the counselor want the student who is just not quite as bright or the student that is lazy? The easy assumption is that both Angie and Brett may be rejected for the student that has high marks in both categories. It is easier for me to work with Brett than Angie.

*We are moving. How does that effect my student's grades?*

If at all possible I counsel parents not to move while your children are in high school. Under no circumstance should a student move senior year. As far as grades go it is not uncommon for the new school to discount class rank for your student. Another common practice is refusing to give honor's credit for honor's classes. Another issue I have seen is the new school or new state requires additional classes for graduation. Students will also have issues getting that letter of recommendation, a club officer position, quality community service or varsity sports team. I have instead recommended students drive to the old school or even live with an uncle or cousin until the student finishes school.

*What is the difference between SAT and ACT?*

Spelling.

Some years ago, way back when I was applying, the common thought was that East coast schools wanted to see the SAT and West coast schools wanted to see the ACT. That just isn't true anymore. Today, almost every university in America takes either. For most students the test scores translate well and a score in one converts nicely to a score in the other. I recommend my students take both. There are some students, and I can not predict which ones, who do significantly better on one or the other. The biggest anomalies tend to be students who do very well in math but not English or vice versa.

One advantage the SAT has is that more schools are willing to super score. What that means is that the college admission's office will take the best English score and the best math score (not necessarily from the same test) and combine the best scores of each section giving a higher composite score. Some schools will also super score an ACT, but the list is much more limited.

I want the student to take the tests multiple times. At the minimum - stress on minimum - take one test spring of sophomore year. Take the other fall of junior year. Whichever test was higher, retake once or twice at the end of junior year. If necessary, retake one or two times fall of senior year. Anything in the spring of senior year will be too late to affect much of anything.

*What score does my student want?*

This is a loaded question. Obviously the best score is a perfect score. The closer to perfect the better. A perfect score is not easy. The numbers will change a bit from year to year, but 24 on the ACT and 1180 on the SAT are about average nationally. 28 on the ACT or 1320 on the SAT makes the student competitive. A 31 or higher on the ACT or a 1430 or higher on the SAT opens almost any door except the most elite schools. Anything below the 24 / 1320, please please keep testing. At this level about the only school that will be affordable will be the state schools.

The number one requirement for both tests is studying. Students are remarkably similar for all their appeals to individuality. Most students end up owning or borrowing at least one practice book. Most students never actually use it. I have cleaned out my own sons' rooms to find practice test books still in the original plastic wrap! Create a study time and be consistent. For example, from 4-5pm every day is for the ACT or SAT study. Turn off the phone and the TV. Put away the music. Do the other homework and chores later. I can almost guarantee that if your student actually devotes an hour a day for two years the scores will be decent. The problem students run into is that the student intends to study - later. And later is always, well . . . later. Other students will spend three hours a night in their room "studying" and never realize that two and half hours was on the phone. Structure the time and demand the time. If this is a problem try making the student study at the kitchen table, and turn off the t.v. for the younger siblings and make your teen read. If the home is too noisy, then start picking junior up from the public library at 6:00 p.m. every Monday and Wednesday (and show up early randomly - just to check). Use an aunt or uncle's house or encourage your student to form a study group with three friends.

Think of it this way. If a student worked seven hours a week at $10 an hour, the earned amount is $70 a week. Over the course of the year we are looking at about $3500 assuming that the student worked on breaks, vacations and birthdays and did not spend a single penny. Over two years (remember he or she can't legally work until around junior year) that is $7000. It is an impressive sum. On the other hand, a merit-based scholarship at a university for a 28 on the ACT can very easily be $20000 a year. Over four years that is $80000. Hmmmm . . . $7,000 or $80,000? There is almost nothing a student can do to make college more affordable than getting good test scores. Let me repeat. It is that important. **Nothing will make college more**

**affordable than good test scores.** If I am working with a student who earned a 35 on the ACT, my job is easy. He can afford college without a problem. If I am working with a student whose highest score on the ACT is an 18, I spend a lot of time worrying. An 18 will require a small miracle for college to be affordable. Make a study schedule NOW. Don't let your teenager procrastinate on this.

*What about classes for test preparation?*

There are a number of private companies that offer test preparation. The average cost seems to be around $1000. I am yet to find the company that offers the magic beans - the class where your student can magically jump to a perfect score. Everything I am going write next is all over simplification and generalizations. The test prep runs a gamut from a single Saturday workshop to a long term relationship involving one on one instruction and Internet help. I have found some really bad deals - usually the shorter ones - where the company gives a practice test that is easily obtainable online and then offers "advice" like, "Bring a pencil" or "Remember your I.D." Even the companies that include direct instruction are simply trying to build on what your student has already learned in school and reinforce good test taking habits.

In the end, there is little that these companies offer that you can not supply with a public library card. The test preparation books that are widely available cover the same basic information. So what is the advantage of the class? First, some students do not learn well from a book. Sometimes an actual class with a real person or an Internet site can be more in tune with a student's particular learning style. Second, having a scheduled class once or twice a week will force your student to do that which he or she is desperately trying to avoid - study. That two-hour class on Wednesday afternoon is two hours a week where your student is doing nothing but studying for the test. No Internet, no cell phones, no drama from the BFF, no math homework, no chores. Just studying. Third, the test - both ACT and SAT - is really heavy on grammar and mechanics. Grammar is not often taught to aspiring English teachers. Aspiring English teachers learn a lot about theory and psychology and methods and testing and data collection and discipline and research but a little about literature and poetry and almost nothing about grammar. If your student has never really been taught grammar, or worse the teacher has taught him or her but gotten the rules wrong, a class may be a good way to learn the grammar rules that were never included in the regular classes.

I know that the fees are often expensive. Before paying anything do some research. Ask the school counselor if he or she has any recommendations. Take those recommendations with a grain of salt. Ask the other parents at the basketball game or the dance recital if the other parents tried any of the test preparation classes and would recommend any. Talk to the company. Any company that makes guarantees or promises is lying. Go to the next one. There are no guarantees in testing. I have found a lot of companies that promise a "money back guarantee," but I am yet to find the company that actually pays it. Ask the company what kind of help your student is receiving? Is it direct instruction or simply workbooks? Is the company teaching math and grammar or simply testing? Where do the practice tests come from? Is there additional help for a student who just isn't getting it? What are the criteria for how the instructors are chosen? How many classes does your money pay for?

If you still can not afford this, speak to the school about finding extra help. Your student is not the unique in the position to need help with the testing. Perhaps the school can contract with a company or offer teachers willing to tutor the requisite subjects. If all else fails, go to the public library, borrow a book and set a specific schedule for your student.

*What test preparation book is the best?*

Honestly they are all about the same. Each book offers practice tests and most offer detailed explanations. What I would recommend is taking your son to the local bookstore some Saturday. Sit him in the café. Buy him a coffee or hot chocolate and have him go through five or six books. Don't worry about the tests, worry about the explanations. Which explanation works the best for your son and how his brain is wired? Which book makes the most sense? Which book emphasizes teaching more than testing? Let him pick one. When he finishes, go back for a different one.

The local public library will often have last year's test books on sale. I have personally picked up about six year-old test preparation books for about $.25 each. There is not much difference between test preparation for 2017 and 2018. I do check to make sure the book is not marked up. For the same reason, I usually avoid getting test preparation books from used book sellers. I don't want a book with eight tests where the previous owner has attempted six of the tests.

While you are at it, sign your son up for the daily Kaplan ACT / SAT question. It will show up as a message on your student's phone every day. Most important, again, is not knowing that the correct answer was "C," but *why* the correct answer was "C."

*Is there a limit to how many times my kid can take the tests?*

No. In the past ACT would only report the tests you send, but SAT would report everything. That is no longer true. With both tests, a student only reports his or her highest score, or possibly the highest English / verbal and highest math. The advantage to the highest of each section is that some schools will super score - highest of each section on different days. Generally, the last test a student can take is about November of senior year. It takes about a month to get the scores. That means to make college admissions deadlines the November test is the last one. Some schools will still accept scores for merit-based scholarship consideration. This is a good question to ask if the student is borderline on the cut offs. Do not be afraid to ask if one or two more points would have an impact on merit based financial need. As of this writing, both test services are looking at a computerized test with about a 72 hour turn around. While I am very enthusiastic about such an option, it does not currently exist. If it becomes reality, there is a possibility that a December test might work.

*My student has really tried to do well on the tests, but just can't seem to do well. My student has just never done well on testing. What can I do?*

Some students just don't test well. We live in a society where everyone is measured by tests. Even the United States Congress has gotten into the testing game with the "Leave No Child Behind" act. Testing has become a mandatory experience in schools today. Most admission's counselors understand the limitations of testing. Grades are far too objective, though. What does an "A" at West High School mean compared to an "A" at North High School? Is an "A" in Wisconsin the same thing as an "A" in North Dakota? Did the student get an "A" because he or she really knew the material well or because the teacher was too easy? Did the student actually earn the "C" or was it a pity grade? Or maybe the "C" was a result of being sick with pneumonia this winter for three weeks. Grades are far more subjective than tests.

The single biggest reason that a student does not test well is that he or she is not ready for the test. I really want to tell a parent that every student that claims to have a problem with testing really does have a problem. The reality is that this has become a convenient excuse for students that have been taking short cuts for four years - or longer. Unfortunately, there really are students who struggle with testing.

Step one, retake the test. Perhaps it was a bad day or a bad test. Step two, if anxiety is really an issue, look for solutions. There is no solution that fits everyone. Some find help from chewing gum, others from taking off their shoes and rubbing their feet across the carpet or counting backwards from twenty before beginning the test. Listen to Mozart (specifically Mozart) for twenty minutes before a test. Also try breathing exercises or even meditation or prayer. If the anxiety is severe, a student might be best served by consulting a health care professional.

Another option for students that just don't test well is the test optional university. There are some universities like Bard in New York or Agnes Scott in Georgia that just do not require testing. I don't want to supply a list as the list changes constantly but feel free to do an Internet search for "test optional universities." Try http://www.fairtest.org/university/optional.

Test optional schools are always a last option for me. Most schools that advertise that they are test optional still prefer to see test scores. All things being equal, the student with test scores - even mediocre test scores - is more likely to be admitted. If no test scores are supplied, then the school is going to ask for evidence that the student really is ready for college because no college wants to accept a student that drops out or fails. One of the primary questions in an admission's process is: "Can this student achieve?" If you are not submitting test scores, how can you show this? Remember grades are not reliable. So, what else is on the resume that speaks to brilliance? One thing I have used extensively is a student's participation in an academic competition like Quizbowl, Academic Decathlon, Math Olympiad, Model United

Nations, Mock Trial or even chess. A student without test scores needs to find a way to shine. Whenever possible, I would rather submit average test scores than nothing. If the test scores are truly horrendous, then consider a test optional university.

One final warning, there are a number of test optional schools that still really want to see test scores. Just because admissions is test optional does not mean that financial aid is test optional. If you really need a test optional school, consider a school that does not accept any tests such as Hampshire College in Massachusetts or Kalamazoo in Michigan. Hampshire and Kalamazoo will require a battery of essays instead of test scores, but a student who needs test optional may really shine here.

*What if I have tried different options, but my student still has a problem with his or her grades?*

My first question is the reason. I have worked with students that actually had a head injury in high school or were unusually ill. Obviously, if a student is tossed from a quad or recovering from lupus then grades suffer. Most teachers are sympathetic but are often impeded by just too much missing work or too many days missed. This can be particularly jarring with advanced classes like AP or IB where one or two days out can be a real setback. One or two weeks can be crippling. I have also worked with students dealing with unimaginable emotional issues like the death of a parent or a divorce. It is no wonder that a student in this situation has a difficulty concentrating.

In these cases write an additional letter to be included with the application. Explain the circumstances. Not every university will make allowances but most will. The primary questions for a school are the sincerity, the length of time and the depth of the damage. Is this a problem that will also affect performance at the university? The answer is different for everyone and every school. Two different admission's officers at the same school can make very different decisions for two students in that same position as can two different schools for the same student.

One final warning. Teenage students often have an unrealistic view of what life events really do cause distraction. Highlighting the wrong event can do more damage than help. For example, I had a young woman argue some years ago that her boyfriend breaking up with her was the reason her grades took a hit - for an entire year! As valid as this may be for the girl, this is an excuse that will strike an admission's office as vaguely pathetic.

If nothing else works and the grades / test scores are simply too low for a decent offer, please consider community college. The good news is that all those negative grades can be erased and the student can basically hit the reset button. As explained previously, this is almost always my last choice.

*My daughter applied to a university and sent her test scores. Three weeks later the admission's counselor called her and told her to resubmit her application as test optional. Should she?*

Absolutely! The admission's counselor is giving her a gift. The admission's office could have simply denied your daughter. Knowing that the odds are not good for regular acceptance, the admission's office was trying to give your daughter a chance to be accepted. Send a thank you note. Do be aware, though, that this is also a warning and the low test scores may be reflected one way or the other in financial aid packages.

*What are the SAT Subject tests?*

Sometimes called a SAT II test, SAT subject tests are similar to the SAT tests except that they test specific subjects. Currently there are subject tests in math (in two different levels), biology, chemistry, physics, literature, US history, world history, Spanish, French, German, Hebrew, Japanese, Korean, Latin, Chinese and Italian. The test is designed to show excellence in specific subject areas.

In general it is top notch schools like the Ivy League that requires subject tests. Many schools are very happy to take subject tests to pad a resume or even to replace poor general ACT / SAT tests. A student with weaknesses in his or her application can go a long way in overcoming these weaknesses with an excellent score in subject tests.

*Does my student need to take the SAT Subject tests?*

It depends on where he or she is applying. Every school has different standards, and the standards change. Start with the most prestigious name-dropping schools on the student's list. If even one school requires the tests, take them. Again, every school is different, but the general rule of thumb is two tests. That means I advise my students to take three tests. I don't necessarily want my students taking all three on the same day. If a university, let's say Amherst, wants two subject tests, taking three tests allows a student to choose the best. By taking two tests one day and retaking one of the tests with a third test the next month, a student has the opportunity to offer the best possible scores. If a student does well on the tests, include the scores with all the applications. Like the SAT test, I would really like a score over 700, but over 650 is workable. Below 600: retake.

*What subject tests should my student take?*

Take whatever the student does best at. Hopefully that will also include the area of study. For example, in the case of a young man who really wanted to be a doctor and just took AP tests receiving a 3 in chemistry and a 5 in United States history, I would tell him to take biology and US history first. Chemistry was a little low on the AP test which tells me that he is still struggling a bit with chemistry. Biology ties directly to his chosen field, and he obviously can do well in history even though it is not his field of study. Take the tests when it is still fresh in the head and be sure to study for the tests. Don't go in cold.

I have a bias against using a foreign language. I feel too many universities will discount a 780 in Spanish from a student with the last name Martinez or slight a 765 in Korean from a student named Park. The same bias does not exist for a Smith who does well in Japanese. All things being equal, take the chemistry and literature. That being said, if you happen to be Hispanic - and speak Spanish well - go ahead and take the Spanish test. If Spanish will be your highest score, a really high score always means something. I would rather see a 780 in Spanish and a 610 in literature than a 480 in chemistry and a 610 in literature. That is also why a lot of schools require two tests, not one.

*What is the PSAT?*

For full details please go to http://www.nationalmerit.org/. The quick and dirty is that this is a test of a student's aptitude compared with all the other students in the country. The number varies by state, but roughly a student needs to be in the top 1-2% or all those tested. If a student is selected, the student becomes a national merit scholar.

What does that mean? There is a monetary award attached. The award itself is not terribly grandiose, especially in terms of the escalating costs of college. More important is the title. Universities love to talk about how many National Merit Scholars are enrolled at the school. Many universities offer special - and significant - merit-based scholarships to all

National Merit Scholars. I can say unequivocally, being named a National Merit Scholar will help a student with admission and will most likely help with financial aid. Remember that the test must be taken junior year to count. A student can take the test prior to junior year, but it is just practice at that point. I actually urge my students to take the PSAT sophomore year to get a base score. The student then sees how close he or she is to what is needed and sees what he or she needs to study.

*Ok. You have mentioned a lot of tests. When does my student take them all?*

This is a SAMPLE schedule. Every student is slightly different.

Freshman fall semester: no testing - you don't know enough yet

Freshman spring semester: no testing - still not yet

Sophomore fall semester: take the ACT (http: //www.act.org/content/act/en/products-and-services/the-act.html)

and PSAT (usually a student signs up at school)

Sophomore spring semester: take the SAT (https: //collegereadiness.collegeboard.org/sat/register)

Junior fall semester: take the PSAT and either the ACT or SAT (whichever scored better)

Junior spring semester: SAT or ACT

Senior fall semester: ACT or SAT (probably twice)

Senior spring semester: too late, don't worry.

If the student gets a perfect score the first time he or she takes the SAT, game over - you win! If less than perfect, retake. Retake. Retake.

When taking the tests, a student is allowed to send the scores to three universities or colleges for free. Send the scores to big in state universities with low standards. Sending a low score to a competitive school could hurt your application. Do not send your scores to a Yale or a Duke or even a University of California - Berkeley until you have seen the scores.

## Chapter 5: Let's Play the University Admission's Game!

Way back when, close to when dinosaurs roamed the planet, I applied for universities. The game then was vastly different. Scores of admissions' counselors freely admit that they would not be admitted to their own schools today. One of the biggest changes has been to activities. When I was applying competitive schools wanted a student who did a little bit of everything: a season on the basketball team, a regional chess trophy, a host of community service with different organizations including the ever touted Thanksgiving meal at the local homeless shelter, a poem in the school newspaper and president of the student body. The more the better. That is no longer true. Today universities want to see a few activities where a student has maximized his or her potential. In contrast to the last chapter, this is not a number's game.

*Why does this really matter? Aren't grades and test scores enough?*

Ummm ... no. Today's universities, and this is especially true of the small liberal arts colleges that I love, want to create a sense of community. A college wants to create an experience that will shape your son or daughter but will also shape the community itself. To this end one of the primary questions an admission's officer will ask is, "Will she fit in?" To be clear, this is very different from, "Can she do well here?" The second question is more academic and is more clearly answered by grades and test scores as addressed in a previous chapter. This question - "Will she fit in" - has more to do with what your daughter (or son) brings to the community as a whole. What unique contributions can she make outside of the classroom? What unique flavor will she bring to the campus? How will she change my school? What direction will she gear the discussion in her freshman humanities class or her senior science seminar? What experience will she offer her future roommate? Will she be an alumnus the school points to with pride in twenty years?

In some ways this part of the application is more important than the grades and test scores. Don't get me wrong. I still maintain that grades and test scores are the first cut. But any counselor worth his salt will steer students toward applying at universities where the student has at least a decent chance to get in. It is cruel to tell a B / C student to apply only at Harvard, Yale, Stanford and Cornell. That is setting the student up for failure - though I have seen this done. Instead most of the admits are about the same level in terms of GPA and test scores. The question of activities and service is where the student really stands out from everyone else. Top notch schools like Harvard always brag about how many "perfect" students are rejected every year. To be blunt, Harvard would fill its freshman class five times over if it accepted every valedictorian with perfect test scores that applied. Harvard just does not have room for all of them. The admits to Harvard are the students who really stand out from the pack.

The ability to stand out in Ivy League schools is not in grades and tests because ALL of your competition has the grades and the tests. Anyone who doesn't have the numbers is an easy cut. You stand out on what you have done, what you can bring to the table that no one else can, how you can impact or change the campus community, what makes you unique, and, yes, how much money you can offer or what your last name is. Is there any world where a George W.

Bush could be admitted to Yale on his own merits? 90% of my students are more qualified, but their last name is not "Bush."

*What activities are best?*

The best activities are the ones that *you* really care about. It is really hard to fake enjoying an activity or wanting to continue said activity in college. But . . . and it is a big BUT, pursue your passion ardently and prove that you love it. The proof is hard. Anyone can say, and I have a half dozen teenage girls a year who say, that she loves puppy dogs. That is cute, but how can you prove it? Have you volunteered at an animal shelter? Have you started working with a local vet? Have you started a program for adopting abandoned kittens or bringing puppy dogs to a children's cancer ward for kids to play with? Have you started a rescue program for birds devastated by a recent hurricane or oil spill? How can you prove that you are in fact passionate about your activity?

I can not enumerate how many students express to me how passionate they are to be a doctor. I usually respond with, "Why?" "Well, my mom says I have always liked to help people. And this would be a really good way to help a lot of people, like sick people. And, doctors make a lot of money. Right?" Does that really sound impressive to you? What about that conversation says your student actually wants to be a doctor? All this flaccid statement tells an admission's officer is that your student likes it when mom gets to brag about how he is going to be a really rich doctor someday. Instead I want to see if your child has taken the hardest science and math classes you can. Has he enrolled in any summer programs relating to medicine? Has he volunteered at the hospital? Has he started volunteering his time as a translator at a local hospital or care center for people who don't speak English? Has he done any original research? Has he published? How can your student show that he wants to be a doctor?

The passion pursued does not necessarily have to tie directly to a major or future career. Neither does the passion always have to be academic. I actually really enjoy when I get to help a student that is genuinely interested in astronomy or Greek mythology, knitting or bass guitar, German existentialism or Spanish realistic fantasy literature, fly fishing or scrap booking. The actual hobby, interest or passion is not terribly important. Just be able to actually demonstrate that this activity is important, for how long it has been important and why your teen chose to pursue this in the first place.

In the end, it does not matter what activity your student pursues or what community service your child pours her heart into. Just do it 100%. Do it well and document that she is actually pursuing excellence. Don't just play chess with dad on the weekend, join the chess team and dominate at state competitions. Don't tell me you love photography. Figure out how the community or local businesses need that talent. Create opportunities. Don't express that you love to watch the political campaigns on t.v. and talk about the campaigns with your older brother. Volunteer to help someone get elected or join a community political organization. Don't bake. Enter baking competitions and win. Write your own recipes and publish. Don't write emo poetry in your dark room by the light of your cell phone. Get published and attend a poetry slam. Find the courage to get on stage and express your voice. Don't just tell me you like to paint. Pick up a book called *Artists' Market* and get your work noticed. Don't tell me that you love to sing. Volunteer at the local opera house and immerse yourself in a type of classical singing that most teens know nothing about. Don't tell me you worry about the environment. Create a local chapter of the Sierra Club at your school and get involved in the community.

Speak at open forums in the community like town meetings to express a need to take better care of the environment and provide concrete plans for how to do that.

Some of the best ideas I have seen begin off beat. This is especially true because admission's officers are desperately seeking someone who marches to the beat of their own drum. Colleges want variety and experiences. Dorky can sell. Drummers in a school band, though not bad, are relatively prosaic. The student who works for the school newspaper is repeated throughout 35,000 high schools. How many students start an astronomy club or knit or teach dance at a senior citizen's home? Dare to be different. Different is a great way to stand out. The best ideas are ones I have not thought about or witnessed yet. Be creative!

Not only should a student maximize the potential of his or her activity or hobby, he or she should do it long term. Every admission's office has seen the student who suddenly is inspired to join a group or start a club or learn an instrument or play a sport first semester senior year. The student who does nothing for three years and is suddenly "Mr. Popular" on campus is not fooling anyone except himself. If you are really passionate about something, show the passion. For example, volunteering in your Sunday school is not a bad thing but volunteering once or twice senior year is lame and obvious. Instead start volunteering as a freshman EVERY Sunday. After three years and some effort the student can move from volunteer in the first grade room to a teacher in the $3^{rd}$ grade room to the one training his replacement for the $4^{th}$ graders, $4^{th}$ graders who will continue to write letters and notes to him the first two years he is at college. Volunteering twice will log maybe four hours of community service. Volunteering once a week for four years - conservatively speaking - is about 400 hours! In this case, more is better. The student has not only shown real dedication, a sincere desire to make a difference and demonstrated his faith; he has also shown leadership, initiative and trustworthiness.

*What activities just don't sell?*

Nothing is "bad." I can take the most boring or oft repeated activity and turn it into something for a resume. There are two general rules. Rule number one: can you show that you are the best or most dedicated at what you do? Excellence is never boring. Being the best is never like everyone else. Rule number two: sell it. Sometimes this comes down to packaging what you are actually doing or getting the publicity for what you accomplish.

For example, some years ago I was working with a young man who struggled to find something for his resume. He was a key part of his Academic Decathlon team and a passive member of the National Honor Society. He didn't have much else, though. After prodding him he finally admitted, a little ashamed, that he also worked. Ok. I can work with that. Work where? He confessed that it was not a company that he worked for. Rather he would build dog houses and sell them at a local swap meet on the weekends. This was better than I hoped. This was enormously better than the local fast food restaurant. Building dog houses made him a business owner. I had him register his business and viola - he was a teenage business owner. He didn't "do" anything extra. The young man just rephrased what he was already doing.

There are however two warnings as well. First, do not do an activity only because everyone else is doing the activity. For example: the time-honored trek to the homeless shelter by middle class teens at Thanksgiving to do their duty serving turkey to the homeless. As noble as this gesture may seem, it is weak and pathetic. The shelter will take almost any help it can get. You are not special. You are not really making a difference. If this is an issue you really care about, why just Thanksgiving? Volunteer four hours a week. All year. What does shelving books at the local library really say about you? Couldn't another teen do this just as easily? And please, visiting Grandma at the nursing home counts for nothing. It is your own grandmother! The same goes for babysitting your little brother. Don't even try to count this as community service.

The second warning is to do something that matters and that you care about. It is closely related to the first warning. One of the high schools I work closely with had a large service project for the National Honor Society. The chapter of National Honor Society made it mandatory for students in the group. It was a major project for the quarter. All the students (60 or so) met at a nearby park after school and picked up dog droppings for two hours. Really! Who thinks that an admission's officer will read that in the comfort of his slightly too warm office with a fresh cup of hot chocolate on his desk and think, "Gosh, those kids are really making a difference in the world." If the local National Honor Society had not done this the parks and recreation service would have asked the local jail to have prisoners come and provide the same service. This kind of activity is simply a waste of time and resources - not to mention slightly disgusting. Do something else. There is no such thing as the best dog poo picker upper.

*Is one set of activities or hobbies actually better than another?*

When in doubt, go big. Think national. For example, especially when we are speaking of top tier schools, best wrestler in the school is nice. Best wrestler in the region or state is better. What I would really shoot for . . . Olympics! No, I really am not joking. Writing a poem for the school newspaper is cute. Performing a poem for a city poetry slam is better. Getting published in a teen poem anthology is best. Go big!

*What if I don't like to do anything?*

This is actually the most difficult student with whom to work. I don't believe that a student cares about nothing. Rather, the student is too apathetic or lazy to take any action. This is just an excuse. Find something. Find something sooner than later. It is okay to try three or four or five activities until you find the one that fits.

With this kind of student, I strongly recommend the parents get more involved. I fully understand about having a busy career and being tired after work. Make the time. Don't take "no" for an answer. If you don't get involved, this light of your life will still be sitting on your couch waiting for inspiration at twenty-six.

Join a gym. Take her to a city council meeting. Pay for guitar lessons or tae-kwon-do lessons or cello or ceramics. If the student likes television, give her acting classes. If the student enjoys reading, encourage him to start a book club - or a comic book club. Have the student volunteer with the local YMCA or church or Kiwanis Club or senior center. Start a business. Take a class together at the local community college on astronomy or cooking or tango or history or creative writing. Get involved with UNICEF or Feed the Children or Habitat for Humanity or Green Peace or the Sierra Club or Amnesty International. Write an article for the local paper on a beached whale or a poem about whale song or an article for a magazine that takes unsolicited research on migratory patterns of the blue whale. Learn scrimshaw or clog dancing or yodeling. Go down to the local senior community and start a living history project recording the memories of the Korean War and the 1950's from the senior citizens. Then write an article about the project and enter a contest or create a presentation for the local American Legion chapter or Elk's Club. Start attending the local church / cathedral / mosque / temple and talk to the pastor / priest / imam / rabbi about getting more involved in the community and finding a spiritual element in your life or starting an English conversation class for members who are still learning

English. Then actually get involved - and not just one day a week. Become instrumental in your church / cathedral / mosque / temple until when your student leaves for the university the religious institution of your choice doesn't know how to continue the programs for which your student has been the backbone the last three years.

And please, in these cases do this with your student. A student that refuses to try or do anything is often in need of attention more than anything else. Find an hour a week to pursue a hobby or sport or event or idea together. On a hunch, one of the first joint activities to pursue might be skeet shooting - with junior's x-box and video games as the first target. Video games while not all bad and certainly entertaining are the biggest leech on many students' time and energy. The second suggestion would be to find a pair of scissors and cut the Internet cable. If none of that works, consider sending your precious child to spend the next summer with a cousin in Guatemala or Albania or Kenya or Laos. Send him to the cousin that lives three hundred miles from the nearest electrical outlet. I can almost guarantee that at the end of the summer the student will have found something to interest himself with - and maybe can talk about his new interest with an acquired facility in a foreign language.

*My daughter plays in the school band. Is one instrument better than another?*

I am delighted your daughter is pursuing music. I am actually a big believer in the link between music and the brain. If your daughter really pursues excellence, any instrument will be superb. I have three preferences when it comes to musical instruments, though. First, I really like the oboe or bassoon. Second, I love the violin. Third, I try to avoid "strange" instruments.

If the goal is simply to allow your child to love music or to better understand her culture or to develop deeper math skills, any instrument will do. If the goal is winning scholarship money for music, then there are really two venues in a university: marching band and orchestra. Most universities have both. Some instruments are wonderfully versatile and can be used in both venues. Other instruments really only fit one type of music. So, what instruments will be the most useful for a university?

Every lunch at every high school in America will sport a handful of teens walking around with a guitar. Jimmy Buffett in his book *A Pirate Looks at 50* speaks of why he first learned the guitar - girls. He witnessed another young man attract a bevy of beauties by simply playing three chords. Jimmy Buffett was hooked, and a legend was born. I am of the opinion that so many of the students walking around at lunch with a guitar have the same fascination. Unfortunately, a guitar is not the most complex instrument to learn and not adaptable to either band or orchestra.

A bassoon or an oboe has the distinction of being some of the most uncool instruments on the planet. Both instruments require quite a bit of effort to learn, have a terribly ungainly sound, and are unique enough to cause great consternation if trying to replicate the sound with another instrument. Both instruments are essential to an orchestra and very useful for a band. Yet, there are precious few students that learn either instrument. On a scale of 1-10 on how "sexy" an instrument is, an oboe ranks about -2. Even a clarinet, flute or piccolo is cooler. Drums are a 10! But drums while essential to band and useful to an orchestra are much easier to learn and have thousands of devoted adherents.

A violin is one of the most magical instruments. I read once that the range of sounds created by a violin are equaled only by the human voice. A violin is also a terribly complex instrument to learn well. If a freshman begins at the University of Rochester and wants to learn the drums or xylophone, she can sound quite good by sophomore year. If a student wants to learn the violin, by senior year she will still need work. A university can't use her. In addition, the violin is one of those instruments that every orchestra needs more. I have never met a conductor for a college orchestra that can't find room for one more violin, especially if she started at 6. If the orchestra is losing its first and second chair violins this year to graduation and your daughter has real talent, which could translate to real money.

I avoid instruments that are . . . strange. Some instruments possess a wonderfully unique sound, are very specialized or reflect a specific culture. None of these are bad. In terms of money for scholarships these instruments are limited. For example, a Theremin. Unique? Yes. Fairly cool? Absolutely! Useful in a school band? Forget it. Another example: the sitar. Super unique instrument. A key instrument if one has an obsession with playing the Beatles' "Norwegian Wood." The sitar evokes complex and rich imagery of South Asia. The sitar does not however have many orchestral compositions. Nor can the sitar really substitute well for a cello or viola.

Again, any instrument has value. If your daughter is choosing an instrument because she loves it, by all means pursue that instrument. If your daughter is hoping to learn an instrument in part for college scholarships, then seek an instrument that is useful in a band and / or orchestra and difficult to learn. The more difficult an instrument, the better.

*How important are the summers?*

There is a mixed response to this. Many books like this advise that the summer should be time for rest and family activities. I disagree. Far too many of the admission's officers I have spoken with want to know how the student occupied himself or herself in the summer. This makes sense as doing nothing requires no effort. Being involved and using the school break shows initiative. Summers are also a great time to delve more deeply into a project that gets pushed off during school. Though I can find support for "family time" in the summer, in the end the question becomes, "What is your competition doing this summer?" "Is there a way to sell yourself better?"

*What summer programs are best?*

The most competitive. The more competitive the summer program the better. Absolute best choice is a class, program or competition that highlights the student's interests or future goals. For example, have your aspiring oncologist do an internship researching cancer pathology with T-Gen. Have your math geek enroll in the MITES program at MIT. Have your legal eagle spend a summer at Notre Dame with a pre-law magnet. The key here is selective.

So, first choice for summers: an extremely selective summer program in the field of interest. As the key is "extremely selective" it is a good idea to apply to more than one. In a perfect world your student will have a choice as to which program to pursue.

Second choice: extremely selective summer program in a general field or outside of interest. (I.E., Creative writing or computers)

Third choice: Class at the local high school or community college for advancement. Be sure this is not a drop back class.

Fourth choice: Pursue community service programs.

Last choice: Please do not, under any circumstances, just allow your teen to sit on the couch all summer while binge watching "Walking Dead" or "Green Arrow" television shows.

I have included a list of some quality summer programs in Appendix 3. Some of these are competitions or contests, but summer programs are mixed into the list. Obviously I have not included every summer program possible. There are so many more. I have tried to emphasize either programs with financial aid available or programs that my students have used in the past.

*I received a flyer in the mail for my son (or daughter) to attend a special program for aspiring engineers at Princeton. How good is this?*

This mailing is a scam. Rather this is simply a way for a private company to make some money feeding on the fears and anxiety of parents. I know this is a scam because it came in a nice glossy envelope embossed with impressive seals and decoration. (The organization is trying to impress you.) I know it is a scam because most universities are very happy to rent out space in the summer. The fact that the program is located at Princeton or Stanford or Duke means nothing other than space was for rent. I know it is a scam because the mail was unsolicited and ends up asking for money. The universities know which programs are open to any that pay and which are actually selective. Though your student will likely have a wonderful experience, the program does nothing to benefit the student attending a university.

*What if I can't afford a summer program?*

The best summer programs will run $2-3000 for about two weeks. I understand fully how expensive that is. If you could easily afford that amount, you probably would not need a book like this. The good news is that some of the best and most competitive programs also have scholarships for which a student can apply. It is entirely possible to reduce the costs or even send your student for free. I would recommend applying to several programs. In a perfect world, your son or daughter is accepted at all programs and in the wonderful position to choose his or her favorite. I don't necessarily recommend trying to do multiple programs like this in a single summer. Alternately, save $800 for three years for a single awesome program between junior and senior year. Just remember, if the program's acceptance is only hinging on your ability to pay, then the program is probably not as competitive as I am looking for.

*Does it benefit my student to travel abroad?*

In general, no. In most cases admission's officers understand that going to France or Spain or China simply means that you have money to spare on a luxury. Students do not glean much from two weeks traveling the highlands of Scotland or the beaches of Costa Rica. I heartily support students going to a foreign country and strongly believe that there are many positives from such an experience. These trips do not serve college applications much. Please do not allow your student to write a personal statement about how much his life transformed while watching a sunset over the Parthenon or how she suddenly found herself while searching for a Caravaggio in Rome. These essays tend to ring hollow.

As with everything else, there are exceptions. A have had a student who traveled to Mexico twice a year - Christmas break and summer. She would stay there for upwards of a week at Christmas and almost a month in the summer. During the time she would help a small community through a mission with her church. It was more manual labor than vacation, and it was a labor that she undertook for three years. This is an experience that I urged the young woman to highlight.

There are programs to send very wealthy students to "feed the starving children in Africa" for a low fee of only $5000. I would again urge restraint. Though the spirit of such a venture seems to closely mirror the student who traveled to Mexico, as the trip is prepackaged and has less to do with generosity of spirit than padding a college application, most schools (not all) see right through it. To be clear, the trip has little to do with the location and much more to do with the impetus. What are the student's reasons for going? If the student wants a vacation, send him to Sweden or Japan or Australia. If the student is looking to pad the resume, then find another avenue. If the student is sincerely trying to give something back to a community, then be sure you can document not only the trip but the reason why.

*Should my student work?*

    Like the previous question, the answer depends on the motivations. As a whole I do not recommend working. Many many many years ago, when I was going through this process, a job was a positive. A job showed responsibility and motivation. A job spoke to my character. Today it is more often a hindrance. I have three specific objections to students working.

    First, with more and more universities, financial aid is subtracted by working. Let me explain in a story. Let us pretend I am working with a student called Andrea. Andrea wants a job. She ends up working at the mall in a clothing store that she often frequents. Andrea figures out that she can afford to work Wednesday night from 6 to close (at 10), Thursday and Friday from 4-8, and Saturday from 9 a.m. to 5 p.m. That is a total of 20 hours - a respectable number in high school. Andrea should still have time to do her homework, only gets home late once a week, still has Sunday free for family and community service, and can still play soccer in high school as most games are Tuesday afternoon. If she is making $10 an hour to keep things simple (obviously she knows the manager somehow), Andrea can make $800 a month. Take 15% off for taxes and deductions. That leaves $650. Andrea takes $50 a month for transportation expenses (gas for the car that Dad gave her). Andrea also wants half ($300) for "spending money." Most of that goes to clothes at the same store she is working and Saturday night movies with her friends. The other $300 she allows Dad to bank for college. At the end of two years, Dad has saved $7200 for Andrea. This seems like a respectable sum.

Senior year Andrea gets into her first choice school - for the sake of the story we will call the school the University of OMG (not a real school but using real numbers). The school, an excellent liberal arts college, costs $65,000 a year. Not to worry, Andrea has earned a merit-based scholarship ($20,000) with a solid 27 on her ACT and 3.65 GPA (weighted). In addition, Andrea gets a small scholarship for soccer at $3000 a year. She also receives a $1000 scholarship for coming from Minnesota, a state not usually utilized by the University of OMG. Finally Andrea receives a need-based aid package of $26,000. That means Andrea can subtract $50,000 from the tuition leaving $15,000 a year for an excellent education. All things considered, this is a decent package. While not free, the offer now makes Andrea's first choice school competitive with large in state public schools.

But wait.

Once the school receives the FAFSA the University of OMG notices that Andrea has been working. By the school's calculation, Andrea should have $24,000 in savings. The university figures that Andrea has saved her entire paycheck - every penny including what is taken out in deductions - for the last two years. The University of OMG, like most schools, wants their cut. Her revised package reduces her $26,000 in financial need to $2,000. Andrea now owes $39,000! The next year, when Andrea's savings have been completely drained and then some, the school will most likely not adjust the financial aid. Andrea will have been expected to have continued to work saving an additional $24,000 a year! Her part time job where she saved $7200 now costs her $92,000.

While not every school deducts money a student makes on a part time job, the trend to deduct is increasing. I have resorted a bit to hyperbole in my example, but I have witnessed such a transaction with at least two applications.

The second reason I don't recommend working is that Andrea is now spending almost 20 hours a week working. While I understand the benefits of learning responsibility and time management, I also understand economics. If Andrea - who remember had 20 hours a week to work at the mall - spends half that time or 10 hours studying every week for the ACT, she can increase her ACT scores dramatically. To go back to our story, the University of OMG offered a $20,000 merit-based scholarship for a 27 on the ACT. After studying 10 hours a week for two years, Andrea has raised her ACT to a 33. This is a monster increase. The merit-based scholarship at the University of OMG for a 31 or higher on the ACT is $30,000 a year for four years. If we add the soccer scholarship and the golly Minnesota scholarship and the $24,000 in need based aid back in, Andrea is now receiving $58,000 a year. That leaves Andrea paying only $7000 a year. Which do you think is a better deal? What high school job will allow Andrea to bank as much money as an awesome merit based scholarship?

There is a third reason I don't like high school students working. Teenagers all seem to apply for the same types of jobs. In most cases my teens work at the mall, the movie theater or fast food. All three types of jobs necessitate a lot of contact with other young people. That of course is part of the appeal for teenagers. I have listened to students gossip for twenty years. The Puritan in me has heard students gush about how many hook ups and phone numbers and first dates have been acquired at work. High school is distracting enough.

*I worry about my student being over scheduled. How much is too much?*

There I no answer that fits everyone. The rule of thumb that I use is how much time is your teen sleeping, texting, playing video games, watching entire television series, or spending time on the Internet? If you suddenly kill the Internet, does your teen suddenly do a good impression of the Incredible Hulk? If your teen has a lot of time for the above activities, then yes, a little more structure would probably be a good idea. On the other hand, if your teen goes from school to soccer practice and then tries to eat dinner while doing homework for three AP classes finally falling into a zombie like state around 2 a.m. on a daily basis, then your teen may already be over booked - at least until soccer season is over.

I have found that much of the problem is that students really don't know anything about time management. Students think they have no time only because they do not know how to schedule their time. Many of the same students who insist they have no time at all, freshmen year in college look back in awe at the amount of time they really did have. I am a firm believer that learning good time management in high school can lead to more success in college - and in life. Any teen that tells me he is far too busy I challenge to work a full time job while going to school for a master's degree and raising two young children while trying to stay married! If your teen says she is really too busy, try keeping a journal for one week: all activities on a 30 minute by 30 minute schedule. The teen might be surprised by how much time she really does have.

Very recently I was explaining to a student how her grades would most likely improve if she had more time studying and less time on her phone. I challenged her to drop her phone in the toilet and see how much time she had. The student vociferously disagreed. As she explained this conversation to her mother later that evening she was waving her cell phone back and forth to illustrate the point - and her moral outrage at the suggestion. About three quarters of the way through the conversation her grip slipped, God laughed and the phone went sailing like a wounded bird across the room. A sickening crack alerted my horror-filled student that her phone had just died a quick and miserable death. Distraught and in tears the teen begged Mom to drive her (speeding if possible) to the nearest Apple Store. The teen then learned that Mom had *declined* the insurance when she had purchased the phone. Repair was impossible. Mom refused, despite the pleas and tears, to replace the phone. Two weeks later the teen's grades had indeed risen considerably. I learned the story when her mother called to thank me about two weeks later.

Another idea. Look for alternative scheduling. For example, instead of coming straight home where the teen is distracted by television and the Internet, noisy siblings and, of course, all the chores he likes to help out with, go to the public library for two hours first. There is a distinct possibility that lack of time is not a problem as much as how the time is being used. Kidnap the phone. Hold it hostage until the math homework is finished. I know a lot of teens that spend four hours a night in their room "doing homework." Every time a parent calls the young man out of the self-imposed exile the teen rolls his eyes exclaiming how these endless distractions - like the fifteen seconds necessary to move his shoes into the bedroom - are why he can not get any homework done. Yet if the phone disappears, the teen finishes the same workload in an hour. When your teen tells you that he has to have his phone to get help from his friends, make him do the homework at the kitchen table.

My younger son really could not concentrate at home. He worked out an alternative schedule where when he came home from school about 3, he went to his room and crashed. About 6:30 or so I would wake him up for dinner. At about 7:30 he would start his homework. At 9:00 or 9:30 he would stop. That is when he would get out his phone and watch Netflix or talk to his friends - all of whom were curiously still awake. He had rarely finished everything by the time he fell asleep around 11 or 11:30, so he would set his alarm for 4 a.m. At that hour the whole house was quiet. He could concentrate completely on his work. The time from 4-6am was usually plenty. When finished, he would fall back to sleep until rising to go to school at 7 a.m. In total he would sleep maybe 8-9 hours. He would do homework maybe four hours. The schedule was a bit disjointed and probably would not have worked for me, but this young man found the early morning when everyone else was asleep to be really productive.

Another possibility is looking for holes in the day. For example, what is the teen doing at lunch? Would it be possible to eat in fifteen minutes and spend the next thirty in the school library? How much time is spent on the bus? Instead of staring out the window, read the novel for English class. There are always minutes that can be recaptured or redirected.

## Chapter 6: Touchdown!

Sports are a big factor in higher education. On one hand the activity shows time management, dedication and a drive to succeed. There is also a very real financial aspect to sports. For the student, many hope to spin a successful college career into professional sports. For the colleges and universities, too, sports can mean big money. A school with a nationally recognized sports team can make more money in a single year from television and commercial rights than anything else that year. That does not even take into account the merchandising and the alumni effect.

The single most important question I have for a student who is interested in sports: "Are you hoping to go pro or is this simply a way to pay for college or are you just looking for some exercise?" The answer changes the perspective quite a bit. If a student has aspirations of going pro, he or she really needs (with a few exceptions) to attend a big state school. For the others a small Division III school might be the best choice.

Keep in mind, just because a student wants to go pro doesn't mean it is in the cards. A few years ago I was working with a young woman - a brilliant young woman - who loved basketball. She (and her parents) loved the game. She was convinced she had what it took to go professional. About half way through sophomore year she dropped all of her honors and AP classes as the classes were taking away too much time for practice. I tried to talk her - and her mother - out of this to no avail. The girl, and I never saw her play, for all of her ambition and passion was only 5'1" and a little less than 100 lbs. In sports there are certain physical absolutes. When I pointed this out, the girl rattled off a series of names - women in the WNBA that were well below the average height. I am sure her numbers were right, but I play the odds. For the same reason when I visit Las Vegas, I enjoy the shows and love the food, but I stay well away from the roulette wheel. I know what the odds are. In the end, the girl's grades were not horrible, but she didn't have anything extra to offer. She ended up going to a community college where she wasn't even able to make the basketball team. Not only would she never go pro, she lost any opportunity at a better school and a better scholarship.

*Do sports still help a student get financial aid?*

Yes. But not as much as they used to. Sports are HUGE money makers for a school. According to *Sports Business Journal*, Arizona State University can expect to clear $8 million for advertising, media rights, and sponsoring in the 2015-2016 season. (Http://www.sportsbusinessdaily.com/Journal/Issues/2016/05/02/Colleges/ASU.aspx) A PAC10 school can clear more than $100 million a year in television rights. (Http://businessofcollegesports.com/2011/05/05/televison-contract-breakdown/). What this means is that a school has a very real financial incentive to attract the best athletes - especially for the holy trinity of football, baseball and men's basketball - also of note are women's basketball, gymnastics and softball. In addition, victory in sports entices alumni and other donors to dig deeper and creates a brand name for the school. All of this is hard to measure in a dollar amount. Is it any wonder that a new football field is a higher priority than new dorms or science labs? Is it any wonder that at many schools the head football coach is paid more than the president of the university?

The sports with the most active high school participation (football, track and field, baseball, and soccer for men; track and field, volleyball, basketball, soccer and softball for women) are not represented in the same proportions in college. Again the reason is primarily economic. It is entirely normal to sit down in front of the television to catch a Pac 10 football game or even a softball tournament. My father can easily list off the top college basketball players this season but would really struggle to name a single soccer player. When was the last time you caught a 500 meter race outside of the Olympics? The colleges, like everyone else, follow the money, and in this case that means advertising dollars and marketing.

Does this translate to more money for students? Not really. Part of the reason is that there are so many students trying to cash in. Part of the reason is that there are caps on how much can be given to students for sports. Part of the reason is economics. The schools don't have to give more. The less the school gives out, the more the school keeps.

The rules vary depending on which conference the school plays in and the school itself. Generally speaking schools are divided into Division I, II and III. A lot, though not all, of that determination is on size of the university. In VERY rough numbers, Division I is most of the big public universities. Division II is medium size schools - both public and private. Division III is small private schools. Keep in mind, this system is more complex than I am explaining here.

Division I and II schools can give scholarships in varying amounts. Division I gives more money. Division III schools can not give sports' scholarships. A Division III school can give a promising student athlete a "leadership scholarship." Though I am certain the school will insist the monies are not tied to athletics. That would technically be illegal. The school despite being Division III still likes to win.

*What are the odds of my child receiving a sport's scholarship?*

About 2%. Only 2% of high school athletes end up with college money (https://www.cbsnews.com/news/8-things-you-should-know-about-sports-scholarships/). In addition, the average amount is less than $11,000 a year. I would go one step further and tell you that the averages are out of balance. There are certain sports - head count sports (football and basketball for men and basketball, gymnastics, volleyball and tennis for women) where a Division I school is obligated to give all or nothing. The numbers given are really not terribly impressive. If the statistics say the "average" package is $11,000, but three students get a full ride at $42,000 per year, that number really skews the averages. More realistic is $2-3,000 per year. Keep in mind: there are always exceptions.

*So, if my son is a real star on the football field can he get a full ride?*

Maybe. First, who says he is a real star? Dad? The coach? A college scout from a small school without a competitive program? The head coach from the University of Texas? Just because "someone" says your son is a star means little. There are maybe a million students playing high school football and only about 20,000 football scholarships available. Even a smaller number of these scholarships are a full ride. A football team has to flesh out an entire team. One star quarterback - who may not start until his junior year - can not justify sacrificing two offensive linemen, a lightning fast running back and a defensive tackle that made three students lose control of their bladder this season. This also brings up another point. What are the needs of the individual team? If a team does not need a quarterback this year, it will be really difficult to get that full ride.

Another very important point has to do with scholarship. A fantastic quarterback - or server or guard - with a 2.0 GPA and a 16 on the ACT is not really wanted. A school can't use a player that can't qualify to play. While many high school coaches will find loop holes and play a mediocre student, colleges are under a lot more scrutiny. Another point on this issue is that many schools putting up so much money will see athletics as a full time job. What grades will your student receive? If he or she is put into "special" classes for athletes, what degree will he or she receive?

*What is the value of a partial sports scholarship?*

Under current regulations, schools are given a specific number of scholarships that are offered for a sport. Often a partial scholarship can be adequate when combined with other incentives like academic merit-based scholarships, other merit-based scholarships and academic need scholarships. The average scholarship amount for students today is less than $10,000 a year. As part of a whole package, though, a sports scholarship of even a moderate amount might lead to an affordable education. Once again, colleges are really looking for the scholar - athlete today.

The days are gone where the best jump shot at your neighborhood court in Brooklyn is sufficient. Athletics can give you a big boost, but what else do you bring to the table? This is probably the best advice for athletes. Think of sports as part of the package - not the whole package. While there are exceptions, and those exceptions will make the local paper, the real advantage is adding something extra to your application to a competitive school. Athletics may be the edge your son or daughter needs to get into that excellent engineering or environmental sciences program that otherwise might be out of reach. While the extra few thousand dollars for volleyball may be welcome, the real money is in the rest of the package at that elite school.

*Is there more money for female athletes?*

Title IX guaranteed that women and men receive the same monies for athletic scholarships. On paper what this means is that if a school has $100,000 set aside for male athletes, the school should have $100,000 set aside for female athletes. To be fair, schools will stretch the limits on this and try to find ways around this rule. The reason is obvious. Men's basketball has the potential to bring in MILLIONS more than women's basketball in television rights, marketing, branding and alumni donations. It may not be equitable, but the imbalance is real. Despite that, there is still quite a bit of money available for women athletes. It seems like there is actually more money for female athletes because of simple math. There are fewer women competing in fewer sports for an equal amount of money. That means your son on third base will most likely get less money than his twin sister in softball. I strongly encourage women especially to pursue athletics. There is a much better chance of getting scholarship money.

In addition, high schools as well as colleges have a distinct bias. Women's sports are just not given the same acclaim as men's sports. While it is considered normal by most schools to have the football team practice four hours a night six nights a week, women's sports will not garner the same dedication. As such, there is less pressure on a female athlete, so that she can do well on the athletic field AND in the classroom.

*What percentage of high school athletes play in college?*

The best answer is found from the NCAA itself. Go to http://www.ncaa.org/about/resources/research/estimated-probability-competing-college-athletics. One can see that the number of students who successfully transfer to college sports is not terribly large. The best numbers seem to be for ice hockey! Also, note which sports are recruiting by division. For example, while the numbers for baseball in Division I and Division II are about the same, there is a small increase with Division III. Football, though, seems to say go big or go home. Division I and III take the lion's share with relatively few going on to Division II. Swimming, both men's and women's, seems to be the same.

When looking at these percentages, keep in mind that high school sports have become increasingly competitive and increasingly expensive. Your son's competition in baseball has had private pitching and batting coaches from the major league, attended summer camps for years, travels with his club to eight different states and plays year round - since he was 6! If the only time your son spends on the baseball field is after his high school day has finished, competition for a few top spots on a university team becomes a challenge for which natural talent alone can not compensate.

*Is there money at a Division III school?*

A Division III school can not offer money directly for athletics. The school can offer a competitive academic package and merit-based scholarships. Many Division III schools still have competitive sports teams. Be careful with this. There is an increasing trend with Division

III schools because of escalating costs or simply the focus of the school to remove competitive sports and just have intermural sports. If a Division III school is pursing national standings with its track team or happens to have a phenomenal coach for a volleyball program that has sent girls to the last three Olympics, the school is very likely to find money in some form for the student. I have never had an issue getting a great student - athlete money from a Division III school. By the same token, just having a baseball team does not mean the school is trying to pursue any excellence in baseball. Many of the smaller Division III schools will pick and choose which athletic programs to actually pursue. An easy question to ask during the tour or college interview is in what sports the school sees itself as most competitive. (Ask this before the admission's officer knows what sport your son or daughter plays.)

*What about more obscure sports?*

I really like obscure college sports like squash, fencing, bowling, archery, field hockey, water polo, ice hockey and rifle. I like these sports because so few students participate. Obscure can really stand out in an application. Just noting expertise or even devotion to an obscure sport can make a student stand out from the pack. If the college or university in question has a program in that particular sport, it can lead to a huge bonus in admissions. Finally while the field is glutted in basketball, very few students can stand out in shooting or golf. One warning. Some sports are less unique and more . . . weird.

Capitalizing on the Harry Potter mania, more and more colleges have begun to offer Quidditch. While an interest in Quidditch can help a student look a bit more three dimensional and make an admission's officer smile, don't expect Quidditch to translate to real money. I heartily endorse interests and hobbies that stand out like Quidditch or rodeo or bass fishing or roller derby, but a parent should not expect this to be a golden ticket to the college of your dreams - unless the admission's officer reading the application is a national champion bull rider. One never knows when a peculiar interest or hobby may strike a particular admission's officer.

*What about crew?*

There are a handful of sports that are hallmarks of a certain socioeconomic group: crew, polo, equestrian sports and - to a lesser extent - lacrosse. These sports are found almost exclusively at top tier universities like Princeton or Notre Dame or Duke. One advantage of the sports is that these activities are a bit more obscure. Just about every public high school, and most private high schools, have a baseball team. How many schools do you know that boast a crew team? Another advantage of the sport is that all these sports take quite a bit of training and skill. A student can not get into a shell or on a horse for the first time freshman year and be competitive by senior year. All this means that top tier universities really value these sports, and that can lead to a distinct advantage in admissions. To be clear, just playing a few competitions or knowing how to ride a horse is not the same thing as actually having skills. Skills are still a prerequisite.

The down side is that these sports are hugely expensive. A hockey family can shell out quite a bit of money on equipment, travel, private coaches, camps and summer programs. Hockey has nothing on polo. Whereas Hockey can cost a car or two, polo may cost an average house or two. This makes these sports naturally selective - only a select few can afford the sports. In addition, because the activities cost so much schools are loathe to have a program. Most programs can only be found through private groups.

*Why should my son / daughter attend a Division I school?*

I generally prefer smaller liberal arts schools. As a whole I feel the smaller schools offer a better education dollar for dollar. One of the biggest exceptions to this is in terms of athletics. Simply put, a student who is hoping to go professional or to the Olympics will have a much more difficult time getting noticed at a Division III school than a Division I school. Keep in mind, just because Dad and the high school coach dream about junior playing for the Dallas Cowboys does not mean Junior can actually get there. That being stated, a young athlete has a much better chance of being noticed by the NFL at the University of Texas - Austin than at St. Edward's (also in Austin). Nothing is impossible, but I do like to play the odds. For the same reason, I don't gamble in Las Vegas. In theory I could win, but . . .

Another reason for a large school is the athletic facilities. Smaller schools will complain that they, too, have excellent facilities, but the fact of the matter is that Loyola - New Orleans does not have the same resources or impetus to invest money in its athletic fields, dorms, coaching staff, programs and facilities that a Louisiana State University possesses. Again this is just money. I don't know of any national networks that will pay millions to watch Loyola play, but an LSU / 'Bama face off can be legendary.

A larger school will also play in larger conferences. A student at Stetson University in Florida will travel around the state of Florida and perhaps in the Southeastern region. A student at Florida State University is much more likely to travel around the country for a game, especially if the sport in question makes it to playoffs or national championships that year. A large public school offers more opportunities not just for travel but for visibility and name recognition.

Finally, there is no experience that a Beloit University in Wisconsin can offer in comparison to walking onto the football field at the University of Wisconsin on a crisp October afternoon when the stadium is awash in red and white as the stadium erupts in a crescendo of a noise and the bass of the school band reverberates through the streets of Madison. The experience of a large stadium on national television before hundreds of thousands of viewers can just not be duplicated by smaller schools.

*Why should my son / daughter attend a Division III school?*

A degree. Division III schools (especially private liberal arts schools) offer an excellent education. A student-athlete can really fill out his or her financial aid packages with a combination of grades, test scores and athletics. A student can still enjoy playing, can still experience the game, and still get some exercise while attending school. He may not ever go professional or be recruited by that team whose banners adorn his room, but he can enjoy the sport and graduate college with little or no debt. The question I began the chapter with was whether a student wanted to be a professional athlete or use sports to afford school? A Division III school is a better choice for the second option.

*What can I do to help my son or daughter pursue an athletic scholarship?*

The single biggest factors are time and money. As to time, the more time your son or daughter has to devote to a sport the better he or she will be. Natural talent is very real, but there are few Michael Jordans in the world. Even for a Michael Jordan, if he did not spend hours and years practicing and perfecting his art, his name would not adorn sneakers for the youth of America. Any sport takes dedication and practice. Start early - like elementary school. Practice often - more than required. If a student really wants to pursue a sport, just the required school practices will never be adequate. Also look at off season sports that will enhance the primary sport, like running cross country in the fall to be better prepared for softball in the spring. In addition, please look into club sports. These are private teams that will practice and play year round. Camps and private coaches are more and more becoming the norm - though these are an expensive choice.

This is where the money comes in. Club sports - and the transportation to and from the practices and games, the insurance, the food you need to bring every other Thursday night, the pizza after a win and the ice cream after a loss, the private coach, the extra fees for time in the batting cage, the new cleats and the $300 bat, registration fees and the day off to help take the team to a game two states away - costs a lot. Teams with a noted coach will help your teen be more competitive, but you should expect to pay for the privilege. If the coach asks for extra batting practice or an additional pitching coach or a summer camp for girls' basketball in Indiana or private rink fees for ice skating, the money really begins to add up. I have met parents that spend around $20,000 a year for their teen to pursue a sport. This price is not even considered terribly expensive anymore!

Find the right school. No club can compare with the clout of a competitive high school. If this is really important to you, consider moving in middle school to the correct high school zone. There are rather strict rules about a school recruiting athletes from other schools. If your all American boy transfers February of sophomore year for baseball, expect him to sit the year out. If you really see this as a priority, moving to the right zip code may come with inherent benefits. It is difficult for the best athlete to be noticed on a losing team.

Start talking with the coaches - high school and club. Express what you are looking for. What program, what school do you have in mind? When can your student start playing varsity sports? Ask for honest feedback. Can your student really compete at that level? Junior year -

not senior year - start calling the universities that are at the top of the list. Talk to the coaches at that university. Ask if the coach is coming out to your city or state?

Record. An increasingly adaptable trick is YouTube. You can record your son or daughter yourself. Post the video on You Tube and invite the coach at the interested universities to watch the video. A coach is much more likely to watch a six minute video on YouTube or on an Internet link than load up a CD or DVD. If you choose to do this, be sure to note which student is yours. You don't necessarily want to promote the kid on the other team. Speak with the coach about what you can and can't show. FERPA regulations have gotten quite stiff about producing video images of students younger than 18 that have not signed off. Don't have a blooper reel attached as a secondary link. Remember you are trying to put your son or daughter in the best light, not the sixteen times she got stuffed the worst in volleyball.

Don't ignore the grades. A student that can't play because he or she is academically ineligible is useless. By the same token, be careful of the coach or athletics program that councils taking the easiest classes or the easiest teachers. This is setting the student up for failure. A high school I worked with was very proud a few years ago about getting three different boys signed to play football at three different universities one spring. The school made a big extravaganza out of the signing event. The principal cancelled classes to showcase the event. Student government made posters. The band played. The local media came. It was a special moment for the school. The next year all three boys had dropped out of college before the first game. All three students had become ineligible in the first three or four weeks! The students had been under the impression that college teachers would cut them the same slack as high school. The students were not academically ready for college. Things did not quite work out that way. In weeks the boys went from dreaming of their pro ball contracts to applying at fast food chains.

Finally, be realistic. I spoke with a father this year who really fantasized about his son getting a football scholarship. His son was not a star in any sense. The boy was still JV as a junior in high school. Worse in my eyes, the boy was 5'6" and maybe 115 lbs. I wasn't as worried about him making the team as what would happen to him if he did. It is nearly impossible to change genetics.

*How can the coach help me?*

Despite my warnings about coaches, the coaches are essential to the process of finding athletic scholarships. If your teen chooses to pursue athletic scholarships, tell the coach early. Ask the coach for an honest appraisal. If the coach says, "Yeah, yeah. Your boy is great. I think with a little hard work he can go pro!" and then never actually plays your boy in a game, then you should have some more questions for the coach. The coach is the first to reach out to schools, the first to tell you if a college scout is coming, and the first that a college team will ask for a recommendation. Also make it clear to the coach which schools your son or daughter is looking into senior year. A coach that only brings the scouts from the local community colleges isn't helping your teen much. Remember that you are your child's best advocate. If the high school coach is less than proactive, talk to the club coach. If that still doesn't work, talk to the university your son or daughter is interested in directly.

*What is a "Letter of Intent"?*

For Division I and II schools, a student signs a letter of intent in the spring of senior year to say, "Yes, I will attend and play at _____ University." The school in turn promises a very specific dollar amount in scholarships. Be very careful about signing this until your student has exhausted all the possible options. If a student changes his or her mind, decides he or she can't afford the school, has a girlfriend or boyfriend that attends a different school and needs to follow, or simply becomes academically ineligible, the contract is binding. Your son or daughter will not be able to play at the new transfer school for some time. Be very clear what is being offered and on what terms. If you are not sure, get a second opinion. Have the conversation with your 18 year old student that he or she is not to sign ANYTHING until you read it first. Remember, once a student turns 18 all contracts he or she signs are binding.

*What questions do I need to ask before my son / daughter signs?*

There are several questions I ask a student to keep in mind before signing. Keep in mind, some of these questions will have no concrete answer.

\*What GPA is required to stay eligible?

\*What support or tutoring is available for my student athlete?

\*How much time per week is expected in practice? How much time in the weight room?

\*Is there an alcohol policy specifically for student athletes?

\*What are the rules on endorsements and commercial contracts?

\*If my son / daughter is part of an award winning team / season, does that translate to more financial incentives (scholarships) for my student?

\*If my son / daughter has ambitions to go professional, does the coaching staff have any contacts?

*At what point could my son / daughter expect to start in a game?

*What are the expectations for my student off season?

*(Probably the most important question for me) What happens if my son / daughter is injured in terms of his / her scholarships?

Many years ago I worked with two young student athletes. Both were injured as freshmen. The young man played baseball. While still in practice, the young man took a fastball to the knee, shattering the knee. The doctor was clear that his college career was over. The very next week the school's business office told him that he needed to leave the school immediately for insufficient funds. Not only was the young man's baseball career shattered so was his college education.

About the same time I knew a young woman who played women's basketball. The woman's parents were from Estonia or Latvia. I don't remember which. The young woman was about 6' 2". In the second game of her first season, she went up for a phenomenal jump shot that seemed to defy gravity. When she came down there was a much smaller girl underneath her. Both girls were hurt rather badly. The girl from the Baltics had enough tendon damage that she never played another game. Her scholarship was not dependent upon her playing but rather on her academics. For the next four years she went to every practice, dressed out for every game, and never got off the bench. She graduated on scholarship four years later. Please find out ahead of time what happens in the event of an injury.

*The pressure of a coach.*

The high school coach has an influence on your teen that is had to underestimate. Your teen will spend four or five hours a day six days a week with his or her coach. The time, the game, the competition, and the emotional roller coaster really creates a unique bond between the student and the coach. In many homes the word of the coach is next to the gospel. This is a double-edged sword. On the positive side a wonderful coach can do much to mold and shape not only the athletic ability of your student but his or her character as well. A great coach can be more than a coach or teacher and become a mentor. There are many teens I have known that stay in contact with their coaches for years and years after high school. A truly outstanding coach can make high school an unforgettable experience. A phenomenal coach can mold and shape your student helping him or her to find the perfect university.

The other side of this equation, though, is the coach that is trying to live vicariously through your child and relive his or her own youth. Maybe worse is the coach who is more worried about winning the next game than where your student will be in four years. I have known athletic trainers who faced incredible pressure to play the kid with a concussion or tape up a broken arm knowing that another hit may require major surgery. I have known coaches who pressure teachers to change a grade on the theory that academics come second to winning Friday's game. I have known students who end up being crushed academically in college because their high school schedule was filled with class after class of only weight training and physical education. I have known students who are used as pawns to form better relationships with universities that the coach likes without considering what school is best for the student.

As a parent, please attend not only the games but the occasional practice. Check on your student's grades. If an "F" in world history suddenly changes to a "C" the afternoon of the big game, ask why. When talking about college, enlist the coach's help and advice, but remember that your son or daughter should choose the school that is best for him or her. Do not ever take the coach's word on how good a school is or how good a financial aid package is. Look into it yourself. In the end, your kid will always and forever be your kid. You will always be "Dad" and the coach, no matter how good, will only be "coach".

## Chapter 7: Where is the Circus?

There are few events more important to learning about a college than a college fair. College fairs come in a lot of different forms. There are fairs that attract 250 universities from all over the country, fairs that attract just 40 of the most select schools, fairs where three elite schools have a unique partnership and events where a single school will speak at your son or daughter's high school. I love the college fairs and the potential that the fairs represent. I encourage all of my students to attend college fairs.

*Why should I attend a college fair?*

College fairs offer unique opportunities. First and foremost the fair gives students a chance to learn more about the university. A major college fair like NACAC (http://www.nacacnet.org/college-fairs/FallNCF/Pages/default.aspx) will attract literally hundreds of colleges and universities. A student will never have the resources or the time to visit all of these schools. The fairs offer an opportunity to speak with ten or twelve universities in more depth about what the specific schools offer and what differentiates the schools from each other. There is no other forum that I know of where a student can meet the admission's staff and introduce themselves to so many colleges at once.

The second reason I really like these fairs is that they offer a unique opportunity for the student to stand out. The admissions staff that "go on tour" will meet hundreds if not thousands of students in a dozen cities or more over the course of a few weeks. Much as the hotels all start to look alike so too do the students. Just as the hotels will all try to offer something unique so too should your student. How does your student stand out from the crowd? Free breakfast buffet? Sorry, been there, done that. Instead he or she should come more prepared, more focused and more "with it" than your competition. Have better questions and a better presentation of *you* than any of the three dozen teenagers that follow your teen like a crazed pack of wildebeests.

The smaller fairs that are threesomes or foursomes like "U. Of Virginia - Duke - Emory" offer even better opportunities to get noticed and have a real conversation. Instead of four or five hundred desperate students in the room there are only 30-40. The odds are in your favor. In addition, you have more time to spend with each school.

*Which college fairs are best?*

To be honest, all the fairs are good, but they serve different purposes and different audiences. I will address three types of fairs that I deal with on the most frequent basis. I am certainly missing some.

*The NACAC Fair:*

The first type of fair, and the one I visit most frequently, is the NACAC Fair. NACAC is a consortium specifically designed to introduce the largest number of students to the largest number of colleges possible. It is very much like a circus. The fair is well advertised on the Internet and through high school counselors. The fair is free and open to the public. Anyone (even freshmen) can attend. Many cities will have large public events attached to the fair. For example: the NACAC fair in Phoenix is often preceded by a large march through downtown Phoenix, a series of tents and informational booths for high school students and local television and radio coverage. The (mostly accurate) list of which schools are attending can be found on their website (http: //www.nacacnet.org/college-fairs/FallNCF/Pages/default.aspx). The list tends to be top heavy with big state universities and has far too many for profit universities for my taste. That being said, there are often some real gems, some smaller liberal arts schools that make the pilgrimage around the nation every year.

The NACAC fairs may attract close to a thousand high school students. No matter how you approach it, that is a lot of teenagers in one very small space all clambering for attention. The fair will encourage students to preregister and fill out an information card. The student will then receive a card with a bar code that can be scanned by participating colleges to instantly upload the student's information onto their mailing list. This will cause many (most) of the students to somehow perceive this as a competition for who can get on the most university mailing lists the fastest. I have witnessed year after year students pathetically running from table to table as exhausted and disassociated college reps patiently "beep" each student with a scanner gun only to watch the student scamper to the next table.

Some basic rules I give my students when the students attend the NACAC fair.
1) Do **not** get a card with a bar code. First, I do not want my students simply running from table to table to get "beeped." What point does that prove? Remember the whole purpose of this fair is to learn more about a college or university - not get on a mailing list. Second, by not having the bar code, students are forced to slow down at the table as they stop to fill out the card. What a wonderful opportunity to strike up a conversation with the person who will most likely be the very first individual to read the admission application! Third, any cards "beeped" are

automatically entered into a computer data base. By doing the card manually, the admission's officer is now required to enter the information manually. An admission's officer will never notice a name automatically added to a computer data base, he or she may notice or remember a name that was entered manually.

2) Look up the universities in attendance and have a game plan. Do not simply run into the room and speak to the very first table or the table with the longest line. To use Phoenix as an example, the longest lines every year are for Arizona State University, which reserves three or four tables if not more, University of California (Berkeley or Los Angeles), and Grand Canyon University. Why waste time talking to Arizona State University or Grand Canyon University? Both schools are in the city, extraordinarily easy to visit, often have school field trips to visit the schools, and visit high school campuses themselves several times a year. UC - Berkeley and UCLA are big public schools in California. An Arizona student can not usually afford either school. The state of California has a state law that students from outside of California can only receive 50% aid as a maximum. At the time of this writing, out of state tuition at both schools has exceeded $50,000 a year. Even *if* your student qualifies for the full amount of scholarships and grants, you are still more than $25,000 short! Most of the families I work with simply can not afford a $25,000 price tag times four years. Avoid any schools that are in state and easy to visit later. Avoid any schools you have no hope of affording (usually large public universities). Avoid schools your student has no intention of ever attending. Look up what schools will be there in advance and plan it out. Rank the schools in order of preference and hit the top of the list first. If there is a huge line for your #3 school on the list, skip it. Go to #4 and return to #3 later. You have limited time to talk with these schools. Maximize the time.

3) Research your schools. Know what questions to ask. See the next sub-chapter in this book.

4) Don't let your student move in a pack. So many students feel insecure in this setting and naturally gravitate to moving from table to table with three or four friends. I do not recommend this. If your student is feeling insecure, let her go to the bathroom as a pack. This is not the time or place to look insecure. I want your student to speak directly to the college representative without the distraction of three friends also trying to get attention. I want the representative fully focused on your child. Later that night when the representative is writing down notes about students, I don't want the representative confused about which of the three girls all in pink sweaters made the biggest impression. Finally, your daughter's college choices probably don't match her friends' choices perfectly.

5) Let your student go by himself or herself. Go get a coffee. Go shopping and come back later. Go get lunch. Anything. Just do not go in with your student. As a parent of two boys I understand completely the urge to go with your children. You want to protect your child. You want to help. You want to make sure that he or she presents himself or herself in the best possible light. Resist the temptation.

Every year I attend these conferences I see the following exchange. Because the exchanges do not involve my students I will provide one I made up with fake people and a fake university (The University of OMG) - but very real observations.

Perky representative whose coffee buzz is just starting to wear off: "Hi. Welcome to the University of OMG. What is your name?"

Overprotective helicopter Mom steps up next to her highly nervous, annoyed and slightly petulant daughter. "Oh, her name is Tiffany."

Slightly less perky representative is looking more annoyed but still managing to paste a plastic smile over perfect teeth. Deep breath. "Oh. Hello, Tiffany. What major were you considering?"

Mom - a bit more forceful. Tiffany looks up but immediately backs down with a withering look from Mom. "Tiffany is going to be a lawyer, just like her father."

Tiffany steps back and slowly wanders over to another girl from her school as Mom continues to have a conversation with the annoyed university representative about "Tiffany's" plans.

In short, the university representative wants to get to know the student. Of course her parents can communicate better and have a better grasp of what to ask, but that is the point. Tiffany needs to be having these conversations. Mom has only insured that the University of OMG no longer considers Tiffany to be a serious candidate - at least not until she grows up. Mom for all of her best intentions is not applying to the school. If you are brave enough to send your daughter half way around the country in eight more months, then have the courage to send her alone into a room with more than a hundred universities. She needs to speak for herself. Have the faith that you have raised a young woman capable of doing that. She will surely make mistakes, but no university expects the students to be perfect.

6) Remember to smile. This is supposed to be fun. At least learn to fake it. No one likes a whiner or a pessimist.

7) Be polite. I can guarantee there will be other students (or parents) that will cut in line, try to speak over your student, insult people around them, or even hip bump someone out of line. Some students (and parents) view college fairs as a contact sport. Others just have no manners. A college representative notices all this. Sometimes the representative will actually say

something. Sometimes the representative will ignore it. I would rather the representative ignore the rude students' behavior than pay attention to your student providing a withering dissection of the rude student's heritage and lack of positive attributes. There are a few times when I have had a student speaking with a college representative, and another student will deliberately cut in line, extend his or her hand and loudly interrupt with something like: "My name is Byron. I attend (insert the name of a prominent local private school)." In most cases the representative will ignore "Byron." If the representative immediately ends the conversation with your student to now focus on "Byron," that tells you something about the school and how the school will treat your student later.

8) In two or three days, have your student send a thank you note to the colleges that he or she spoke with. Have your student send an actual hand-written note. I know. Nobody does this anymore. That is the point. It is also a good idea to follow up via email in a week or so with another good question. In addition to just being polite, it is a good way to be remembered.

*What should I ask?*

General rules for asking questions (and I will repeat these later as the questions are rather important):

*Don't ask anything you can find on a website in two minutes or less. "How much do you cost?" Stop being lazy! Look it up.

*Don't ask anything you do not really care about. "What is your school mascot?" Really? Are you really not going to attend Tulane because the mascot is the Green Wave? Does the mascot really matter to you?

* My absolute favorite stupid question: "Do you have my major?" Do you expect the college representative to be psychic? How are they supposed to know if they have your unstated major preference? In addition, isn't this a question you could just look up? I don't expect an admission's officer to have the entire list memorized.

*Ask what would actually make a difference to attending that school. "Do you have any specific companies that are used every year for internships?"

*Ask what you actually care about. "I'm a vegan. Do you have options other than a salad bar for vegan and vegetarian students?"

*Ask something that you found on the website and want more information on. (For Hendrix College) "I noticed you have a program called 'Odyssey of the Mind'. I'm not sure what that is? Can you give me details about it?" (For Goucher) "I noticed that you require all students to do a study abroad. Why?"

I can not over emphasize the effect a really good question can have. Remember these representatives see hundreds of teenagers in four to six weeks. By far the majority only look for "the beep." The rest will ask predictable lame questions that are meaningless or can be found pretty easily on the website. I can not tell you how many times I hear a student standing in front of a table for the University of Minnesota asking, "What state are you in?" There may be entire cities where a representative does not get a single well thought out question. If your student is well prepared, he or she can really stand out and make a positive impression. That is how to get a more in depth interview - a topic I will return to shortly. Finally, when your teen has done the research and found some really excellent questions, encourage him not to share those questions with his best friend since third grade. I really superb question and the impression that question creates is ruined when three or four students start asking the same question to the same schools.

*The CTCL fair:*

This may be my favorite college fair. Some years ago a pioneer in the field of college admissions, Loren Pope, wrote a book called *Colleges that Change Lives*. In the book, Mr. Pope highlighted 40 small liberal arts schools that focus not so much on the bottom line but on being a school that transforms your student's experiences and shapes his or her future. This particular fair is composed of 37-40 of the schools mentioned. As such, it is a truly wonderful opportunity to meet with some really outstanding small liberal arts colleges from all over the country. I tell my students that they can not go wrong in this room. The colleges represented are all really quality schools. That being said, a student still needs to do research, make a good impression and be aware of time management. There is no way to speak to all 40 schools. Pick five or six before attending and concentrate on those schools first. Not every school will fit every student (or every budget). The biggest downside is that the CTCL fair only visits a limited number of locations and some locations may only be revisited in three or four years. The easiest way to find out is to visit the website: http://ctcl.org/info-sessions/

*High school sponsored college fairs:*

Many high schools, especially private high schools, will invite universities. If the visit is during school hours, the visit is usually closed to outsiders. Many times, though, two or three universities of similar caliber will ask a school or district to host a public event in the evening. To find out about these events, check the university website. Duke University for example will post exactly where and when the school representatives are traveling. Get on a mailing list. If you are not sure if the event is open to the public, call or email the university. I do not recommend calling the host school. Many hosting schools will discourage outsiders on the theory that this will offer competition for the host school's students. I have even seen host schools try to turn away people at the door. If you have already spoken to the representative from Duke, you can then smile and say Mr._____ from Duke invited me.

The disadvantage of these fairs is that they are not advertised well and many will try to make your student feel unwelcome. The advantage is that the fairs tend to host a very small defined number of schools that tend to share similar characteristics such as academic rigor or selectivity. A student has a wonderful chance to speak to a representative one on one in a much smaller, quieter and more intimate session. The smaller environment also helps to reduce the stress of some students.

*How soon is too soon to attend?*

I took my own sons freshman and sophomore year. I did not expect too many schools to take either boy seriously, though some were impressed that the boys had started looking so early. I took the boys at such a young age so that the boys would get the practice speaking to colleges and asking questions. In this manner, junior and senior year both boys ended up having a lot more confidence and had a better idea of how the system worked. Junior year it is almost essential that your student attend. I want the student to start considering schools. It is possible, though not common, for a student to get an interview with a university even as a junior. What a fantastic way to make an impression. If your student follows up over the next year with contacts and questions, I can almost guarantee an advantage in the admission's process. Senior year the college fair is an absolute must. Your student must get out and meet schools and make a positive impression.

*What should I bring?*

I recommend bringing 10 copies of a scholastic resume and transcript. If the ACT /SAT scores are solid, list them. If the scores are less positive, leave the scores off. Dress well, but not too well. Wearing a full suit or tuxedo screams that your child is trying to compensate for something. Be sure to wear a smile.

*How do I follow up?*

The ultimate goal is to get a one on one interview with the college representative. Keep in mind two things. First, the college representatives have limited time and space. Not every student who wants a one on one interview gets one. Second, your student has limited time and space. He or she may very well get an interview with two or three or even four schools. More is just not practical.

How does one get that interview? That is the trick. A college representative will see over a hundred students in a two-hour meet and greet session. A representative may only have time for six to eight students. To be in that top tier a student needs to have the right numbers (grades and test scores) and ask the right questions. Questions and visible interest are the key. An excellent question or two shows a university that you have actually done research in the school beyond a poster in the counseling office. A well placed question shows that the student is a good prospect for the school. If an interview is not offered, ask for one. Worst case scenario - the representative says no and your student is exactly where he or she started.

Finally, after the fair - two or three days later - send a thank you note. Make it an actual note, not an email. Email is too impersonal. Take the time to write a real thank you note to the representative. The representative may have been stumped by a question like, "What companies do the university typically use for accounting majors?" In most cases the representative will follow up with an urge for your student to contact the accounting or business department directly. Have your student do so.

*Do I want to be on the mailing list?*

Absolutely. When first researching a college, if the college looks promising get on the mailing list. I would even say to do this as early as sophomore year. Being on the mailing list expresses interest. Will Princeton notice? Probably not. Will Union College notice? Probably. This can be key to not only showing an interest in the school but to receiving an interview or a fly out or a tuition voucher. Getting your student on the mailing list puts the student on the school's radar. The schools will then start sending big glossy brochures full of pictures of beautiful people doing happy activities and laughing on a gorgeous sunny day. Interestingly, Carleton in Minnesota and Colby in Maine almost never show pictures of the snow. The pictures imply that Minnesota and Maine are always sunny and warm. And happy. These flyers do a great job getting your student more enthusiastic about a specific college and many times can clue a student into specific programs or features that he can ask about in an interview or college visit.

*What are fly-outs?*

One of the great advantages of speaking directly with a university representative is to learn about fly outs. This is an invitation to have your student fly out to the university your student is interested in. I can not do enough to recommend a fly out. I want the student to take advantage of a fly out whenever possible. There is no better way to see if the university in question is the right fit. How does your student feel about the campus? The dorms? The other students? The demographic mix? What are the classes like? It is also a fantastic way to get a more in depth interview with the admission's office and show real interest in the school.

A university will usually have three options for fly out. My absolute favorite - and relatively rare - is where the university agrees to fly out your student on their dime. All expenses (flight, transport to and from the airport, food) are covered. The universities that are the most flexible about this are those that know they offer a unique experience like College of the Atlantic and those that are struggling to get interested candidates outside of their immediate region interested like Juniata College. Many schools will offer this opportunity to the best prospects that have already been admitted. Even if a school tells your student in October that the school does not pay for fly outs, ask again in February after your student has been admitted. When offered, I urge students that have any interest in the school to take advantage of the opportunity.

The second option is where the university is willing to defray part of the costs (for example: half the flight, room and board) and have the family pay the other part. Realistically, this will run around $200-500. Again, I strongly recommend it. If a family is really interested, but just can not afford the $300, speak with the college. Many times an arrangement can be made. Just don't embarrass yourself by pleading poverty and have your teen show up with a $700 cell phone and a $1500 purse. That tends to leave a bad taste in the school's mouth and can come back and haunt you in the financial aid process. Alternately, a school may not pay anything up front, but will deduct $500 or so from the first year's tuition is a student chooses to attend that school.

The third option is when a school says that the school would love for your student to come and visit, but all the school can offer is room and board for a weekend. This does not necessarily mean that the school is not interested in your student. A much more likely scenario is that interest is just far too high to accommodate every student. If you can afford the trip for your student ($500-750 / person), I would strongly recommend this for the first or second choice schools.

If fall fly outs don't work, a student can also ask for fly outs for admitted students. In this case the first two categories are actually much more common. The game has changed at this point. Instead of your son or daughter trying to impress the school, the school is now trying to impress your son or daughter. At the very least I would recommend your student visit his or her first choice school. I really want your student to see if the school is the right fit. There are few experiences worse than having your son attend the university he fought for admission only to find out in the first three weeks that he hates the school and wants to transfer. In addition, giving the university a face to match the name can be really beneficial on a financial aid application. Showing a genuine interest can also help with a financial aid application.

Remember that a school does not always fit every student. The school that can be a perfect fit for Zach is not necessarily the right school for Manuel. The school where Juanita finds a second home might send Jennifer looking at the transfer process after just one semester. And a school that offers a stimulating academic challenge to Taylor may completely crush James. Going to see a school where your student comes back with an "Aww, heck no!" is not really a waste of money. At least you know now. Attending a school that your son or daughter hates and needs to transfer out of is a waste of money.

*What should my student bring for the fly out?*

Simple is better. Start by asking the host school. Ask about the weather but also ask if your student needs to bring a sleeping bag and / or pillow. Often when a student is put up in a dorm, the hosting student does not actually have "extra" space. That can mean sleeping on the floor. (Oh, to be 17 again.) Bring a towel. I might recommend a cheap pair of plastic sandals for the showers. Toiletries, extra socks, sleep wear, medicine, inhalers, chargers. Bring one nice set of clothes for the interview at the college. Long sleeve shirt and tie for men, nice blouse or dress for women. Bring about $100 cash. Though most schools will promise to pick up your teen at the airport, I always like to have a "Plan B" and bring money for a taxi or Uber. Bring a current resume, letters of recommendation if possible and a current transcript.

Most important, remember that your student is always under observation even when he or she thinks otherwise. I know of a case where a student on a fly out managed to get completely drunk. The next morning, 8:00 a.m., she had an interview for a full ride scholarship. About half way through an interview that was not going well to begin with she deposited the source of her inebriation all over the Dean's carpet. The good news is that the Dean's decision about who was to get financial assistance just got easier.

Be positive. Don't let your student talk badly about his or her high school or family. This reflects poorly on the student. Tell your student not to complain, even when everything that could go wrong does go wrong. What does it say about a student's character when the student's plane is delayed six hours, the airline loses the luggage, the admission's office forgets to pick the student up at the airport, the hosting student forgets the compromise and is nowhere to be found and your student is still cheerful, positive and uncomplaining? How does that contrast with the other student flying in on the same flight who complains the entire morning and begs to get on the next flight leaving?

Like a college fair, this is an experience that your student should have on his or her own. Among the items to be left at home are "parents." Let your student experience this for himself or herself. If you can not trust your student to make good choices for one weekend, then an entirely different conversation about the merits of going to college at all needs to be addressed.

Again, a few days after the fly out, have your student write a nice thank you note and follow up with any professor to whom your student spoke. After returning, have your student jot down some notes and impressions of the school. Especially if your student has the option of seeing several schools, the colleges start to blend together.

*Should I drive out to visit the university?*

This is personally one of my favorite options. It is also the favorite of colleges as it costs the college nothing. The biggest drawback is the financial cost to you. What I have recommended to my students is over spring break or summer break plan a family vacation. Don't bother going during winter break as the campus you want to see is also closed. Spring break is better than summer break as you and your student can see the school in session and visit some classes.

Pick a major city with many universities in the vicinity. My general rule of thumb is a two-hour drive. My personal favorites are Philadelphia, New York, Boston, Chicago, San Antonio, Los Angeles, and Seattle. All the above cities have a large number of smaller liberal arts colleges nearby. That is not to say that Cedar Rapids, IA or San Francisco, CA are bad choices, just more limited. I love small Midwestern schools, but the schools just are not as closely packed. This makes it difficult to see so many of the schools. I do not worry about the large public universities. I ignore the larger public schools because the large public schools won't really note that your student visited and don't generally make any accommodations beyond a basic tour. I stick exclusively with smaller liberal arts schools.

Turn the trip into a vacation. How many more chances will you have to actually spend time with your teen before he or she embarks on a radical departure from life as you have both come to know it? In a week's time, you can visit maybe three or four universities without much stress and probably enjoy yourselves in the process.

Sample itinerary 1: (and keep in mind, this is just a sample. It can be modified to almost any city or interest.)

Day 1: Drive from . . . Colorado to Los Angeles. This is a long drive -about 14 hours. You will need to leave early in the morning to arrive late at night. If your teen has a license, practice some Zen meditation and allow him or her to do some of the driving. It is not often that teens get real highway driving experience. Stop at a hotel in Anaheim, California near Disneyland.

Day 2: Spend the day at Disneyland. Relax. Be a kid again. Laugh and take way too many pictures. Make your sister in Nebraska jealous with all the Facebook posts of you and your teenage daughter actually seeming to communicate.

Day 3: Wake up early. Drive out to the University of the Redlands (about an hour from Anaheim.) Tour the campus. Have lunch on the campus. Stop at the Getty Art Museum for the afternoon (also about an hour from the University of the Redlands). Head back to your hotel.

Day 4: Go visit Pepperdine University in the morning. Put an extra change of clothes in the trunk of the car. In the afternoon, stop by the beach and eat dinner on one of the piers overlooking the ocean.

Day 5: Go see Universal Studios with a new Harry Potter exhibit in the morning. In the afternoon take a stroll down Hollywood Boulevard. Eat dinner in China Town or be adventurous and try Little Saigon.

Day 6: Back to Colorado with a sun tan to make your neighbors and co-workers jealous. Keep in mind, I specifically mentioned two schools. I could change those names four times over and never leave the Los Angeles area. More schools could be added at the cost of an extra day or sacrificing another activity like Universal Studios.

Sample itinerary 2:

Day 1: Fly from St. Louis, MO to New York City. I have always found flights to be exhausting. I also know what New York traffic is like. No matter what time you arrive you will spend time in traffic. Once you check in ask the concierge at the hotel for suggestions and walk to a local restaurant. One of my favorite activities in New York is to find small family owned restaurants that are not part of a chain outside of your local mall.

Day 2: Wake up early. Go visit Barnard on the upper west side. (This is an all girl's school, so you may have to go across the street to Columbia with your son.) After touring the school take a subway south, transfer to a cross town bus and visit the Metropolitan Museum of Art in the afternoon. (I have a thing for art museums.)

Day 3: Rent a car and drive up to Fairfield University in Connecticut (about two hours). After visiting the school, go to the Seaside Park and stroll the beach or shop in the little tourist shops that line Captain's Cove Boardwalk. Get back in time to take in a Broadway Play. (Book these far in advance or you will never get the play you want.)

Day 4: Visit New York University in the morning in downtown Manhattan. Bring good walking shoes. After touring the school - which is inescapably part of the city - tour downtown New York. The entire city is closely packed. One can walk from end to end of Manhattan Island with relative ease. The subway system is efficient and fantastically well organized. Try something adventurous for dinner. New York is one of the best places in the world for some really great ethnic food that simply can not be found in most cities. (I also love food.)

Day 5: Back to Missouri which suddenly looks a lot more provincial.

Start with the schools that might interest your teen the most. If the University of Chicago is high on his list, then go to Chicago and hit Loyola and Northwestern or catch the train down to Illinois Wesleyan or rent a car and visit Coe or Beloit or Earlham or Knox. If Loyola - New Orleans is number one, then fly into New Orleans and visit Tulane as well. Or rent a car and drive to Houston to see Rice University or go the other direction and visit Samford University in Birmingham, Alabama and then fly out of where you stop, returning the rental car to the airport you fly out from.

Once you have picked the city, then match your interests and your teen's interests. If the two of you (or three of you) love hiking, then when you visit the Los Angeles' area rent a car to go just outside of the city. If you love the water, then when you visit Seattle, take a boat tour. If you love baseball, then go during baseball season and catch a game at Fenway Park in Boston. If shopping is your thing, be sure to include the Riverwalk in San Antonio. In short, make the experience a vacation.

Warning: if you visit two schools in the same day (i.e. Boston University and Boston College), don't wear the Boston University sweatshirt you just bought in the gift store to the Boston College interview.

Some other dos and don'ts:

| Do | Don't |
|---|---|
| Do ask questions. | Don't be negative. |
| Do ask to see the dorms. | Don't ask about tuition costs. |
| Do be personable and charming. | Don't follow your student into the interview. |
| Do get a business card. | Don't write the thank you note for your student. |
| Do go on the tour. | Don't forget your student needs to be the star. |
| Do take notes. | Don't treat your teen like he or she is still 3. |
| Do take lots of pictures. | Don't take the call from your boss on the tour. |

*A few observations when visiting a school.*

When visiting a school please note that the school will always put themselves in the best possible light. A few things that might pop out. If a school promises that the student / faculty ratio is 8:1, but all the classrooms you see look like auditoriums or have 45 desks crammed in, you should be aware that the ratios are a bit skewed. Second, the dorm rooms on a tour are often "model dorms" much the same way a new housing community may have model homes. The rooms may be slightly larger than average or have been designed by a professional stager. Any dorm on the tour will be the newest and the nicest. Take everything with a grain of salt.

Some other questions to consider (though this is not a check list):

"My freshman drives. Can she bring a car on campus?"

"My son is really interested in a semester abroad. If he chooses to do this, what impact does it have on graduation? Is the experience covered by his current financial aid?"

"What kind of Wi-Fi access is there?" (Actually a good question for a student tour guide.)

"What is your favorite place to eat off campus?" (Also good for the tour guide.)

"What types of meal plans are available?"

(For schools not in the city) "Are there any shuttles available for students that need to go into town for shopping?"

"What are the library hours?"

"Is there a separate fitness center for non-athletes?"

"Are dorm rooms available all four years or is the student encouraged to live off campus?"

"Can freshmen do research?"

"What is the job placement rate?"

"Are there any graduate schools that this university has a special relationship with?"

"What percentage of students pass the MCATs (for pre-med) or LSAT (for pre-law)?"

"Do you have a winter term? Does it cost extra?"

"Is there a price guarantee? How much has tuition risen in the past five years?"

"Are there jobs on campus that are not part of work study?"

"Does the school have its own health center?"

"I know this college is affiliated with the church. Are there any religious classes or chapels that are compulsory?"

"What makes your school unique?"

"Would you send your own child here? Why?"

Don't ask questions where you know the answer. For example, if you ask, "Is your school safe?" What answer do you expect? Even if unsafe, what school is going to advertise that? Similarly, "What happens if my freshman is caught drinking?" Ummm ... your freshman is under 21. Don't be stupid. "Can he bring his gun?" NO! "Are the students here sexually active?" How do you really expect the school to answer that? "Are there drugs here?" Of course not. "What if she doesn't like her roommate?" Cut the cord. Time for her to grow up. Before asking a question, think about what answer you expect.

*I saw the school, and I think the neighborhood is unsafe. Now what?*

Many universities and colleges are in neighborhoods that are ... less than perfect. This is particularly true of colleges on the East coast where real estate is at a premium and the cities have morphed and evolved around the colleges. Two of the worst neighborhoods I have seen were around Temple University in Philadelphia and Yale in New Haven. Both were in or right next to very seedy places. I have never felt bad about sending students to the schools. No matter how "bad" the surrounding neighborhood is, I have found the schools to be very safe. To use Yale and Temple as examples, every building is locked. All the dorms are controlled entry and exit. There are numerous safety features around both campuses. I really do not worry about a student's safety on campus. If the student goes off campus, the student does need to use common sense. By that measure, Rice University in Houston, TX - a beautiful and "safe" campus in all respects - can be just as dangerous or more dangerous at the bar five blocks away than Colombia in the heart of New York's upper west side.

*My family is African American, is it safe to send my daughter to a university in the deep South?*

As I stated above, I have found campuses in general to be bastions of safety, education and tolerance. There are always individuals that are just poorly educated no matter where you attend school. I am usually less worried about the school than I am the community in general. In other words, if your 19 year old African American daughter is driving back to campus after a day trip downtown, is she likely to be stopped by local police? Is your 21 year old son likely to be followed around a store as he shops? These are issues that no one is immune regardless of geographic location. In general, large cities are more tolerant than small towns.

As with everything I write, there are caveats. This has a huge caveat. Though every school I look at has individual incidents, there are few that seem to have institutionalized the incidents. There are a handful of schools though that have seen an unstated mission of keeping the campus white. The easiest way to determine this - Google it. Type in the name of the school followed by racism or racial incidents. Some results may surprise a casual researcher. For example, Duke University in Durham, NC shows many more problems and incidents than Mississippi State University in Starkville, MS. I have personally spoken with more admission's officers than I can remember. Only twice has a school - both very prestigious schools and none in the deep South - made outright racists comments about not wanting to accept students of a certain ethnicity. I have chosen not to name the schools here as I hope both are changing the focus and attitude of the admission's office.

### Chapter 8: The Advantages of Charm, Wit and Preparation

The interview is one of the best, and one of the most overlooked, ways for your teen to really stand out. So much is judged by a teen's ability to speak clearly and eloquently. Sadly, few high schools offer any real preparation for a professional interview. Time to start practicing because this is one area any teen can really stand out from his or her competition regardless of grades and test scores.

*So, my son has an interview at two this afternoon at a nearby coffee shop. Now what?*

Congratulations! I love interviews! Think of it this way. The University of OMG representative will read the applications for more than one hundred students. The representative will have to make hard choices about which students are a good fit for the University of OMG - not only who will fit in academically and be able to handle the rigor of the university classes but who can handle the transition to college emotionally and socially. Academic decisions are relatively easy to make. Grades, test scores and class rigor make that decision.

"Does this particular teen fit my school?" "Will this teenager make positive contributions to my campus?" "How will this student fit in? Will he join clubs and create interactions? Will he be able to form a study group for the engineering class that is breaking everyone? Will he start an intramural Quidditch team?" Those questions are so difficult to answer from a series of numbers. An interview puts a face to a name and answers some of these questions. Not only can a great interview move your teen to the top of the list for admission, but the admission's representative may be impressed enough to hand deliver the application to financial aid with the invective, "We need this kid. Please make sure he is taken care of." Given the choice, ALWAYS take the interview.

*What are the different types of interview?*

I will begin with my favorite. My absolute favorite is a face to face interview with the admission's representative in charge of your region. Second best is a face to face interview with a representative from the school but not necessarily your region. After those two choices my enthusiasm wanes. Next best is a Skype interview followed by a phone interview. I do not like this option as much because it is harder for your kid to sell himself. So much of the personality is lost when the interview is done remotely. That being said, a phone interview is still better than no interview at all.

*What is an alumnus interview?*

I am not a huge fan of alumni interviews. A student can more easily make a mistake than add something that will help his file. Schools that have an inordinate amount of applicants or are more prestigious use more alumnus interviews. For example, Stanford University has so many great students interested in an interview that the school just can not accommodate everyone. An alumnus interview may be the only interview offered. Every once in a while, especially with more rural areas, the admission's representative may not be willing to travel to your city or town and will instead refer you to a local alumnus instead.

The first reason that I am not a fan of alumni interviews is that the alumni are often doing this as a favor to the alma mater. Not all alumni are terribly enthusiastic about the interview and some even see this as an unwelcome distraction in their day. I much prefer an admission's officer who sees this process as part of the job description.

The second reason I am lukewarm is that the interview often has little impact on the admission's process. At the conclusion of the interview the alumnus will submit a report to the school in question. A really bad report can hurt your student's chances to gain acceptance. A really great report does not often sway a committee much. Obviously, there are exceptions to this. There is an attorney in Phoenix that I know gives alumni interviews for a particular Ivy

League institution. He has been doing these interviews for so many years and such great accuracy that the school puts quite a bit of emphasis on his recommendation. Additionally, there are times that the alumnus goes above and beyond in his or her effusion and praise of a particular student. This can really stand out. Effusive praise just does not happen often - even when the alumnus tells you that he or she will do so.

The biggest advantage of an alumni interview is to get a better idea of what the school is like. This knowledge of the school is the best advantage of these interviews. As such, make these interviews personal. Ask the alumnus: "What did you like about the school? How was the food? What did you get involved in? What advice would you give an incoming freshman? How can I improve my application?" An alumnus can give you an uncensored insight and let your student know if the school is the right fit. Do keep in mind, the 24 year old anthropologist may give more insight than the 73 year old physician simply due to the fact that the anthropologist just graduated. Like everything else, the school and the climate at the school changes with time. At the same time, remember that you are getting one individual's response to the school - not a comprehensive view.

*How should my teen dress?*

Casual. No jeans, shorts, short skirts, t-shirts, anything low cut or anything stained. Do iron the clothes and polish the shoes. Don't wear a full business suit. Jeans and t-shirt say that the teen is taking this lightly. A full suit says that your teen is trying to compensate for something. Long sleeve shirt and a tie work well for dudes. A dress or slacks and a blouse work for a dudette. No party dresses. Go light on the makeup and jewelry. As one of my students asked me, "So, dress like a teacher?" Yes! Perfect. Just not the gym teacher.

*What should my teen bring?*

Keep it simple. A resume and transcript are the most basic. Make sure the copies are clean and not your final copy. Put both in a folder so the papers are not torn, stained or smudged. If your student is applying for an art scholarship or major, I would recommend bringing a portfolio of art work (don't let the representative take the actual portfolio) or at least pictures on his phone. If a student is applying for a music scholarship or major, I would recommend bringing a burned CD of her greatest hits or a flash drive that you can part with or at least an MP3 recording on her phone. If the student is applying for an athletics' scholarship, bring a link to a YouTube video with a highlight reel and maybe a laptop so the representative can actually see the highlights.

Your teen should also bring some cash. If meeting at a Starbucks or a restaurant I fully expect the representative to pay, but I always like to have a plan B.

*Basic rules*

1) Be on time! I can not stress this one enough. Nothing sets a bad impression more than showing up ten minutes late for a twenty minute interview. Worse, many interviews are back to back. It is entirely possible that if your teen is late, he will lose his time slot or at the very least cut into the time. With that in mind, have your teen bring the representative's phone number just in case your teen is caught in traffic or can't find the right location.

2) Confirm the interview the day before. Have your teen send an email or text verifying the time and place. If meeting at a Starbucks or another chain restaurant, make sure you have the right one. Remember that there may be three Starbucks on Central Ave. A confirmation also works

well to remind a very busy alumnus who may have agreed to do this two weeks ago and forgotten to put it in her schedule.

3) If the representative offers to order something for your teen, go light. This is not the time or place to get an extra-large café mocha with extra whip, soy milk, a coffee cake and a slice of cheese cake. A small coffee or mocha or tea will do. If it is a lunch interview, talk with your teen about what foods are easier to eat and still be polite. There is no graceful way to eat crab or spaghetti and meatballs. Gorging on an enormous hamburger dripping with special sauce may not leave the impression you want. When in doubt, go with the salad. By the same token, if meeting for a lunch interview do a crash course review with your teen on table manners.

4) Stay home. The interview is the time and place for your teenager to shine. If your teen does not drive and the location is too far for the bus, then drive your teen but drop her off and come back when she is done. Whatever you do, do not go into the coffee shop or restaurant. Despite your best intentions to sit at another table, the temptation is often too much. Without realizing it you may find yourself staring uncomfortably at your teen or simply making your teenager more nervous than necessary. Do not even go in "just to say hello."

One of the worst examples I have ever witnessed involved an overprotective father and his 17 year old daughter. Unfortunately, dad did not look much like his daughter. He took his daughter to an interview and then stood ten feet away glaring at her. Twenty minutes into the interview the police showed up. Someone thought he was stalking this poor girl and was worried for her safety. I am fairly certain that the only thing the admission's officer remembered about the girl was her interrupting the interview to speak with the police.

5) Have your teenager do some research on the school before the interview. Your teen should definitely use this as an opportunity to show his interest in the school and ask real questions

about the school that apply only to that particular school. It is his one chance to impress the university. Do not let him throw that opportunity away.

*What do I ask?*

There is no one answer. To be blunt, this is why your teen (not you) <u>needs</u> to do research on the school. The first questions should be things your teen is actually interested in. Ask about academics and food choices, intramural sports and clubs, dorm life and parking. Be careful. The websites are usually beautiful. The romantic in me was recently besotted by a beautiful photo of Allegheny College on a gorgeous fall day with the trees in an explosion of colors. The photos neglected the pictures of students wading through two feet of snow on a bitterly overcast day. Similarly, Eckerd College is quick to highlight (and rightly so) that the college is actually right on the beach. Less mention is made about mosquitos the size of small birds or recent hurricanes. Dig deep. Don't ask the College of Wooster, "What merit-based scholarships do you have?" Instead ask, "Can you tell me what the requirements for the Clarence Beecher Allen Scholarship are?" Don't ask the University of Puget Sound what the dorms are like. Instead ask why the dorms are thematic and what the themes are. What choice do you have as an incoming freshman on what dorm you are in?

Also useful is to get the interviewer talking about themselves. One of the great ironies for me about interviews is that the interviewer often thinks the interview went really well when the interviewer spent a lot of time talking about themselves. Especially if the interviewer attended the university in question, ask about his or her experiences at the school.

*What will the college ask my teen?*

The sky is the limit, but the most common questions I hear are:

1) Tell me about yourself.

2) Why do you want to attend _____?

3) Why do you want to major in _____?

4) Why should I choose you?

5) Questions on the resume and on hobbies.

6) What are your greatest strengths?

7) Tell me about a time you failed and how you overcame it.

The first question is one of the most common. It is also a tricky question. Plan this out. Two great strategies:

A) Think of a specific story that highlights the attributes your teen most wants to highlight. Everyone loves a good story. Practice the story so that the answer looks spontaneous, not scripted.

B) Flip a favorite application question. "Well, if I was to describe myself in three adjectives they would be ........" And then explain each adjective. Pick your adjectives carefully. Whatever you choose, do not include "nice." The interview is the wrong time and place to list all the student's activities. Highlight one or two only. Hand a resume to the interviewer for the rest of the activities.

Don't go to these interviews cold. Practice and be prepared.

*What if my child is not a good public speaker?*

Most students are lousy public speakers. Even if the student is normally gregarious and outgoing, public speaking is a very different animal. One of my great regrets about secondary education is that public speaking is not usually taught. Anything not "on the test" is not usually taught. Far too many students leave high school and never have any real experience with public speaking or professional interviews. This is tragic as so much depends on one's ability to communicate effectively. I would argue that the first impression is certainly dominated by appearance. The next impression is based on one's ability to communicate well.

One of the favorite stories I tell my students is that of Robert Oppenheimer, the lead scientist on the Manhattan Project building America's atomic bomb. General Leslie Groves was the overall commander in charge of the Manhattan Project. General Groves picked Oppenheimer as the lead for the Manhattan Project. General Groves did not pick Oppenheimer because Oppenheimer was the most senior, or the brightest, or had the best references or security clearance. General Groves picked Oppenheimer because Robert Oppenheimer had the unique ability to take a very complex idea - nuclear physics - and put the science in terms that General Groves could more easily understand. Oppenheimer had a singular gift for making the complex appear to be simple and for getting to the root of problems. Oppenheimer is the most famous scientist to come out of the New Mexico desert because of his communication skills.

The good news is that communication skills can be taught. My first choice is to see if the high school has a club or program that highlights public speaking such as debate or Model UN or Mock Trial or Academic Decathlon. Involvement in one or more of these programs, especially if your student is shy, may be a wonderful introduction to public speaking skills. Additionally, all these programs emphasize reading, writing and critical thinking skills. All these programs are wonderful on a resume and would help your student get more involved in school. Finally, one of the most underutilized merit scholarships is forensics or debate. Far fewer students apply for forensics scholarships than music or art or athletics. A recent student of mine was really struggling with finding the money for college. She was a few thousand dollars short of what her parents thought was affordable. Upon visiting the school she learned that the school had a quality debate team. The student arranged a last minute interview with the debate coach and went home with $6,000 more in scholarships (partly from the visit itself and partly from being the newest member of a debate team). As an added bonus, the young woman was pre-med. The interest in debate - especially if she gains attention or merit - will be an outstanding asset to her medical school applications in four years.

If these programs are not an option, another choice is to self- teach. I strongly recommend learning by example. Your student is surrounded by professional speakers on a daily basis, his teachers. Have your student start noting what works and what doesn't work. Use Ted Talks, a wonderful Internet resource of professional and amateur speakers on a varied topic list. Spoken word poetry can also really be useful in hearing inflection, tone and voice variation.

Finally, there is no substitute for practice. I do not recommend having your student practice with her parents or siblings. There is too much sub text to these interviews. The family relationships and knowledge of strengths and weaknesses make the interview false. I would recommend starting with teachers. I do not want the "nice" teacher. I want a real experience, not smiles and platitudes. By the same token the "mean" teacher may raise stress levels beyond where they need to be. Another suggestion, ask your boss or co-worker to do an interview. I like this option because your teenager does not know the interviewer well and the questions tend to be more genuine. Practice. Practice. Practice.

*How does a teenager do a resume?*

In many ways an academic resume is similar to a professional resume. Templates can be found online and with popular word processing programs. I tend to shy away from these as because they are templates, many others use the same template. In the absence of any experience, though, the templates can offer a good starting point. Try very hard to keep everything to one page. Manipulate the spacing, font and font size to accommodate.

At the very top put the student's name, address, phone number and email address. A small photo is not a bad idea. I like to have the name offset, in a different color or different font to stand out. When changing fonts or colors please remember that a little goes a long way. You want to get attention, not add a flashing strobe light to your resume.

On the subject of emails, please make sure the student has a professional email. Some of the worst examples I have ever seen run the gamut from extremely juvenile (unicornsparkles@gmail.com) to slightly creepy (hotmama6442@htomail.com). Something very basic and boring works really well for college. In addition, a separate email account may make it easier for your teen to keep all the college notifications and contact in a separate place where it doesn't get lost in spam about a sale on carpeting or coupons for a favorite restaurant.

The next paragraph should have the academic record. Put the most recent experience first. Mention not only which school, but also add a notation about AP or IB or honors' classes. It is a good place for class rank (if above 10%) or ACT /SAT scores (provided they are at least close to the target). Only mention high school and any college class taken. Elementary school where your child was the shining star of the 3rd grade is no longer relevant.

I follow the academic record with clubs / activities. I want a special emphasis on not only a title, but what that means. For example:

National Honor Society                                         2014-2016

(BORING!!)

Better:

National Honor Society                                  2014-2016

    Vice President 2015

As a member I participated in community service activities like helping at a local marathon and school tutoring. When I was elected the vice-president, I started a program to tutor elementary school kids as a mentor at a local elementary school. The program was so successful that the elementary school is seeking to expand the program to include our Student Government class next year. I also organized a trip downtown for 32 students to volunteer at a local Special Olympics.

A student needs to explain not only what he or she has done, but what that means. A national organization like National Honor Society or Key Club or Girl Scouts may not need much explanation, but what is an admission's officer from Ohio supposed to make of AP Club or Anime / Yu-Gi-Oh club or Earth Rangers. Additionally, be very careful of abbreviations for the same reason. While an active membership in a club may make an abbreviation obvious, the acronym may not be so obvious to an outsider. An admission's officer may assume that NRA stands for National Rifle Association while your teen was actually involved in New Reading Activities.

If your teen has a depth of leadership positions, then you may consider making "Leadership" a section in and of itself. The next section for me would be honors and awards. If this section is empty or nearly empty, that should send a message. By the same token, if you have to dig so deeply that honors like "Perfect Attendance Award" and "Principal's Honorable

Mention" make the cut, then the list needs to be reevaluated. If the student has nothing or nearly nothing for this section, don't use it. I do not want to highlight the fact that the student has not received any awards.

Almost done. The next section is skills or hobbies. This really depends on your teens specific talents. Please be concrete. Not everything works equally well.

<u>Bad Ideas</u>

Computer skills

Speaks more than one language

Running

Reading

Playing video games

<u>Good Ideas</u>

Designs web pages using HTML (see the link to my latest page)

Bilingual Bosnian / English

Run half marathons three times a year

Reading Harry Potter and J.R. Tolkien

(I just can't make endless hours of video games look good.)

The more specific the list is, the better the chance it will spark a conversation. What if your interviewer loves to run marathons or is a huge Harry Potter fan? Warning: do NOT lie. This is too easy to catch. Your application takes a decided hit if you brag about being bilingual and you are not. I knew an Asian student once, not Chinese, who bragged about being fluent in Chinese. Her interviewer switched to Chinese in the interview. The girl could only count to ten in

Chinese. It was rather embarrassing to admit the lie. Absolutely put a positive spin on whatever the activity is but never lie or exaggerate to the point of incredulity.

Finally, I usually recommend ending with three references. Do not use a reference without asking the individual in question first. Similarly, do not use a reference with an incorrect phone number or email. I want the interviewer to follow up.

*Can I get a sample resume?*

Umm ... no. That defeats the whole purpose. I want the resume to be original to your student. I want the resume to stand out. I don't want your son's resume to look exactly like the next student who also read this book. Be creative. Be professional. Dig deep. Find your own style. There is no one "right" way to do a resume.

### Chapter 9: My kingdom for a horse - or at least a good reference

Because colleges expect teens to sell themselves, and possibly to exaggerate a little, much emphasis is put on the references. This should not be a casual process or a last minute thought. Teens should begin to think about who to ask for a reference as early as sophomore year.

*What references are best?*

As a general rule I tell students to get three references. The first reference needs to be from the teacher that adores your son or daughter. I would prefer a teacher that has known your student for more than one year. You do not want a teacher your student first met two months ago. By the same token, that really nice English teacher from freshman year or the 7th grade teacher that was awesome just doesn't cut it. In a perfect world, I would ask the teacher your student had freshman and again junior year. In that way the teacher can also address how much your student has grown. Your first recommendation should be a content teacher: math, English, science or history. Do not ask the PE or art teacher here. You really want this teacher to be concrete and address not only the academic qualifications, but also the personal characteristics that make your son or daughter stand out.

The second letter should be someone that your son or daughter has done the community service or an extended extracurricular activity with. This could be a coach, a minister, a community leader. If your daughter was doing community service at the hospital, ask her supervisor or the doctor she worked with most closely. If your son spent hours and hours at the animal shelter, have the director of the shelter write a letter. If your daughter devoted considerable time to her synagogue, have the rabbi or the adult she worked with most closely write the letter. If your son was the star of this year's baseball team, have the coach write a letter. Once again, multiple years that are relatively recent are best. Have this individual write to your student's personal character and motivations. This is a really good person to talk about goals.

The third letter is usually extra. Most schools ask for two letters. The third one serves two purposes. First it will act as insurance in case one of the first two letters falls through. Second, the third letter can highlight something that the first two did not. For example, if your student was active in band for four years, have the band director write a letter. If the student was an avid art student, have the art teacher write a letter about your son's latent talents. If your student was involved in multiple activities, highlight a different activity. Do not get a letter that basically repeats the first two, though. There is no need for two letters from the same church or two letters from different math teachers. Emphasize a different skill set. Remember these letters are key to a university getting to know your student who at this point is a series of letters and numbers. This is a personal introduction.

If your student gets all three letters but the school only asks for two, send three. One more can help an application. Do not, however, operate on the theory that more is better and send five or six. In addition to looking desperate, five or six letters just annoys and frustrates the admission's officer that has to read way too many applications in way too short of a time frame. Alternately, you could always hold the third letter and submit it if your student is wait-listed by a school.

When asking for a letter of recommendation, please ask early - at least two weeks. Students all seem to like the same six or seven teachers in a school. Those teachers get bombarded by requests for a letter of reference at about the same time. Try to beat the crowd and give the teacher time to actually consider the letter and the reference. I can not tell you how many times a student has run into my room at 3:30 p.m. for a letter that needs to be submitted by 5:00 p.m. that day. I regretfully tell the student no.

When you ask give the recommender a copy of the student resume and if necessary an addressed and stamped envelope. The resume is to remind the recommender who will see the resume on her desk until she finishes the letter of recommendation. In addition, the resume may fill in some blanks. The math teacher may realize that your son is part of the percussion ensemble at school, but she may not have known that your son placed $2^{nd}$ in a state competition this year or that he plays at six community events throughout the year. Seeing how much emphasis your son places on the drums may spin the letter the math teacher was planning to write.

About a week after asking for the letter of recommendation give the people you asked a thank you card. This thank you card will show gratitude, but it will also serve as a valuable reminder to finish the letter while putting the recommender in a good mood at the same time. For teachers or community leaders that are inundated with requests, this may move the right request to the top of the pile. It is not going too far to include a ten-dollar gift card at a local coffee shop that your recommender always visits or a bar of chocolate for the chocolate addict. Don't spend too much and never give cash, but it is a lot easier to write that letter of recommendation full of wit and wisdom while sipping on a fresh cup of coffee.

A few warnings about letters of recommendation:

*Be sure you know whom you are asking and what that person's opinion of your student really is. I worked for some years with a teacher that would laugh in the teacher's lounge about crushing students in their letters of recommendation. This teacher really loved the betrayal made sweeter by hand delivering the sealed letter with a smile. Ask the right teacher.

*Be careful of the form letter. I know teachers that have two files on their computer: letter or rec. boy and letter of rec. girl. When asked, the teacher simply hits print for the appropriate gender. These letters do nothing for your student as they are too generic. A letter that can be equally used by two students in the same class fails. For this reason, I have had several sets of identical twins who are involved in the exact same activities and have basically the same grades. I tell the twins that I can write one a letter, but not both. The two letters would be far too similar.

*Beware of time lines. In general, colleges are far more patient with adults writing a letter of recommendation, but there are limits. Do not feel bad about reminding a recommender that a deadline is approaching. If you have to remind the teacher or community leader more than once, you probably need to ask someone else. It is not a bad idea in the case of mailed letters to call or email the university a week later and verify that the letter was received.

*Be aware that no usually means no. I work with a lot of very nice individuals. Some of them can not tell a pretty young girl whose eyes are pregnant with tears that he / she will not be able to write the letter requested. Instead the teacher will say something like, "I would really love to, but I am far too busy right now," or "I'm not sure I know you well enough to write the letter," or "I heard you want to be a lawyer, you should ask your government teacher." This is all code for, "You don't want me to write this." Take the teacher at his or her word. I am usually blunt and not very tactful. When certain students ask me to write a letter, I will actually tell the student, "You really don't want me to write this letter." Often the student still insists. I can only imagine the pressure students bring to bear on teachers much nicer than I am. If a teacher or community leader still writes the letter your student could receive a letter than burns the student or is never actually submitted. At best the letter is lukewarm or a form letter and does not help.

*Be mindful that the letter can not come from a parent, grandparent, sister, brother or other immediate relative. Colleges generally discount such letters as too biased. The letters are often too emotional or go into cute vignettes about the time junior skinned his knee learning to ride the bike. This really does not serve a purpose and in fact can raise the question about why no one else was willing to write a letter.

*What can I do if no one wants to write a letter of recommendation?*

This can be a huge problem and should definitely be a warning sign. One solution is to test the waters junior year. Ask for a letter for "a job" or for a recommendation for National Honor Society. An astute student could even ask to use the teacher or community leader or coach as a job reference (that the student really doesn't need) and watch the body language.

Another option: if your student really hits it off with a teacher freshman year, keep in contact. I don't want the letter that starts, "I first met Ashley four years ago as a freshman in my biology class. I don't remember much about Ashley, but I think she was a decent student." On the other hand, the letter that begins, "I first met Ashley four years ago as a freshman in my biology class. The last three years Ashley has come in on her own time to help my current students with the major lab project I do every March," is solid gold.

Another option - and it is a last option - is asking a family friend that has known your student for years. An "uncle" that is best friends with dad and has gone on numerous camping trips or Wednesday night tacos with the boys who can speak to your son's character or aspirations can help. It is never my first choice, but I would prefer this to nothing or to a form letter. I mostly use this recommendation when a student had to transfer schools junior year or later and has not had an opportunity to form a bond or connection with any adults in the new location.

*Do I need a counselor to write a letter of recommendation?*

Maybe. This answer is dependent on the university or college. Most simply want a form filled out. For example, when doing the Common App, a student will be asked for his or her counselor and the email. The counselor will then receive a request to fill out a form about class rank, class rigor, GPA, attendance, and disciplinary record. In many cases there is no written statement.

I am always nervous about counselor statements. Large public schools often have counselors working with 500 students at once. Many of my students have had four or five counselors by senior year. Smaller schools do a better job with this. Either way, I would recommend your student going in to speak with the counselor at the beginning of senior year. Have your student talk about future career plans and majors. Have your student ask for advice about college recommendations - even if not needed. After that have your student make the effort to walk through counseling once every two or three weeks just to say hello. As with teachers, send a thank you note after filling out the Common App or realizing that the counselor will be asked for something.

If a counselor absolutely refuses or your student has had too many run ins with her counselor, try the head of the department. If all else fails, contact an administrator and ask if the administrator can write the letter. I once set up one of my best students as the girl who read the school announcements with the principal every morning. After a year of five minute conversations the principal had actually gotten to be very fond of the young woman and was very pleased to step in and write a letter in lieu of the counseling office.


*I know _____ (someone famous or influential). Should I have that person write a letter of recommendation?*

In general, no. Having mom's golfing buddy or dad's former boss write a letter usually says nothing. In the end the point of the letter is to introduce your teen to a university or college. If your teen was going on a first date, would a letter from the mayor or state congressman about your teen's attributes and favorite foods come off as interesting or creepy? It is the same for colleges. Very prestigious schools see this quite frequently. It usually appears that the student is trying to compensate for some failing. Mom's golf buddy can probably go into great depth on Mom's golf handicap or even Mom's acumen at closing a real estate deal, but what can the golf friend really say about the teenager that maybe waves hello as Mom pulls out of the driveway?

An exception would be if this person actually had direct contact with the teen. For example, if your friend is the state congressman and your teen has worked at the congressman's personal charity for the last three summers, then the recommendation makes sense. If your teen wrote his own play that your famous actor friend volunteered to direct, then the letter makes sense. If your friend is only doing this as a favor to a friend, though, or worse as a favor to a friend of a friend, there are better avenues.

The biggest exceptions are the military academies. The military academies are some of the most difficult schools to be accepted to. The application process is probably the most rigorous. By the numbers, it is easier to get into Harvard than West Point. One of the key obstacles for the military academy is that your teen will NEED a letter of recommendation from a US (not state) senator or representative - or the current Vice President of the United States or Secretary of Defense. There is a component for sons and daughters of active military but listing everything will take more space than I want. This is the website for West Point. The other military academies are similar and should be consulted.

http://www.usma.edu/admissions/SitePages/Apply_Nominations.aspx

These letters are highly competitive and limited. If everything else is in order, but your son or daughter is missing this particular letter, the application is pretty much dead. I strongly recommend that your teen approach this early if a military academy is the goal. A year early is really not too soon. If at all possible, have your teen start working with the senator or congressman as a volunteer, perhaps in his or her campaign office during an election year. The more the congressman or senator knows your son or daughter, the better the chance is that your son or daughter will receive one of these coveted nominations. Of course, your teen could do everything right only to have the nomination that year go to the senator's wife's cousin's son at the last minute.

## Chapter 10: Defining Who You are in 700 Words or Less

*Do I really need a personal statement?*

Yes! The only schools that do not require a personal statement are ones that do admissions by the numbers. For example, Arizona State University has so many students that ASU does not even pretend to ask for a personal statement. Acceptance is totally based on raw numbers. All competitive schools require a personal statement.

*What is the personal statement?*

Think of it this way. Applying to a university is sort of like a blind date. All the school has is a list of numbers, sort of like your cousin saying she knows a guy. The first question you should have - and the first question the school has - is, "What is he like?" When a university is first introduced to your student, all the school sees is a set of raw data: GPA, test scores, class rank. Unfortunately, the numbers are not that far off everyone else's numbers. Everyone that is significantly higher is an easy accept. Anyone significantly lower is an easy reject. Most students are in that gray area in the middle. How is you student unique? How is your student different? Why should a university accept your student over some nice girl from Sheboygan, Wisconsin or that kid from middle of nowhere Montana?

When crafting a personal statement there are a couple of rules I like to use. Obviously, I want every personal statement to be unique, so the rules are more like vague guidelines. This next section is really written for your teen. Under no circumstances should the parent, counselor, teacher, well-meaning friend, boss, significant other or family dog write the personal statement. First, it is far more obvious than most realize when someone else has written the personal statement. Second, it is very common for the personal statement to come up during the interview. Though your teen may have read the statement penned by another source, he or she will not really know it. Third, one of the primary reasons that a university wants to see a personal statement is to ascertain whether the school is a good fit for your teen. How can a university make a good decision if the voice heard is not in fact genuine? Remember, **have your teen read this part**:

Rule 1: Work backwards. What is it you want the admission's office to know about you? Make a list of three characteristics or parts of your personality you want to highlight. If you decide that one of your best characteristics is your ability to work with others, then how can you show that? Most students begin writing and hope that the audience will eventually pull the right kernel of insight out of a rather convoluted personal statement. Instead start with your ultimate goal in mind - in this example your ability to work with others - and find a story that drives that narrative.

Rule 2: Tell a story. Everyone gets sucked into a good story. Have your ultimate objectives embedded into a story that highlights your attributes. So, find a story about the new girl in your sophomore history class that just transferred from Nigeria. Focus on how you really enjoyed working with the new girl not just on school work but in helping her fit in better in a new school and a new environment. Then talk about how you grew or changed as a person - maybe a new appreciation for the djembe (look it up). Remember, you can not fit in every detail about your life in 700 words or less, so focus on one idea - one story - and work with the word count to maximize the message. Every school is different, but many operate on a principle where the student's application goes into a manila folder. On the front of the folder the admission's officer will write a short phrase or word or code for each file. The most common I have seen is "BGK" - basically good kid. This is generic and says nothing. This says that there is nothing wrong, but there is nothing . . . right. You didn't sell anything that stands out from the crowd. You may still get into the school, but you will be filler - if and when space is available. I would rather see something like, "aspiring veterinarian who started an adopt a pet program" or "computer programmer that started his own business" or "cheerleader - national championships" on the front of your manila folder.

Rule 3: Never begin with "My name is _____, and I am a senior at _____." That intro is sooooooo boring and overdone. As someone who has read way too many personal statements, this is too stereotypical and says absolutely nothing about YOU. I know that when I get a personal statement like this I roll my eyes and moan about reading yet another one. This is not the mind set you want to encourage. An admission's officer will get a veritable mountain of essays to read around the first week of January. The pile seems endless especially because a lot of the essays are read by at least two counselors. If you are exceptionally lucky, your essay will cross the desk at 9:00 a.m. right after the first cup of coffee. If you are unlucky, your essay will be read by a very tired and cranky counselor from her bedroom at 11:00 p.m. with the mantra in her head "just one more." In the second case, how much do you think the counselor is really paying attention? If you start the same as everyone else, the admission's representative unwittingly goes into autopilot. Everything else is lost. This of course is also part of the reason for rule #2. The first line is everything. The first line is what hooks a reader. Let's try. I will give you some samples. You tell me what makes you want to keep reading.

"My name is William Kibler, and I am a senior at Basic High School."

Boring!

"It was the big game and there were three seconds on the clock."

Predictable and overused.

"It was a dark and stormy night."

Don't copy Snoopy.

"All I remember from the hospital is the sickly smell of too much bleach and antiseptic."

"There is a moment when the sea spray hits you square in the face, when the salt clings to your skin, and the sun warms the back of your neck that you truly feel alive."

"The first explosive gunshot ripped apart the night - and ripped apart my childhood."

I hope you can see the difference a good first line makes.

Rule 4: Be careful of the sport's analogy. "Sports is life." "I understand life better from sports." "I learned so much from winning the big game," or the ever popular twist, "from losing the big game." There is a time and place for the sport's story, but only use this as a last resort. That is not to say the story or analogy is not valid, but it is overdone. If I read ten personal statements, two will probably be a twist on the sport's analogy. If your point is to stand out from the pack, this is not how to do it. There are students where this is the best possible narrative, but I try to avoid sports' stories.

Rule 5: Be positive. Highlight your best. This is not the place to give excuses, whine, complain or display how disgruntled you are. To use my original analogy of a blind date, if your first date is three hours of the boy complaining about his last girlfriend, will there be a second date? There are two personal statements that I have read that really stand out as awful. The first involved a student talking about child abuse. It was horrible; it was graphic; it resulted in a call to child protective services - not admission. The second was a student who spent every syllable complaining about how awful his teachers and his school were. After reading a page one began to wonder if the school was so bad, why would the university ever want a student from that school? Denied. One of the biggest qualifications being sought is how will you impact my campus? My classrooms? My other students? If all you do is vent, what image am I getting of a future student? Overcoming diversity is a good angle. I use this angle a lot. But, end on a positive note and stay focused on YOU.

Rule 6: Be careful of the sob story. There are places for violins and roses. The personal statement is not necessarily one of them. The single biggest reason is that the story often gets sidetracked and you end on a note other than planned. I read an essay not too long ago where a student's mother was battling cancer. It was a battle that the mother went through - and ultimately lost - for the majority of high school. The essay was well written, passionate, heartfelt, and tragic. In the end I received a profound vision of mom's struggle, mom's endurance and courage, mom's efforts to beat an insidious beast lying dormant in her cells. I would have admitted mom in a heartbeat. The essay told me absolutely nothing about the student, though. There are times when I urge a student to go this route, but it needs to be done with care. Be sure the end result is about YOU. Be sure that the story is genuine and not pathetic. Just because your girlfriend of eight whole months broke up with you and crushed your spirit under the stiletto heels of heartache doesn't mean the admissions representative will see the episode with the same drama and heartache. You may just garner a snicker of derision. Think in the end what does this story say about you, your qualities and why a university wants you. If you talk about a failing or a major issue, you must address how you overcame it. Why would a university want the student who confesses he really struggles with the English language and admits he has never really learned it?

Rule 7: English. Do not write the essay in Korean, Spanish, Hebrew or Klingon. Even if you are applying for a foreign language major, you can not expect the admission's staff to run to the building across campus to translate the letter. In addition, the admission's office wants to know if you can handle the course work at their institution. Writing the letter in Chinese - especially from a student whose last name sounds Chinese - raises the question of whether you are actually fluent in English. Not a question you want the office asking.

Rule 8: Weird is good, but do not be too weird. I personally love creativity and thinking outside of the box. Especially after reading essays all day, the one that is quirky can be a welcome relief. I love when a student can combine their own insights, passions, and intellectual glitches into an essay that gives me more insight into the student. A few warnings. First, most students are not nearly as funny as they think they are. Your sense of humor is unique and not always appreciated by those outside of your immediate circle. Some humor in the wrong setting can be seen as racist, sexist or off color. Second, other than the fact you are different does this essay convey a sense of you? Is the essay comprehensive in the traits you are trying to display? Third, does the essay tell me you will do well in college - academically and emotionally? I have seen some big fails in the area of creative. One student submitted a letter written in the voice of a four year old sister and written in crayon. This one screamed for a psychological evaluation.

Another student began by bragging about a facility with poetry. The entire essay was in iambic pentameter - and done really badly. Do keep in mind that everyone reads these letters with different eyes. I may see an essay that seems really creative. Someone else may look at the same essay as over the top. More and more universities are accepting video "letters" or allow alternative media. Especially if you have specific talents, look into the options.

The last word on this issue: be very careful of anything that shows anger issues, an obsession with guns or violence, domestic abuse issues or suicidal tendencies. Universities are extremely sensitive to these issues and likely to instantly reject the student.

Rule 9: Word choice. First rule: do not use expletives. At the right time and in the right place such words can give a gritty punch. A personal statement is not the right time or place. Choose your words wisely. You will be judged by the words you choose.

At one point I taught English for some years. I have always been fascinated by how rich the English language truly is. The English lexicon is far more developed than any other language. As such, you have a unique ability not available to most language groups to choose the exact right word. For example, how many words can you think of to replace "beautiful?" How about pretty, cute, amazing, awe inspiring, like a goddess, scintillating, alluring, bewitching, attractive, wow!, amazing, sublime, angelic, gorgeous, exquisite or comely? I am certain that with the aid of a good thesaurus you could name even more. As such, don't use boring words. Make every word count and find the exact right word to convey the emotion for which you are grasping. If you get set up on a blind date and all your cousin says is "nice," that should cause some small degree of panic. What does "nice" mean?! Is she stunning? Will all my friends be jealous? Or does she have a third eye and a hunchback? "Nice" is far too vague for a first date. Don't use it for a personal statement. Also, don't use: a lot, stuff, etc., things, big, small, fast, slow, wanna, gonna, hafta.

Rework your essay and find the exact right word. She isn't nice - she is angelic with a face that inspires poets. The hill wasn't big. It was enormous or gigantic or awe inspiring or monumental. The flip side of course is that you can go too far the other direction. One or two ten-dollar words are excellent. Ten or fifteen ten-dollar words make it sound like you are pretentious. Be very careful to use the words correctly. I always got a sick thrill from emasculating students who used the fancy vocabulary incorrectly.

Rule 10: Grammar. This essay should be one of the most important in your life. If you do not take the time to edit it, what does that say about you? I tell the students I work with to expect to go through three or four drafts. It is not unusual for me to tell a student on the first draft that the essay just won't work. Start over. This is one of the reasons you can not afford to procrastinate on these essays. The essays will need more than one draft and will need editing. You don't want your parents to edit the final draft. Your parents know you too well and are too invested. Some parents won't be critical enough. Other parents will want to write the essay themselves. Neither helps. Find someone who will give you a serious edit. Teachers and counselors tend to be good choices, but you are not looking for "nice." Find the teacher or counselor that will do a serious edit, not just glance at the essay and say, "That's really nice." The same is true with a letter of recommendation, follow up with a thank you note. Don't try to tailor the essay to what "X" university wants as it probably won't work for "Y" university. Instead, use your own authentic voice. Finally, remember that editing takes time. Do not expect a favorite English teacher to give you the edit you need over his lunch break.

*I found a really good personal statement online. Can I use it?*

Never. First the essay was written by someone else for someone else. If this essay fits you, too, the essay fails. Of course there is the issue of academic integrity. More importantly college representatives speak and email and call and write and visit each other. If you have a college fair and 38 schools attend, they all stay in the same hotel. The representatives often go to dinner together or rent a car and visit the local tourist sites. Some of the competing schools are on the same tour for weeks at a time. What do you think they talk about?

Some years ago a young man wrote a truly outstanding and original essay. It went viral. Every college admission's officer I know was aware of it. Dozens and dozens of students copied it over the next several years, some word for word. Admission's officers I know still have a good laugh at the expense of the unwitting student who submitted a copied essay. I am not including it for fear that some student will copy if not the essay itself, the format. If you can find the essay in a book or on the Internet, so can the university. Particularly stupid is to use the exact same essay as an older brother who applied at the exact same university two years before.

*Should I list my clubs or my achievements?*

No, you have another place to do that. Your space is really limited. Somewhere else on your application is a place to list your clubs, sports, activities, hobbies and awards. Don't repeat it here. If there is one club that really matters, use that club but don't just rehash your list of "stuff."

*I can't fit it all in. Is the word limit really a limit or just a suggestion?*

Back in the day, when the essays were mailed in, you had more latitude. No one would sit and count words. You still needed to be close, but you could at least finish the sentence.

Today almost everything is done online. The essay prompts lock when you reach the word limit. While we are on the topic, be careful about sending admission's offices extra stuff. There are advisors that will recommend sending grades and extra letters, photos and videos, Internet links and hometown newspapers, music tapes and essay samples, art portfolios and letters from Mom, and the list goes on. There are times and places to send something extra, but as a whole sending lots of extra material just annoys and slows down the admission's office. If there is one emotion you should try to avoid in college admissions, it is annoyance.

*In the end what needs to be in my essays?*

Each essay is different and each should convey a unique perspective. There is no single answer. When you think you are finished go back and reread your edited essays to answer the following questions.

1) Does this actually answer the prompt? You have some latitude with this, but the prompt is still the prompt.

2) Does this really tell about you? If your best friend or your brother could use the same essay, you failed. Open up. Reveal who you are and what makes you different. This is an introduction to you! Show your humor, your quirks, your imperfections, your desires and your ambition.

3) Does this essay tell or does it show? Anyone can say that she wants to be a doctor - and lots do. Why? How can I know? How have you proved it? Anyone can say he wants to attend Harvard - and lots do. Why? How can I know? How have you proved it? Do some research. Give details in the essays that you have actually done some research. Don't write something prosaic like, "I really like the value of the education I will receive at Harvard." Duh!

What separates you from everyone else? Why does Harvard want you? What do you really know about Harvard?

*Can I get a sample personal statement?*

No. That defeats the purpose. The key word here is "personal." By the same token, there are lots and lots of books that have compiled personal statements. I have read maybe a half dozen of them. They are not bad, but none of them are you. I really don't recommend books on college essays much. The biggest reason is reading someone else's perfect personal statement that got that individual into Stanford makes it too tempting to copy some phrases, ideas or structure. If you are really stuck, then go ahead and look at some, but absolutely do not have the book on your desk when you start typing.

*My English teacher made a class assignment for the personal statement. She is asking all of us to follow a format.*

Ugh. Remember this is individual. If what you can say fits a format, you failed on the individual part. I believe your English teacher has good intentions, but good intentions can pave the way to . . . well, you know. My recommendation is to do what she wants and then submit something different.

## Chapter 11: Your Life in Someone Else's Hands

Everything to this point was preparation. The real game starts senior year. One of the biggest issues I have had with students is fall of senior year. Fall semester of senior year is not the right time to become angsty, apathetic, fearful or simply bored with the idea of college. I can work with and fix almost anything. I can't fix students choosing not to turn in applications or missing deadlines. I can say from experience, as a parent don't trust that everything is done and submitted just because your son or daughter tells you it was submitted. You must double check everything. There are times for privacy and letting your teen have responsibility. I'm not convinced this is the time. I have had experiences before where a student kept telling his parents everything was turned in when he was in fact procrastinating. He missed some deadlines. I have had experiences where a student told her parents that she was done when in fact she submitted nothing because her boyfriend wasn't going to college, and she wanted to stay with him. The girl stayed at community college, and the relationship ended around September. I have also had situations where everything was submitted on time and properly, but for whatever reason there was a glitch in the system and Common App did not upload some essays. The parents caught this two days before the deadline after double checking everything.

*What is the first step senior year?*

Summer of senior year I need your teen to do two things. First, finish the personal statement and have it edited over the summer. The first quarter of senior year flies by faster than anticipated. Every senior I have ever talked to says that it seemed as if school started, they went to sleep the first night and woke up in November. There is so much going on senior year that your student will have far less time than anticipated. As the personal statement is one of the most important on the to-do list and one of the most time consuming, have the statement completed and ready to submit by August. Do not wait until Christmas break to start! I can not tell you how many times I have had procrastinating students thinking it is okay to call a favorite teacher Christmas Day to edit a personal statement that needs to be submitted two days later. You do not often get the answer you want. Get it done early!

Second, make a list of colleges that you will be applying to. I recommend doing this in a spreadsheet format to keep track. Something like this:

|  | Location | Deadline | Extra essays | ED/EA | Submitted | Missing docs | Accepted | Total costs | Fin. Aid | Final Costs |
|---|---|---|---|---|---|---|---|---|---|---|
| In State School | | | | | | | | | | |
| University of | | | | | | | | | | |
| OMG | | | | | | | | | | |
| School 3 | | | | | | | | | | |
| School 4 | | | | | | | | | | |

On the left side list your schools. On the top I list the location - it matters, deadlines - put the final due dates, extra essays - are any extra essays needed and at what date, is the school early decision or early action - I'll explain shortly, date you submitted, are you still missing documents, date you received acceptance (or rejection / wait list), total costs - I will explain later what to include, financial aid - more details later, and final costs - subtract the last two columns.

I suggest a list because it is difficult to keep all the schools straight. After the seventh application it is easy to forget if the materials have been sent into all the schools, if school 6 still needs a transcript or school 5 needs an application fee. I would go one step further and print it out. Hang the copy in junior's bedroom or even on the bathroom mirror. Then the list will act as a constant reminder of what needs to be done still.

I recommend applying to 10-12 schools. I know this is a lot. Most of the other individuals and companies offering college advice recommend far fewer. I ask for so many because of financial aid. Financial aid packages have become more and more unpredictable. An increasingly difficult factor for families is that schools have been raising prices yearly, but the same schools do not raise their merit-based packages. Let me give you an example. Two brothers applied to the same liberal arts school in Pennsylvania recently. The older brother had a 24 on the ACT, decent grades, lots of community service and wonderful leadership. The younger brother had a 29 on the ACT, considerable community service and leadership and was the valedictorian. The two brothers applied exactly three years apart. Neither qualified for financial need. By the numbers the younger brother should have received more money. He in fact did receive a higher merit-based package. In the final tally, though, the older brother would have owed close to $9,000 a year. The younger brother, with the bigger merit-based package, would have owed around $26,000 a year. Over four years that is a difference of $68,000! I don't really blame the school or hold anyone at fault, so I am not naming the school. It serves as an example of why I like to cast a large net, though. I am never sure year to year where the financial aid numbers will come out.

    I want one school to be an in state public school. There is always a chance that the public school will be cheapest. I rarely see this, but it is possible. I know a lot of the college services that "guarantee" acceptance at "one of your top two schools" usually insists that one of the schools be the in state school. This is almost a sure bet as acceptance rates at the in state public schools are usually far more generous than liberal arts colleges (with the notable exception of the state of California). In addition, I can not predict what factors will change senior year. Some years ago I had a young man set to go out of state. In the course of senior year his father had a massive stroke. The student decided it was in the best interests of his family to stay in state and help provide care and emotional support for his father.

I want one school to be what I call the OMG School. This is the school that the student has been dreaming about since he or she was 9, the school that the well-meaning uncle bought a sweatshirt for at Christmas, the school that may be a bit of a reach. I will never tell a student not to shoot high. There is always the admission's office that will see something not apparent to others in your student or maybe the school really needs one more archaeology major and your son is the only other applicant. I can't predict it. I know what the odds are, but sometimes I am pleasantly surprised. To be clear, I am not trying to get every student to apply to Ivy League schools on a whim. There are schools that are a reach and schools that are a fantasy. There are students I work with where Brown is a reach. There are others where Brown just isn't in the cards.

The last 8-10 schools should be about the same level and about what the student can get into. Remember, the big state universities are rarely affordable to out of state students. The easiest way to tell if this school is reasonable is to look at the average ACT / SAT scores. Go to College Board at https://www.collegeboard.org/. Under "college search" type in the name of the school. Under the tab that says "applying" go to the SAT /ACT scores. I am going to use ACT in my example for simplicity, but SAT works just as well.

If your student's scores are above the average - you can get in and get money.

If your student's scores are exactly average - you can get in but money will be more limited.

If your student's scores are below average - you may not get in and there will be little money.

I am oversimplifying this, but this is a good place to start. Remember that the first cut is on grades and test scores. Of the two, test scores matter more. Obviously, a really outstanding candidate can overcome bad test scores and a mediocre candidate may be crushed even with good test scores. The test scores give me a baseline, though.

To give a concrete example, at the time of this writing Coe College in Iowa was looking for a 22-28 on the ACT. That means that a student who has a 33 is not only in a really good position for acceptance but is also competitive for their highest merit-based scholarships. Could the same student get into Notre Dame in Indiana? The University of Notre Dame wants an ACT of 32-35, so a 33 would be competitive. That student - depending on a lot of factors - may find Coe College to be more affordable, though.

If another student had a 23 on the ACT, Coe College is still possible, though not as confidently. Merit based scholarships will be more difficult to obtain - though possible. Notre Dame becomes a real stretch, and depending on the other factors in the application, a fantasy.

I know many students are planning to retake the ACT / SAT in senior year. That is fine, but as a rule of thumb I say three points as a change. I don't encourage students with a 23 on the ACT to apply to Notre Dame in the hope that the next score will be higher. Going from a 23 to a 26 (or a 23 to a 20) is completely reasonable. I do not usually see a student jump ten points on a single test - though I had one student prove me wrong.

To recap, create a list of 10-12 schools. One school in state. One school as a reach. The remainder should be about the same level dependent on a student's ACT /SAT scores. Parents, weigh in on the choices. Students seek advice from you parents, a respected teacher or a counselor who has experience with out of state schools.

*I was told that in state schools are always cheaper. Is that true?*

Sometimes. Rarely in my experience. In theory, as a resident of Mississippi you have been paying taxes for years that in part subsidize the Mississippi public college / university system. As such many of the in state schools will offer you a better price. If your student decided to go to a public school in Alabama, where you did not pay taxes for the last eighteen years, the state of Alabama will charge an additional surcharge for the privilege. As such, when attending a school out of state, private schools are almost always cheaper in the final calculation.

The complication is that Mississippi State University has a very large number of students. By the same token the school has limited funds, a relatively small endowment and priorities that include very expensive athletic programs. To give you some real numbers, at the time of this writing, Mississippi State charged about $25,000 a year for residents of Mississippi and $41,000 a year for out of state residents. The average student sees 41% of his financial aid (merit based and need based scholarships combined) as loans and the school on average only covers 78% of the need to begin with. To use real numbers - based on averages - if a student has an expected family contribution (EFC) of $10,000 (to use large round numbers), which leaves an in state resident with a debt of $15,000 a year. The school offers 78% of that or $11,700. Of that 41% is loans or $4,797. That means the school actually gives the family - playing average numbers - $6,903. The family pays about $18,000 a year. There are other scholarships available at the school, but considering the size of the student body, the amounts available are actually quite limited.

To give a comparison, Millsaps College is just down the highway in Jackson, MS. To be fair I will use averages again. Millsaps College costs about $56,000 in state or out of state. Because the college is private and never received money from the state, the school charges everyone the same price. (Well, international students probably pay more.) I know that is a big number, but it is sticker shock. Very few students actually pay this. Let's assume the same expected family contribution of $10,000 a year. That leaves a need for $46,000 a year. Millsaps on average gives 79% of need or $36,340. Of this 19% are loans or $6904.60. So, a family at Millsaps is looking at an initial need-based package where the family pays $26, 564.60.

On the surface it appears that Millsaps will cost about $8,000 a year more. I can make an argument about the costs of education and the value received, class sizes and the quality of the faculty, reputation or rigor of the classes, but $8000 a year is still significant. Millsaps, though, also offers merit based aid. Students can get money for art or music scholarships, for being Methodist, for living in certain counties within Mississippi, for being part of the scouts, leadership, drama or most importantly for good grades and test scores. Using the official website (http: //www.millsaps.edu/financial-aid/scholarships-grants-loans-students.php), if your student has an ACT score of 28 the student is now eligible for an additional $27,000 - $30,000 in aid. What this means in practice is that a good student is almost guaranteed more money at Millsaps than Mississippi State. When I add the merit based and financial need scholarships together I would estimate a payment of around $10,000-12,000 a year. Mostly what a family is paying is expected family contribution, though it rarely works out dollar for dollar. With some effort, interest, the right factors and a little luck the student will pay quite a bit less than this.

To be fair, Mississippi State also has merit-based scholarships (http: //www.admissions.msstate.edu/freshmen/money-matters/scholarships/academic-scholarships/). The same student will have earned up to $4,000 in merit-based scholarships. Millsaps should still be more affordable.

Are there exceptions? Always. That is why I urge students to apply to at least one in state university in addition to the rest of the schools on the list. I simply encourage families to think outside of the box and apply at some good quality liberal arts schools as well.

*Are there any public universities that are affordable?*

In general public universities have more students and less money. The in state tuition offered is usually not unrealistic, though I maintain a family can usually do better. It is also more difficult to bargain over price with a public university. Generally speaking, you get what you get. One item to research is regional compacts. These are deals that offer reduced rates to states within the compact. For example, being from Arizona, my students can usually find competitive offers in New Mexico or Hawaii or a few other states. The catch is that the schools still cost more and are loathe to put more financial aid on top. The argument is something like, "We already gave you a HUGE discount. What else do you want?" Other times the most prestigious schools opt out. For Arizona students Washington state seems like a really welcome change. Eastern Washington University - close to Idaho and freezing cold in winter - is on the list, but University of Washington in Seattle is not on the list.

Ask schools as the schools do not like to volunteer the information. Ask if the school is part of a compact like Academic Common Market, Midwestern Higher Education Compact, New England Board of Higher Education or Western Undergraduate Exchange. All the compacts work a little bit differently and the governing agreements are subject to change as are the members.

*How do I know if it is a good school?*

Most people judge a school by name recognition. This is imperfect at best. Some of the schools I love to use the most - and schools that I use with dozens and dozens of teenagers - are schools that are not often "heard of." There is absolutely nothing wrong with asking around. Please ask your co-workers, the parents of your son's friends, your boss, a high school counselor or teacher. That is a rather limited list, though. I know most of those on that list will mention the big state schools, schools with prominent athletic teams or schools that are "Ivy League." I'm going to put aside the Ivy League for now as most students just can't get in. The big state schools and well known athletic schools are obvious as to why they make the list. I urge you to go beyond that list, though. One great list to begin with is the "Colleges that Change Lives," named after a book some years ago written by Loren Pope. You can find the list of these schools at https://ctcl.org/ . Another good resource is, again, College Board. https://www.collegeboard.org/

Let's go back to the search. This time let's try a big "sports" school - Arizona State University. Due to the supremacy of its athletic programs, it certainly has name recognition. ASU in Phoenix, AZ is a school with an excellent reputation and "a name." Look at the numbers, though. Under "Majors and Learning Environment" - the first numbers that should stand out are the percentage "Returning Sophomore Year" and the percentage "Graduating in 6 Years" - 87% and 63% respectively at the time of this writing. 87% isn't bad, but 63% leaves me with some concerns. In general I want these numbers to be higher than 80%.

I don't expect a school to be at 100% on these numbers. There is always some attrition because the school was harder than expected, the student had family issues, the student made poor personal choices, finances change or a pregnancy side tracks the student. If either set is below 80%, questions should be raised. Why do less than three quarters of those that begin at

ASU not finish? To be fair, there could be some reasons that are completely valid. The most common I find is that many schools admit students that are marginal. ASU for example is only looking for a 22-29 on an ACT. In the scheme of things, those scores are relatively low. So, my supposition that the school let in students that were not ready yet plays out. Another factor that I find frequently, and one that is less benign, concerns financial aid. For many schools normal operations mean giving more financial aid to incoming freshmen and slowly withdrawing that aid as the student progresses on the theory that it is too late to transfer. A university that was affordable freshman year can become completely unrealistic by junior year.

So, look at another school - Morningside College in Sioux City, IA. Their retention rate sophomore year is just 70% and their 6 year graduation rate is just 56%. That raises some serious concerns for me. Grinnell College, just down the road, is at 96% and 87% respectively. Does this mean that Morningside is a "bad" school and Grinnell a "good" school? Nothing is quite that simple, but I would certainly have concerns about Morningside over Grinnell. There might still be some good reasons to send a student to Morningside, but as a parent I would certainly want to address some numbers first.

Additionally, while still on the web page with Grinnell, click on the small blue print on the left column that says "see similar colleges." Grinnell's list is composed of Cornell University, Boston University, New York University, Brown, Oberlin, Vassar, Carleton, University of Chicago, Kenyon, Northwestern, Harvard, Amherst, Macalester, Columbia and Swarthmore. This is supposed to be a list of where else students apply. It is not a bad starting point and often gives really good comparisons including some schools under your radar, but it is not perfect. One example, if you look up Cornell College (in Iowa), the list of similar schools does a poor job of matching Cornell College and instead matches better with Cornell University in New York.

A final option is U.S. News and World Report's rankings. I am always hesitant to use US News and World Report as the ranking system is highly contentious and weighted towards schools with low acceptance rates. Low acceptance does not always mean a better school. US News is not a bad resource, but one should use the ranking with a grain of salt. Similarly, Forbes has a list of best value colleges. Forbes' list is not a bad list to peruse. One might also try the Center for College Affordability and Productivity (http://centerforcollegeaffordability.org/) on which the Forbes' list is based. Also have your teen search Niche (https://www.niche.com/colleges/search/best-colleges/) which offers a student perspective. College Week Live (https://www.collegeweeklive.com/) can connect your student directly to admissions counselors. I often like to reference several lists just to get a head start on where to look.

After much hesitation I have included a list of schools I have used in Appendix B. The list is certainly not every possible school. This is simply a starting point. Anyone with some experience will note that there are some notable omissions. Some omissions are my fault. I just have not used the school or am not aware of the school yet. Some omissions are intentional as I just didn't need "X" when I had "Y" and "Z" and both "Y" and "Z" did an excellent job. Some omissions are due to interactions I have had with admissions and or financial aid. These negative interactions are my own experiences and do not necessarily reflect everyone's experiences. Instead of putting a school on blast, though, I have simply omitted the school. For example, one such school came off my list when the dean of admissions told me in a phone conversation with a note of derision in his voice, "We at _____ will never accept a student from a high school called Martin Luther King, Jr. or Cesar Chavez." Another school that is omitted asked me in a conversation where I was inquiring about a number of students, "Don't you have any white students?" Another I omitted because the financial aid office lost tax returns and some very sensitive financial information - twice! I advised the family not to send it a third time and took the school off my list.

Also, please be aware that schools frequently change their focus and change their admission's staff. A bad experience one year may be very pleasant three years later (and vice versa). Take any list - from me or anyone else - as starting points and suggestions only.

*Should I worry about class size?*

Colleges love to talk about class size. I never pay any attention to what the schools say about class size. I believe that class size can be a huge indicator of success. I am in a unique position where the majority of students I have worked with are with me for three or more years. By the time senior year approaches I really like the students. As such I really want the student in a program where he or she is noticed and has an opportunity to stand out. I love small classes where every student is involved in discussion and debate. I love settings so intimate that when a student does not show up for a class, the professor calls her on her cell phone to make sure she is doing okay. Conversely, I despise large stadium seating where your student is never more than row 46 seat 17. This venue does not encourage questions or discussion. Professors often seem aloof and unavailable. There is far too much emphasis on the student's own drive to succeed with little external support.

I recently had a student attend a small liberal arts school in Iowa. She made a tactical error. The student called Mom early in the morning to ask what insurance plan she had and then hung up and turned off her phone. Still struggling to wake up, Mom snapped into consciousness with the realization, "Why would my daughter need her insurance information? What is wrong? What happened?!" The teen had turned off her phone. Mom called the roommate, some friends, campus security, campus administration and just about everyone else who mattered. In addition to taking Mom seriously, the entire campus began searching for her daughter - who was in class with her phone turned off. Despite the embarrassment, this serves as a lesson for me. How many schools would take the effort to find one student who may or may not actually need help?

Despite this I never ask about class size. The simple reason is that the numbers given are rarely accurate. A school can choose not to include part time students. A school can count all the professors including those that do not teach, teach only one class or are on sabbatical. A school that boasts a graduate school where class sizes are smaller by nature will include those numbers. I do not believe I have ever found a school where class sizes are reported to be larger than 35. I know of plenty of schools where the first year introductory classes like Psychology 101 or English 102 or introduction to calculus or first year philosophy can number in the hundreds.

The best gauge I have found for a class size is a tour of the campus. If you tour a campus and the student guide is explaining the class size, look at the rooms. If all the classes you see hold twenty students or so, the class size is relatively small. I have had the experience, though, where an admission's officer proudly boasted that the class size was a maximum of 25 while we were seated in a lecture hall that held more than 200. Another time I toured a school that promised "very small classes" and yet room after room was crammed with so many chairs that literally the only way to get to the back row was to climb over another chair. Not only was the school exaggerating class sizes, the school was probably in violation of several fire codes.

Small schools generally have small classes. Large schools will have at least some very large classes, usually for freshmen and sophomores. As a student's schedule gets more and more specialized the class size tends to fall. A large school's small classes will still be 20-30 students whereas a small school's small classes may be 6.

*Should I apply Ivy League?*

Most students (and parents) feel that Ivy League schools (Harvard, Princeton, Yale, Cornell University, Brown, Colombia, Dartmouth and the University of Pennsylvania) are the best schools that the United States offers. In fact, the schools are internationally famous. Ivy League schools simply are not for everyone.

On the positive side, these schools certainly offer a name recognition. Every first employer takes note when the candidate is a graduate from the University of Pennsylvania or Dartmouth. The name does mean something. The second job interview does not see quite the same benefit. After the first job much more important than the school is what a candidate did in her last position, the experience and the skills a candidate is bringing to the table.

The alumni's network is not to be discounted. The University of Illinois is an excellent school with a well-deserved reputation. There are U of I alumni all over the country. Yale still trumps U of I. The alumni's network is much more developed. There is also a sort of "club" mentality. One of the first questions a Yale graduate will ask will be what house the recent graduate lived in. The house provides a sort of insider's code that few if any schools can replicate and the connections that come with that not so hidden fraternity are not to be overlooked.

As I explain to my students, if a student attends the University of Connecticut, the roommate can hook you up with a great discount at Subway. At Yale, your roommate might own Subway. Obviously, I am using hyperbole, but the point is clear. A graduate from an Ivy League school can see doors opened at a higher level and faster than elsewhere. Due to the name recognition and the contacts it is possible for a new graduate to start in mid-level management. A graduate from the University of Connecticut will most likely begin in a cubicle. In time, the second student can climb the ladder, catch up to and even pass the Ivy League alum, but everything is made easier when a new graduate starts higher on the ladder. A quick search online will provide lots of stories and some data that Ivy League graduates also suffer in the job market. Just because a student graduates from Harvard, there is no guarantee that he will get a job or get paid what he thinks he is worth. Even Harvard grads can be passed up for the boss's nephew that just graduated from the local state school with a "C" average.

The research opportunities are unequaled by almost anyone else. The Ivy League schools certainly attract a wealth of talent and intellect. The Ivy Leagues have a reputation to preserve and are quite good at making sure the faculty helps build on that reputation. Funding for experiments or studies is nearly inexhaustible. Equipment for research is also unprecedented. If your physics student wants to play with a cyclotron, she needs to attend Harvard or University of California - Berkeley. Cornell University and Stanford boast some of the only access to an electron-positron collider.

Another boon that Ivy League schools possess is the ego factor. I have yet to meet the mother who does not casually drop, "Yes, my son is trying to decide between Princeton and Dartmouth," or "I can't wait until my daughter gets home for Christmas from Colombia." There is certainly a status symbol around these schools. If you are unsure about this, visit the bookstore on campus. If an object can be branded, it is. I know that the University of Wisconsin brands as well, but Colombia could teach them something.

Finally is the cost. Cost is a double-edged sword with the Ivy League schools. For families of means, a student should expect to pay full price and then some. There is a common belief - not entirely unfounded - that donations can help your son or daughter be accepted. Officially, the universities would probably deny this. Unofficially, I encourage families of a certain tax bracket to donate - and it is a substantial amount - beginning about ... birth. A middle class family will be asked to pay on a sliding scale. I have found that though the school is actually reasonable, it is not often as generous as the family was expecting. Can Princeton compete with ... Juniata financially? Of course! Will Princeton match dollar for dollar? Sometimes. There are many variables here. The best advice I can give is try to use what another school is giving you as leverage. For a family that is financially strapped - a marker lower than most expect - Ivy Leagues can be great. These schools have endowments that other schools can only fantasize about. If Harvard decides that your son is a good fit and you are truly broke, score! I can virtually guarantee that your family can afford Harvard. Just keep in mind that "broke" for Harvard is considerably lower than what most families count as "broke."

Now the reasons against Ivy League. First of course is that the costs can be prohibitive. For middle class families in particular I like to balance need-based and merit-based aid. Cornell University will insist - and not wrongly - that 100% of its students qualify for merit-based aid. As such, no student receives merit-based aid at Cornell - at least not for grades and tests. That means these schools at least initially have the potential to cost more for middle class families.

Ivy League schools are notoriously difficult to win admissions at. I will be the first to tell you that the schools have a lot of clearly unqualified candidates inflating those numbers, but not all of it is inflated. For your student to be accepted to an Ivy League institution he or she truly needs to stand out. I promise that the university is asking itself reading your son's admissions file if this young man will really stand out in ten or twenty years. Will he write a Pulitzer Prize winning novel or win a Noble prize in economics? Will she find the code that finally cracks cancer or create a multi-billion dollar company at 24? Will he find the missing link on an African plateau? Will she be elected president of the United States? How will your student increase the prestige of the university later in life? It is a guessing game, but the university is looking for students that already stand out as an 18 year old applicant. The only schools harder to get into are the military academies.

Another negative is that the "teaching" at these universities often suffers. While not exclusive, popular thought says a professor can research or teach. At Ivy League schools the emphasis is certainly on research. Class size is another good indication. Princeton's freshman classes are much larger than many of the liberal arts colleges within an hour's drive. Whereas a freshman class at a big state university might number several hundred, Princeton's freshmen classes will be much smaller at only 40-50. Muhlenberg College in Pennsylvania may not have any classes larger than 20. The small liberal arts schools really make a concerted effort to keep classes smaller and connect with students. That is not to say that every student has equal access at Muhlenberg, but it is easier to get noticed, get help and find a mentor at a school like Muhlenberg.

In the same vein, though a school like Harvard has immense resources and access to the best internships and job markets, many of the best resources are reserved for graduate students. Smaller liberal arts colleges don't have graduate students and as such farm out the best opportunities and the best access to the undergraduate students. An exemplary student at

Harvard is among a large group of exemplary students and will have a more difficult time getting noticed. An exemplary student at Simpson College in Iowa will most likely benefit from the maximum assistance the faculty can give. Perhaps a Harvard professor has better contacts, and that is not always a given, but the student at Harvard may never hear of the choices that a Simpson College student eagerly follows up on. To use a sports analogy, if the Chicago Cubs announce a season internship, do you want your son trying out at the same time as the players on his local baseball team or the players of the Lowell Spinners, an affiliate for the Boston Red Socks? In which group can your son better stand out?

My final reservation about Ivy League schools comes back to money. A student from a family that struggles financially will often find himself out of place and at times in a socially awkward situation. There may be three or four unintentional slights per day. To give a concrete example, a young man I knew attended an Ivy League school and made friends with students in a very different social class. They would often go out on the weekend. Each student in the group took turns paying for the evening's activities. At the end of one Friday night, the young man received a bill for slightly more than $1000 - or about three weeks' pay for his father. It was with much embarrassment that he had to ask his friends to cover it - which they did with no hesitation. It is not always easy being the poor kid in a group of very wealthy and entitled students.

Ivy League schools offer some great opportunities and often deserve the reputation they have worked so hard to build. The schools are not ideal for every student. I am much less besotted with Ivy League schools than many of the parents I speak with. The name does matter, but it is not always the most important factor. Most important, beyond the brand, is if the school is indeed a good fit. If accepted, all the Ivy League schools will make every effort to have your son or daughter visit the school. I believe that is an absolute must. I have known individuals who get accepted to Ivy League schools, attended elsewhere and were very happy with the decision. I have known others who were accepted, attended, and still very happy. Everything comes down to the individual.

*That's nice for those other kids, but I simply will not feel validated unless my son attends an Ivy League school. What can he do?*

There are three well known back doors. First is try to find out what majors are actually highly in demand. Every school is glutted with biology majors. Most are really hurting for some of the smaller ones like theology. I had an acquaintance once that tried twice to get into Harvard's business school unsuccessfully. The next year he applied for the school of divinity. He was accepted and then changed his major to business. These loopholes are closing very quickly.

The second option is a 3:2 program specifically for engineering but increasingly for law as well. Your son will begin at a lesser known university as an engineering major. After completing basic classes and keeping the GPA over a certain point, he will then transfer at a much higher acceptance rate to far more prestigious school to finish his education with a master's in engineering. I have also seen several schools that have begun similar pre-law programs. I am a huge fan of these programs as a B.A. in pre-law garners nothing. This helps students get into far more selective institutions. For example, I know that the University of Southern California and Washington in St. Louis have a number of relationships for a 3:2 program. The downside is that the transfer usually loses all or most financial aid.

A third option is community education programs. Many of the prestigious Ivy League schools have old charters where the school has guaranteed community education. It is entirely possible to move to let's say Cambridge, MA and then begin taking classes at the same revered institution with some of the same professors. Your son would not usually be able to live in the dorms and would not have access to all the athletic and social events. In addition, the final diploma is often written in simple English as opposed to the archaic Latin for the regular diploma. Many of these programs are actually quite affordable, though living expenses in a nearby town can be exorbitant.

*Should I consider HBCU schools?*

A HBCU school is a historically black college or university. The best among them, in no particular order - and at the risk of leaving some off a rather extensive list - include Spelman, Howard, Xavier in Louisiana, Florida A & M, Jackson State, Tuskegee, North Carolina A & T, Morehouse, Winston-Salem, Clark-Atlanta and Elizabeth City State. There are many more than this. The schools are public, private, big schools, medium schools and small schools. Some of the schools are women only, others male only. Most schools are coed. As a whole, the schools have an excellent reputation for academics. Some of the schools like Spelman are still 96% African American. Others like Xavier are only 79% African American. No matter what the percentages, the schools offer a unique educational experience.

As a whole, I have a great deal of respect for HBCUs and the education that is offered. I still evaluate the schools just like I do every other school I use in terms of graduation rates, matriculation rates, average test scores, financial aid and location. Some of these schools will simply not work on that rubric; others will work really well.

One factor that must be considered though is that the school offers a very different experience based on the racial makeup. For Caucasian students it can be quite a culture shock to suddenly be the minority. Even for African American students the experience is a culture shock. The best advice I can give, try to visit with an overnight experience. These schools are really good schools overall, but they all offer a very unique experience.

*My daughter wants to be an artist. She is a free spirit. Should she attend a school just for the arts?*

I am always hesitant with arts schools. Some, particularly when we reference schools of music, can be excellent schools. Most of these are for-profit institutions, though. I have a special disdain for for-profit schools. The school's stated purpose is to milk your teen for every last penny and leave her drowning in a morass of debt at a far too high interest rate. In addition, though I understand your daughter is a "free spirit" at 18, what happens if she faces an existential crisis mid-way through sophomore year and wants to switch to social justice or even accounting? An arts school is usually severely limited in the majors offered.

In the end, I would advise adding one or two to the college list. Evaluate the schools in terms of graduation rates, acceptance rates and financial aid the exact same as you would another school and see what the numbers say in March. In my experience a small liberal arts school can often do as well as or better than an art school. The exception to all the above is an acceptance to Juilliard. Juilliard is special - an elite school of the arts that I just can not compare to any other school. See Appendix 2 for a more complete list of arts schools.

*Should I consider the military?*

The military is rarely my first choice. I must confess I am rather perturbed every time I watch the army van loaded with popular video games pull up to a school at lunch. "Sure you can play. Why don't you just fill out this form giving me your name, phone number, address and email?" The marine recruiters surely create an imposing image in their dress uniform. I have known far too many young men who joined the marines just to wear dress blues to the senior prom.

My problem with the military has several origins. First, the military tends to disproportionally recruit from low income - high minority schools. I understand that these schools tend to yield the best results, but I still find the practice vaguely predatory. Second, I have known far too many recruiters that say whatever a student wants to hear. My personal favorite line is, "No, I don't think you will go to Afghanistan. We really need people in Germany right now." Five months later I get a postcard from Kabul. Third - and most important, entering the service right out of high school seems to be . . . a stall.

When a student enlists right out of high school he or she is usually entering as enlisted. The young man or woman has no real rank. He or she will say "Yes, sir!" fifteen or twenty times an hour. The student will learn few marketable skills. Private first class really does not impress universities or employers. Master sergeant is impressive, but I wish any student luck attaining a rank that most people who devote their life to the military do not obtain. I much prefer my students who enter the military do so as an officer.

A student who enters as an officer does so with more responsibility, more privileges, a higher paygrade, better benefits, a stronger peer group, and a better chance to train in skills that transfer to civilian life more easily. A young man or woman who leaves the military and applies as a captain or second lieutenant will garner attention from colleges and from the job market. The question is how to enter as an officer?

The easiest route, and the one I endorse the most, is the official military academies: West Point, Annapolis, Air Force Academy at Colorado Springs, Merchant Marine Academy or Coast Guard Academy. All of these schools are fantastic institutions. The education and the rigor are unparalleled. Though I rarely see the military as a first choice, I would be delighted to see any of my students enter the military academies. The positives are that students get the honor of attending some of the best institutions in the world, receive a fantastic education, leave with leadership skills and prestige, and pay nothing. The negative is that these are schools to which it is very difficult to gain admission. It is actually easier to gain admission to Harvard than West Point. To be accepted a student MUST obtain a letter of recommendation from a United States congressman, senator or vice president. Please see: http://www.usma.edu/admissions/SitePages/Apply_Nominations.aspx . And, of course, the academies require a minimum of five years military service upon graduation. Most of the graduates end with the military as a profession.

The second route is through a military school other than the academies: University of North Georgia, Norwich, Texas A & M, the Citadel, Virginia Military Institute, or Virginia Polytechnic Institute and State College. The list is alternative military academies. As with the big five, these academies offer an excellent education in exchange for military service. The military schools are not free, but often the schools are cheaper than other university options. While still difficult to gain admission, the schools are far easier than the five large academies and do not require a Congressional recommendation.

Mention should also be made of NAPS (Naval Academy Preparatory School), USMAPS (United States Military Academy Preparatory School) and New Mexico Military School. These schools are designed for students, many of them athletes, who desire admission to one of the larger military academies but do not have the academic qualifications to go directly to one of the academies. The intent is that after one or two years the students will have improved their academic qualifications enough to transfer to an elite military academy. The catch is that this transfer is not guaranteed. There are also a number of preparatory high schools (boarding schools) that promise admission to an elite military institution. I have not seen very positive numbers coming from these high schools.

A third option is ROTC (Reserve Officer Training Corps) http://todaysmilitary.com/training/rotc. Most branches offer some sort of ROTC. With ROTC a student will attend a participating university, and the list is quite extensive. While at the university, a student will also participate in training for the military. The first two years in the program does not generally commit a student to military service. The first two years are generally a trial period. The biggest misconception, though, is that this will mean a "full ride" in college. To be clear ROTC does have scholarships, but the scholarships are competitive and in different amounts. It is entirely possible to go through the university, enter the army, and never receive one penny. It is also possible to go through the university, enter the navy, and never pay a penny for school. It all depends on a student's merits. Academics still matter. The military is happy to take students with questionable academics and unrealized motivation, as enlisted men and women - not officers.

*What classes should I take senior year?*

Far too many counselors I know will encourage students to take an "easy" senior year. I strongly do not recommend this. If a student has followed my advice to this point and taken honors and AP or IB or Cambridge classes, to suddenly drop back and take photography or weight training or student assistant, sends the message that the student is giving up. This makes a student look lazy at precisely the time a student does not want to look lazy. By the same token, I do not encourage having a period or an afternoon off. Missing classes sends the same message. Continue to take challenging and academic classes.

*My counselor told me I have all my credits and can graduate in December. Should I?*

As I was saying above, the last thing you want to do senior year is to look like you are taking it easy. Schools often have an incentive for a student to take a half day - the school still gets federal monies and doesn't need as much staff or as many classes. I know the temptation to leave school at noon is really strong, but in the end this tells a university the student is not serious. By the same token, if a student graduates first semester, then the first question a university will have is, "What did you do second semester?" If all a student does is sit at home and binge watch his favorite television shows, what message is sent about future motivation in school. Very few schools will allow January admittance. If a student is working for that second semester, there is a really good chance that the financial aid will be decreased. The best option in most cases is just to stay in school.

There is one exception to that rule. Some years ago I was working with a young woman. She was in my junior class (mostly 16 and 17 year old students). This particular young woman was 20. When she was in middle school she had some very serious health issues and as such entered high school at 18. I completely understood how she had a decided interest in leaving high school as soon as possible. We worked on a schedule that included evening school and independent study, so she could in fact graduate early. She went to community college for the second semester and then transferred to a four year institution the following year.

*Do I want the same school for my BA as my MA?*

"I wanna be an architect." Or an attorney, or a doctor, or an engineer, or . . . More and more professions require more education than a simple B.A. or B.S. An increasing number, like a B.A. in general business, can get you in the door, but the profession really requires an advanced degree to go beyond an entry level position, generally an MBA in this case. This begs the question if a student should pursue the undergraduate degree at the same institution as he or she wants to pursue the advanced degree.

There are several different ways to look at this and no easy answers. Let us look at a few case studies. One of the most sought after medical schools in the country is Baylor College of Medicine in Texas. Baylor College of Medicine has become so popular because of its sterling reputation and the fact that as medical schools go, Baylor is one of the most affordable. A student decides to go to Baylor University in the hopes that will help her get admitted to Baylor College of Medicine later. This theory has a few flaws. The first problem is despite the similarity in name, Baylor University and Baylor College of Medicine are now two very different schools. Second, all indications are that if any school is favored - and BCM will insist that none are - it is Rice University that is favored with around 30% of the admitted class. (http://www.baylor.edu/prehealth/news.php?action=story&story=40545) Third, even when an institution is actually linked (like the University of Pennsylvania) the graduate school usually makes independent decisions and prefers students from outside of the institution. This is not to say that Baylor University is not an excellent school with a great program of preparation. It is a school I have recommended. Just do not allow your student to fall under the illusions that the search for medical school will somehow be easier.

On the other hand, another student may have his heart set on the medical program at Johns Hopkins University in Maryland. It is one of the preeminent medical schools in the world. That student may not have the grades, test scores, or anything else that stands out for an admission to Johns Hopkins as an undergraduate. The student may instead attend Dickinson College in Pennsylvania to study biology. If the student applies himself at Dickinson College and does well on the MCATs, then it is very possible he can then finish his medical degree at Johns Hopkins.

In the scheme of things, where a student attends for his or her undergraduate degree has little bearing on where he or she will attend graduate school. Just like with high school, the student needs to stand out from the pack and show his or her dedication and scholastic efforts. A student can attend Dartmouth and think of the experience as a four year vacation mostly centered on the manifest of a bar. That student, despite the pedigree of the institution, will find the application difficult to attend any graduate institution of merit. A student at a local community college that transfers to a mediocre state school but really applies herself and demonstrates that her education is indeed on par with the other candidates will have a much better opportunity for an A+ education in graduate school. Attend the undergraduate school that is best for you individually. Tell your advisor freshman year where you want to be in four years and turn the goal into a reality.

*What about colleges that are women only or men only?*

I am terribly fond of universities and colleges that are not coed. The biggest single reason is that the schools are not widely popular. Most of these schools have been around a long time. As such they are well established, have usually garnered an excellent reputation scholastically, and often have sizeable endowments. Your daughter can receive a phenomenal education at a price she can afford at a school where if coed she may not be able to gain admissions. The biggest objection I hear from teens is the fear that he or she may not be able to date. I have found that to be ludicrous. Do you really believe that if there was an all girl's college in town that every single man within 50 miles is not aware of where it is located or when the social functions are planned throughout the year?

Again I am really fond of actual comparisons. Years and years ago before the world was more enlightened, top notch schools were often gender segregated. One hold over of that age can be found on the upper west side of New York City. A tale of two schools if you will - and two mythical students, twins. Sarah and Samantha. Both Sarah and Samantha are enchanted with New York City. Sarah wants to major in biology, Samantha in political science. Both girls took the ACT and received a 31 - respectable, not amazing. Both girls graduate in the top 3% of their class - a very good place to be. Both have shown initiative in beginning community service programs highlighting their respective interests. Both have participated in Mock Trial and Academic Decathlon and won individual awards in the programs. Both played soccer for three years but chose not to play senior year. Both girls are well rounded and above average candidates on paper.

Sarah applies to Columbia University - a coed institution. Columbia of course has a sterling reputation and is a superb institution in the heart of the city. Only 6% of applicants are selected. Columbia is really looking for ACT scores a little higher than Sarah's scores. In addition, Sarah has chosen biology with a pre-med track. This is a major that is glutted and tends to attract the very competition that makes Sarah's respectable 31 look inadequate. Her community service, activities, and initiative certainly help, but in the end, Sarah is turned down. She ends up attending Northeastern University where she does very well.

Samantha applies to Barnard College literally across the street from Columbia. Barnard is in fact all women. Samantha's 31 is actually middle of the pack, though. In addition, Barnard has a 17% acceptance rate. Samantha is terribly excited to share the good news with her family when she is accepted in mid-February. All throughout the next four years Samantha takes some classes at Columbia and some classes at Barnard. She attends athletic events and cultural events at both schools. She crosses between the campuses freely. At no point does anyone look down on her for being a student officially enrolled at Barnard. In fact, after four years she receives a degree that says "Columbia University." Probably the unique experience that would have been different for Samantha as opposed to Sarah is that her entire dorm consisted of women. At no point did she leave her room to see a young man in desperate need of a gym strut down the hall clad only in a wet towel.

There are a number of really good all girls schools still - and several more that have only recently gone coed. In addition to Barnard I would highly recommend researching - and I realize I am leaving some good schools off the list - Bryn Mawr, Mount Holyoke, Mills, Simmons, Smith, Spelman, Scripps and Agnes Scott. As far as schools that are only for men, the list is really short. There are few I really use. One is a very non-traditional school called Deep Springs. Also look at Wabash in Indiana and an HBCU - Morehouse.

*What is the Common App?*

The Common App (http://www.commonapp.org/) is one of the most efficient ways to apply to universities. Over 700 schools subscribe to the service. The beauty of Common App is that a student has one stop shopping. He or she can fill out one application instead of seven or eight. The biggest drawbacks for Common App are that Common App is now limiting the number of schools a student can apply to twelve and not every school is using the service. Despite the draw backs, I strongly recommend this be the very first stop for applications. One feature I really like about Common App is that the navigation system is wonderfully transparent about due dates, fees and essays. Do note which extra essays are required. Keep in mind, if a school says the essay is "optional," it is not actually optional. DO IT!

If a student really really wants to attend a certain school, the clear number one choice, I usually recommend not going through Common App for that top school. Take the time and effort to complete the separate application to show your specific interest and perhaps stand out from the crowd.

Two warnings about the essays. Once again, double check if any extra essays are needed and then double check that the submission went through successfully. Second, be sure that the essays you submit to all the schools fit all the schools. It is rather embarrassing to submit an essay that is specific to the University of Chicago to eleven other schools. The other eleven now know you really want to be in Chicago and may help you make that decision more easily.

Senior year, about the end of August, begin filling out the Common App. Start by listing your top twelve schools. Include one in state school. Consider doing your very first choice on the individual school application. If the list of schools is far too long, start cross referencing which school only accept the Common App and put those on your list first.

*Are there other applications like Common App?*

There are several competing services. Most of the other services I hesitate to recommend yet as the other services have not really established their reputation yet or service a very limited number of schools. The biggest exception, and one I have been using more and more, is the Coalition App (http://www.coalitionforcollegeaccess.org/). One huge positive for me about the Coalition App is the service is really designed to give an overview of a teen's entire high school experience, not just senior year numbers. The Coalition App only services about a quarter of what Common App services, but the schools tend to be much more selective. At this point Common App is used by just about every major university and college - though there will always be exceptions. The Coalition App, at the point of this writing, is more selective. I can recommend just about every school that utilizes the Coalition App. Finally, the majority of my students have reported that they prefer the lay out of Coalition App to Common App. I have used Common App for years and still recommend it, but the Coalition App is worth a look. Especially if reading this book sophomore or junior year, I would recommend starting a file on Coalition App.

*There is a box on the Common App asking if I will be able to view the application later. What do I check?*

Check no. Always opt to keep the recommendations private. If the review or recommendation is public, the university may assume that the reviewer was more positive than he or she would have been otherwise. A good recommendation should not be discounted by a student's insecurity. If a student is not 100% certain on the recommender and on what the recommender may say, rethink asking this individual. At the least do some major but kissing the two weeks before asking for a letter.

*What's in a major?*

The major a student chooses really makes little difference to me. I have found two truths about majors. Truth number one is that students often pick a major because it is high profile or is encouraged by the parents. For example, until recently forensic science was relatively unknown. Even for someone in the business, I had to research to find schools that offered quality programs in forensic science. Then several television shows hit about the same time. All the shows glamorized the career. Within just two years colleges and universities saw a relatively rare program glutted by young students who were certain this was their long dormant passion. The cynic in me thinks that the passion had less to do with real passion and more to do with some really good television.

Truth number two is that most students change their major. There is absolutely nothing wrong with changing majors as long as it happens in the first two years. Students change for a lot of different reasons. Perhaps my young CSI fan got into the first lab with a cadaver and realized that she could never ever get past that smell. Perhaps the course work was harder than expected. Perhaps the new psychology student thought his freshman anthropology professor was so awesome that he developed a new passion for a subject he had never considered. Or maybe the freshman psychology professor was so bad he never wanted another psychology class again. Maybe she got bored or challenged by something else. Maybe she just realized that art history was an actual major and had never really considered the profession before. Or maybe *she* just walked into *that* building and it doesn't matter what it is, *that* is his new major! Whatever the reason, changing majors is perfectly normal, natural and expected by the college.

Most students do not finish with exactly what they start out to study. My own son is a good example. He was sure he wanted to study architecture, specifically green architecture. Architecture of course is a graduate program, so his BA was a double major in art and environmental science with a minor in physics. The environmental science was too much science and was changed in the first few weeks to environmental studies. Then the physics classes never really took and were replaced by a minor in economics. Taking so many art classes encouraged him to add another minor in art history. The economics minor was going to be short one class, so it was replaced by a major in public relations. He ended with a triple major in art and environmental studies and public relations and a minor art history. If the college would have allowed it, he would have added another minor. He is no longer looking at architecture as much as he is looking at graphic design. All of this is rather normal.

As a whole I don't worry about the major. The biggest exceptions: medicine and engineering. These are exceptions because the programs are so intense it is really difficult to transfer in at a later date. If a student is set on becoming a doctor, start with a biology or pre-med track. If a student begins with a mathematics track and tries to change to pre-med at the beginning of junior year, the student may be so far behind he will never catch up. By the same token, many of these pre-professions have separate schools or colleges within the college which have a separate admissions process. I have seen students run into problems with trying to transfer into a professional program after general admissions.

Certain majors are glutted. Biology, social science, political science, English, philosophy, psychology, general business and engineering are all glutted. Far too many students apply for these programs. Take one specific university, Johns Hopkins University. Johns Hopkins is an elite school with a superb reputation in biology, engineering and music. The school enrolls around 1300 students a year, but receives around 27,000 applicants. In theory, Johns Hopkins could split three majors: biology, engineering and music into thirds and fill the entire freshman class with these three majors relatively easily. But what about all the other classes and programs? What about African-American studies or bioinformatics or communications or English language and literature or cartography or art history? Does the university just allow those programs to whither? Of course not! Instead the student applying for a degree in cartography may be one of a half dozen applying this year whereas the student applying for biology may be one of 10,000 or so. In which group does your student have a better chance? The university may not need six students in cartography, but I can assure you that 10,000 is far more than needed for biology.

If a student tells me he has a passion for biology or she wants nothing more than engineering, I will tell the student to pursue that passion. If a student is torn between pre-engineering and . . . statistics, I would tell the student to begin with pre-engineering as engineering is hard to change into it later. All things being equal, if a student is torn between psychology and economics, I would go with economics every time - even faster if the student is a minority woman (largely unrepresented in economics).

One warning. Don't lie. One of the most popular interview questions is, "Why _____ (pick your major)?" If your cartography major doesn't even know what cartography is let alone why he wants to pursue it, what message does that send to the university?

*Should my student put "undecided" on his or her major?*

I never recommend this. I have spoken with several different admissions' officers who swear it does not hurt the application, but I have two specific reservations about this. First is that the choice - though real and valid - makes the student look indecisive. This is not an attribute I want on the application. Second, if I am right about trying to build and support programs at the university, "undecided" doesn't help any program.

If your student is really undecided try going through the list of majors at a big public school like Arizona State University or the University of Illinois or Ohio State University. The big public universities have just about every major possible. A perplexed student can just peruse the list of majors and start making notes on which majors sound intriguing or possible. There are some books like *What Color is Your Parachute* by Richard Bolles or *Do What You Are* by Paul Tieger, but I put little faith in them. Similarly, there are computer programs or tests like the ASVAB test through the military that offer career advice. I also take these with a grain of salt. I am not convinced a book or test can accurately predict what I am passionate about. Finally a relatively new website http://collegemajors101.com/ seems to be promising for helping students understand what is actually available.

*What factors affect admissions?*

This is a loaded question, and a really long answer. In the end, what sells really depends on the university and depends on the admission's officer reading the individual application. The more a student stands out from the pack, the more a student can be seen as an individual, the more a student has demonstrated *excellence* in anything, the better. Obviously, a student that has done egregious damage to his transcript prior to senior year has problems. A student that is vanilla and never really tried to stand out in anything also has problems. Big state universities are very happy just to fill seats.

Some of the big state universities do not even bother with the illusion of having the student write an essay. The university will not read the essay anyway. The universities I like to use are more discerning. All of these schools want a student that will make a difference - a difference not only as a student but make a difference after graduation as well. What should also be apparent is that every school has different standards and is looking for something different or has different needs. A student that may be an ideal candidate at Allegheny may not be so ideal at Hamilton. A student quickly accepted at Colgate may, through no fault of the student, be rejected at Colby. Two students who seem nearly identical may receive very different answers.

I also approach this process as somewhat of a realist. If an admission's counselor is arguing for acceptance before the entire admission's office for his region's students and has two nearly identical students, isn't it plausible that one student strikes a chord the other does not or that by the time the second student is argued someone at the table says, "We have enough music majors this year. Don't you have anyone else?" I maintain that there is no magical formula. Again, please cast a wide net. I have had too many students who should be accepted and are rejected and others that should be rejected and are accepted. Make sure the list is varied. I have had students apply at eight schools - all Ivy League - and think a list of only Ivy League is a varied list. It is not. It is setting the student up for disappointment. That being said, there are some common factors that show up again and again. There is no exact number and the individual school applied to makes a huge difference.

A) Grades and test scores: These are still the first cut. For top end schools a student really wants almost all "A's" and an ACT of at least 31, SAT (New) of 1450. For second tier schools and a decent financial aid package, a student still wants more "A's" than "B's" and an ACT of at least 27, SAT (New) of 1300. Anything less than this and there are still options, but the student is no longer a sure bet. In addition, financial aid becomes trickier.

B) Class Rank: Best is top 1%, then top 3% and 10%. I really want all my students in the top 10%. If not in the top 25%, a student will have real issues getting accepted.

C) Activities, service, sports: A student wants to have at least two activities (band, knitting club, choir, soccer, basketball, softball, Academic Decathlon, Mock Trial, church service, or so many other choices). Having the activities is not enough. Keep the activities for 3-4 years consecutively. The student should ideally show leadership by senior year and be in the position to demonstrate his or her personal impact. Be able to talk about the activities. Just saying, "Yeah, I played baseball for four years," doesn't work for me. Why did you play? Why four years? What position? What awards or recognition did you receive? Were you able to get on the varsity team by sophomore year? If you started a yodeling club, why? What inspired you? What did you hope to accomplish? Offbeat and unique interests can really sell well - but you must develop them. I have seen knitting be a home run.

D) Major: As previously stated, a major can matter. I would never counsel changing a major simply for admissions.

E) Essays and personal statement: There are few factors at selective schools that matter more than an essay or personal statement. Make the writing count. In most cases the essay is the one chance to really introduce what makes a student an individual. Would the student fit into *my* university? What contribution to the climate of the campus will the student make? Please avoid clichés and hyperbole in an essay. Admission's counselors have read it all. Be genuine. Show your best assets. Do not provide a list of activities. Do not lie or plagiarize. If the final product can be used by a brother or sister or a best friend, the essay fails. Dare to be unique. You may not impress everyone, but that is the point of the essay.

F) Recommendations: Next to essays this is probably the biggest factor. Make sure the student has three high quality recommendations. The recommendations need to be genuine and specific. Do not take these for granted. A vanilla recommendation that is given to multiple students will be wasted.

G) Geography: Every school I know wants to represent every state. A student from Montana has a very slight advantage over a student from California simply because fewer students from Montana apply. There is little one can do to change this, so don't worry about it. Geographic diversity is one of the reasons I really look beyond the immediate area. An application by a student from Milwaukee to Concordia - Wisconsin doesn't garner much attention as Concordia is just twenty minutes north of Milwaukee in Mequon. An application from eastern Oregon may get some attention, though. I have had several universities call me asking how a particular student first noticed the university. This has a bigger effect on schools like Concordia - Wisconsin or Simpson in Iowa or Knox in Illinois that don't have huge name recognition. Schools that regularly get out of state applicants really don't notice much. I once visited Illinois Wesleyan and Loyola -Chicago in the same week. There was such a remarkable difference in how the two schools treated me. Illinois Wesleyan gave a guided tour by the admission's director and did everything possible to make me feel welcome. Loyola - Chicago, which gets many more applicants and has a bigger name recognition, did everything possible to make to feel like a number. I was not even granted the "privilege" of meeting with admissions despite a previous appointment. That is not to say that Loyola is a bad school, just that the experience by one person on a random day in June was very different.

H) Unique attributes: Similarly, every school wants to know that the freshman class is "diverse". Racial diversity is certainly part of this. Native American actually gives the biggest advantage. (Warning: I mean someone with a tribal identity, not a story that great great grandpa might be part Cherokee.) Latino and African American can help. Asian or Caucasian actually have a slight disadvantage. Whenever possible I would use "mixed" or simply put that the student prefers not to answer. Diversity also entails disability, life experiences, religion, neighborhood and obstacles overcome. Is the student the first generation to go to college? Has the student overcome any great obstacles? Has the student ever been homeless? What is the socio-economic background? Did the student grow up on a rural farm or in the inner-city ghetto? Did the student attend a school where no one goes on to the university? Do not invent anything, but do point out what circumstances and events were present. If a student has nothing to offer along these lines - white, middle class with no real struggles - that is okay. Remember that this is just one factor.

I) Interviews: Interviews are fantastic for showing a school what makes your student an individual. It is so much easier to argue for a specific student's admission when a counselor can picture the face or hear the laugh or recall a specific vignette that seemed trivial but actually gives a good insight into the student. My oldest son, a student whose grades were far from perfect, had a natural and innate talent for interview. This gift was his biggest asset when applying to colleges. A really good interview can really save an otherwise mediocre student. By the same token, a really bad interview can sink an otherwise stellar student. I promise that one of the thoughts in the back on an admission counselor's head is, "Do I want to see this student on my campus next fall?"

J) Demonstrated interest: Schools routinely accept more students than there is room available on the theory that some students will choose to go somewhere else. A school like Boston University knows that many applicants also applied to Harvard and see Boston University as a backup or "safety" school (though I might take exception with that idea). As such Boston University will accept many more students than needed. If your student can show that he or she really is interested, that Boston University (or Northwestern or Oberlin or Pitzer) is not just a backup, your student's application is much stronger. Show interest by visiting the school. Go to college fairs and speak to the admission's officer. Follow up a meeting with emailed questions that mean something. Request an interview. Show a school that research has been done. Be concrete. Don't tell the University of Puget Sound that you like the dorms. Ask how the themes are chosen and explain which theme you see yourself following. Don't tell Yale that the campus is beautiful. Talk about Maya Lin's sculpture in front of the library and how it really struck a chord within you. Don't tell the school that you like the academics. Explain that you have been following Prof. Mayann Bylander's research on Cambodian migrants and why this is a field of inquiry that attracts you to Lewis and Clark University. When you speak to Seattle University talk about the little coffee shop you found just two blocks away and how the coffee, though $8 a cup, was the best coffee you have ever had. (There is no bitter after taste.) Make the school see your student there. Help your student imagine himself or herself meeting with an art professor at her house for brick oven pizza or strolling across the bridge connecting the College of the Atlantic to Bar Harbor or attending a senior seminar taught by Prof. Northrup on the Atlantic slave trade at Boston College. The more genuine enthusiasm the better. A genuine interest also can have a huge effect on a student's financial aid package.

K) Legacy: A common aid for students is being a legacy. Specifically, that means that Mom or Dad graduated from the institution in question. The more elite and famous the school, the more likely this will help a student's application. To be blunt, Iowa State University doesn't care if dad graduated in the class of '94. If Dad graduated from Princeton and Mom graduated from Yale, a student is in a much better position to apply at both Princeton Yale - though that might lead to some interesting discussions around the dinner table. In this case I strongly recommend that parents who want to use this angle have been active in the respective alumni networks and have donated on a regular basis. Unfortunately, a grandparent or aunt or cousin or brother who graduated from a specific institution does little for a student's application.

The exact opposite can be true as well. A student who is first in his or her family to attend college can have an advantage in admissions. If neither *mom nor dad finished at a four year institution* (pay attention to the wording) then the student is first generation. I will always find a way to mention this if applicable somewhere in the student's application. In some admission's conferences this can be a bigger benefit than a legacy student.

Of course, the inverse is also true. A student who had both parents attend a non-prestigious university may suffer for it. Ironically, being middle class is a negative to many admission's offices. I personally don't believe this is fair, but I don't make the rules.

*A random note on email and social media.*

One last factor I like to check with my students is their email address and social media accounts. Every resume and usually somewhere on the application itself a student's personal email is noted. Please be wary of inappropriate email addresses. I have had students use something way too juvenile for an account created when the student was seven like "purpleunicorns@gmail.com" (not a real address but similar to one I have seen). I have seen email addresses that are slightly pornographic where the innuendo is not exactly subtle like "bigdaddy69@gmail.com" (also not real). I have also seen pathetic such as (also not real) "IloveBobbyD@gmail.com." Review what email your teen is using. It may be time to update.

Also check your student's social media accounts. If you mention this and your student starts yelling about first amendment rights and violation of privacy and how his best friend's mother who is way cooler than you would never do this, the protests might actually be a warning sign that the account really needs to be checked. As with many job interviews today, colleges routinely check a student's social media. Many of the admission's counselors I have worked with, especially admission's counselors that just graduated from the university themselves, send an invitation to school social media accounts. That can be a two-way street.

What am I looking for? Take off anything regarding drugs or alcohol. While most campuses are not dry campuses, the school knows that an 18 year old student should not be drunk. Repeated references to drugs and alcohol can be a good sign that the student may need counseling more than admissions. Take off any references to guns or a fetish with assassinations or mass shootings. The girl who is an award winning skeet shooter or the boy applying for next year's Olympics are exceptions. Schools are hypersensitive to any chance that a student may do something to put the school on the news in a way that the school does not want to be on the news. Similarly, take off anything that shows some real anger issues or suicidal tendencies. This is also a giant red flag for a school. In short, approach this with the eye, "Would I want Grandma to see this?" If the answer is no, then why would you want a school to see it?

*What does first generation college student mean?*

A first generation college student is one whose mother or father did not finish a four year degree. If an older brother or sister graduated, a student still counts. If mom finished her associate's degree (two years) at a local community college, a student still counts. If dad started at the University of (insert your favorite state), but he didn't finish yet, the student still counts. In any case where a student is actually a first generation college student, please find a way to insert this information somewhere in the application. The insight about first generation college can be included in a personal statement, in the form of the application itself, or in one of the letters of recommendation. Make sure that the knowledge is disseminated, though. Far too many universities put an emphasis on this situation. Look into the following website if you are first generation college: http://www.imfirst.org/#! .

*What about "test optional" schools?*

Not too long ago the dean of Bates College, William C. Hiss, completed a long term study trying to tie ACT / SAT scores to college success. In a surprise to many, there was no real correlation. There are lots of information sources that reported on this, but the Washington Post is one that broke the story to a national audience. (https://www.washingtonpost.com/news/answer-sheet/wp/2014/02/21/a-telling-study-about-act-sat-scores/?utm_term=.886b6e65c702)

Since the report, more and more schools have been experimenting with test optional. What this means in a nutshell is that the school does not use standardized tests as a factor in admissions or de-emphasizes standardized tests as a factor in admissions (not the same thing). A complete list of which schools no longer require standardized test scores can be found at http://fairtest.org/university/optional.

If I have a student that simply can not break a 24 on an ACT or 1110 on SAT (New), then I strongly start looking at test optional schools. This does have drawbacks. First and foremost, if a school is not using standardized testing how does a school know that your student stands out? The grades, the class rank, the essays, the letters of recommendation, the activities, and the leadership all become that much more important. A student that has a low GPA, a low class rank, no real leadership and low test scores has a major problem. There is little I can do. This student needs a miracle. I can work with admission, but financial aid is going to be bloody. If a student is excelling in all areas except test scores, though, a test optional school may be an option. Do expect extra essays. Do keep in mind, there is a difference between a student saying he or she is in fact phenomenal and proving he or she is phenomenal.

The second drawback is that a lot of "test optional" schools still want to see the test scores. To me this still seems like double speak. I can not express how many times a school representative has said that the school is "test optional" but that the school still wants to see test scores. Even if a school does not see scores for everyone, but does see scores for some, the assumption is that your student's unreported scores are awful. In some cases, the imagined scores are lower than the actual scores.

The third drawback, and it is a common trick, is that the school will say test optional for admissions. The school is in fact test optional for admissions. But when your student is accepted and applies for financial aid, the family needs to supply test scores. The scores are then usually so low that financial aid is not awarded in an amount to make the school affordable.

I only use test optional as a last chance scenario. When I use it, I am very careful to find out which schools still use the unsubmitted test scores for financial aid. Though there are a lot of schools now claiming test optional, the best I have found are Bard, Kalamazoo, Hampshire and some specialty schools like Juilliard.

*How do I defuse bad test scores?*

In a perfect world, your student began testing early and had the chance to retest - and retest - and retest. The last chance is typically October or November of senior year. Anything after this might be useful for financial aid, but the scores will come too late to affect admissions. If a student is an excellent candidate with the exception of test scores, see if a teacher will address the issue in a letter of recommendation. Sometimes - stress on sometimes - a really good letter of recommendation explaining that the student really does suffer from test anxiety can overcome some of the deficiency. But remember, admissions and financial aid are two different animals.

I have also recommended having students add a supplemental essay - not a replacement for the personal statement - explaining why test scores (or grades sophomore year) are lower than they should have been. This is really a hail Mary pass. It may or may not have an effect. As with so much else, a student needs to have a real reason. "I was playing too many video games and the games melted my mind," won't really sway anyone. "I moved from on level to all AP classes my sophomore year and had a hard time adjusting at first," or "My junior year my little brother was diagnosed with leukemia, and I couldn't focus on anything," are more what I am thinking.

*What is ED and EA?*

ED is "early decision." EA is "early action." This is one way to show a school interest. Both programs ask students to submit an application early - around mid-November. The idea behind the programs is that a student expressing interest this early may really be captivated by a particular school. As a result the admissions rates for ED and EA tend to be significantly higher than general admissions. This is a really good option for a first choice school.

There is a catch. Two catches actually. First, a student applying "early decision" is bound if accepted. What that means is that a student who applies "early decision" to University of Pennsylvania, assuming she gets in, *must* attend the University of Pennsylvania. Second, because it is binding a student may only apply to one school "early decision". A student will receive an answer by Christmas and know if she is attending the University of Pennsylvania or applying at other schools.

"Early action" is not binding. I recommend my students apply to five or six schools as "early action". If a student is accepted via "early action", though, he may still opt to attend a different school.

As a whole, I love "early action" and encourage my students to apply to their first choice school "early action". This expresses a definitive interest in the school and usually increases the chances of acceptance. Additionally, a student who knows by Christmas that his first choice school really wants him is so much more relaxed not only through the holidays but throughout the rest of the college admission's process. What better Christmas present than that email from Stanford saying welcome to sunny San Jose, CA?

I am more reticent about "early decision". The primary reason is financial. Hypothetically, if I have a student who applies "early decision" to Brown and gets in, she will receive the financial aid package at about the same time as the acceptance letter. The financial aid package at this juncture is really not negotiable. You get what you get. This may not always be the best deal. I have known schools that will say, "Don't worry. If the decision is based on finances, we will release you." That is up to the school to determine at that point, not the family. What is affordable for the school may not be affordable to the family.

Let me break this down in terms of finances. Obviously, I am using really rough numbers and there are always exceptions.

A) Student A is from an upper income bracket. Student A's parents are not even planning on applying for financial aid. Writing a check for $70,000, while significant, is still just one check. No financing or selling of homes is necessary. Early decision or early action are both wonderful choices. These programs can help Student A get acceptance and money is not a factor.

B) Student B is middle class. Student B's parents make enough to have a nice home and car, but the parents have precious little in a college saving's account. I strongly endorse "early action" but really would not urge "early decision." The exception is the student that has been set on Duke all her life. Student B and the parents have talked about it, and Duke is really the first and last choice. If accepted, the family is willing to take money from Grandpa, refinance the house or sell stock in order to afford Duke. If a family is all in, then go ahead and apply "early decision." Otherwise, I really counsel middle class families against "early decision." Early action is a definite yes if the family passes on early decision.

C) Student C's family is just broke. The family has been working and working and yet the money never seems to pay the bills. Be careful here. A lot of families feel broke. Feeling broke and being broke for a university are just not the same things. Numbers vary depending on the school, the tax year, how many children in the family, how many in college and several other factors. I use $40,000 as a family income as safe. This means that mom and dad together, yes even if divorced, make an annual income before taxes of $40,000. This will qualify almost all families as "broke" in the eyes of a university. If a family is truly "broke" then early decision *might* be a possibility. Early action is again a safe bet and a good bet. "Early decision" would work for universities that provide a great deal of financial need. To use the universities I have mentioned: University of Pennsylvania, Brown and Duke, all three universities would work with the family to make the university affordable. If I have a student in such dire economic straits, I will from time to time use "early decision." Be careful. Make sure the school will actually provide financial assistance. Many of the great liberal arts colleges that I love simply do not have the funds to be as competitive as some other schools. I suspect some schools deliberately short a family financially with early decision as the admission is binding.

I am urging my students to use early action more and more. There is an increasing trend in colleges to only allow students accepted for early action or early decision to apply for the top tier scholarships. Even if a regular decision student is accepted and meets the other qualifications, the regular decision student will not be invited to apply for a top tier scholarship. Additionally, some schools are beginning to fill their freshmen class entirely with early action and early decision. There are no spots left for regular decision students.

*Should my student apply at an honor's college?*

I love honor's colleges. Given an opportunity I will always recommend a student apply at an honor's college. The first and most obvious benefit is that the student will graduate with the honor's college designation. Remember, if your student is planning on going to graduate school, the whole game starts over. Just as the university now is asking how your student stands out, the university in four years will be asking how your student stands out. While the most important factors will be internships, research projects, and published writings, an honor's college designation can help.

Much more important for the student is that the honor's college often comes with hidden perks. Many of these perks are just not advertised up front. The three most common perks are unique dorms, separate dining facilities and / or more money. Many of the honor's colleges I use will house the students in a separate dorm. I can not say that this separate dorm is always better. In some cases, the dorm was the best, but all the other dorms were updated and the honor's college is still waiting. In almost every case, though, the dorms for the honor's college are smaller and allow a little more freedom. One of my favorite perks is the separate dining facility. One of the greatest criticisms of colleges is the food. In every case I know of, the separate honor's cafeteria is really a step above.

Most important for a family is what the honor's college offers financially. Many of the honor's colleges I work with require the students enrolled to take an additional one or two classes. Those costs are offset by increased financial aid. Other schools promise full tuition to any student in the honor's college. Other schools have full tuition scholarships that only the students in the honor's college are eligible to receive. Acceptance to the honor's college can often be a financial boon.

In addition, especially true of large state universities, it is not uncommon for the best professors - the famous ones that have published - to only teach in the honor's college. Students often receive more or different advising, job placement and internship opportunities. I can not find the down side to an honor's college. In the end, if your student is accepted at the honor's college and decides for whatever reason that he or she does not like the option, the student can still attend the university and decline the honor's college.

## Chapter 12: Take a Deep Breath and Hope for the Best

Once the decisions have been made about where to apply and the applications have been submitted, everything becomes a waiting game. By mid-March to early April a family should have all the acceptance or rejection notifications. That is when decisions have to be made. Do not pay much attention to the initial numbers on an acceptance letter for costs or financial aid. This is another step of the process, and rarely do schools provide their final offer up front. In some ways college shopping resembles car shopping. How many salesmen put the final offer up front?

*So when does my student need to send everything in?*

Thanksgiving. Obviously, if a student does "early decision" or "early action," that application may be a bit earlier. Everything else I want completed by Thanksgiving. I realize this is early. I am asking students to complete everything this early for several reasons.

First, by completing applications this early a student relieves himself or herself of a tremendous stress or burden. The college admission's process has become terribly stressful. What better way to greet the last real holiday at home than to know that all the paperwork and applications are completed? In addition, by getting everything done so early there is little chance for procrastination - a disease that afflicts many of today's teens. There is no stress about if the January 15th deadline is using Eastern Standard Time or Pacific Coast. There is no stress about checking to see if that supplemental essay for the sixth university on the list was submitted.

The second reason is being a pragmatist again. Let's take two hypothetical students, Robert and Regina. Robert gets all of his applications completed early. For his first choice school, he does early action. The other nine schools on his list are all completed by Thanksgiving. To be sure, some of the nine schools will wait until mid-January before looking at his file. Other schools will get a head start on the coming avalanche of applications and make a decision early just as if Robert had applied "early action." Robert's application will be compared to a much smaller pool. In addition, should Robert be a marginal candidate, it is much easier for an admission's counselor to argue for admission of a marginal candidate when there are 310 of 400 spots in the next year's class still open.

By Christmas Robert is pleased to learn that he was in fact accepted at his first choice school and four others on his list. By February 1 Robert has heard back from three more schools meaning that well before financial aid packages roll out Robert has heard back from eight of his ten schools. He has a really good idea which schools to focus on for financial aid now.

Regina is one of the many afflicted teens. She suffers from procrastination. Regina, like Robert, does get her "early action" application done on time. The other nine schools are submitted twenty minutes before the deadline of January 15. Regina spends most of her Christmas break working on college applications and making her family miserable. Realizing that she was one recommendation short, Regina ended up calling three teachers at home to beg for a last minute recommendation before one finally acceded. Her applications were received and promptly buried in a veritable tower of other applications. There is nothing at this point to show a real interest in any of the schools Regina applied at. At three of the schools on her list Regina's essays had the misfortune of being read by a rather bleary eyed admission's officer who had been reading essays for the last seven or eight hours straight. At the point Regina's essays were picked up, the admission's counselor was only half focused.

By Christmas, Regina did find out that she was accepted by her "early action" school, but the other nine schools didn't start rolling in until mid-March. If Regina is a marginal candidate, there is a good chance that by the time her admission's counselor is making the plea for her acceptance, there are only seventeen spots remaining in a class of 400. It is really hard to argue that a marginal student should get one of the last 17 spots. The last admission's letter was not received until the second week of April. Regina has precious little time to decide or to argue financial aid packages.

*What if I have everything submitted except for one thing?*

In the end, a student usually needs a complete package to be considered. It is not uncommon for an application to be delayed because a piece is missing. Most schools understand that a student can only control so much and getting that last letter of recommendation in on time is not usually a deal breaker as long as it does get in. In addition, there are lots and lots of pieces of information on a student coming into an admission's office. Services like the Coalition App and Common App have streamlined this process, but there is still a lot of paperwork. It is really easy for an admission's office to misplace a letter of recommendation or a high school to forget to send out a transcript or ACT scores to be put in the wrong student file.

Step one, about two weeks after you have submitted everything - admission forms, personal statement, extra essays, test scores, recommendations, resumes and official transcripts - email or call the admission's officer. I prefer email as the office is usually really busy. Something simple like, "Good afternoon! I just wanted to verify that you have received everything for my application for admission. Let me know if there is anything else you need from me. Thank you." Be sure to include your name and contact information and have your student do this - not the parent. If your student has not received an answer within a week, call. Do wait a week and wait until you are certain that everything should be in. This is the busiest time of year for admission's offices. There is a fine line between checking on application status and being an annoyance. Don't cross the line.

Step two, if the school says it is still missing . . . a recommendation letter or a transcript . . . go back to the source. Tell the source, "I just heard from the University of OMG. They said that they never got your letter (or the transcript). Could you resend it please?" I have had problems with the letters of recommendation on Common App. The way the system is set up a teacher uploads a letter and then hits submit. There have been a number of teachers that upload but don't submit. In the case of the teacher that just missed it, a reminder is enough. In the case of the teacher that is a technophobe or is computer illiterate I have asked a guidance counselor or computer technician at the school to find the time to help the teacher submit. This needs to be done delicately.

If the school is missing standardized test scores, you should have a record of where the scores were sent on your account. Double check. Resending the same scores to the same school should not be an extra fee. The most common problem I have run into is that a student sent nine sets of scores to ten schools and accidently missed one. Other times the scores for Jennifer Martin were put in the file for Jennifer O. Martin - not your student. Especially when a name is relatively common it is easy for a school to mix up scores. Just resend.

If mid-March has come and you have not heard one way or another from a school, it is time to check. There is always the possibility that the school is releasing acceptance at a specific date and time, there is the possibility that the school is just late sending out letters, and there is the possibility your son's letter was lost in the mail or not sent. Every year I hear about at least one school where a stack of acceptance letters was lost or not stamped or fell behind the counter in the post office. My own son had one school notify him in July that they had "forgotten" to send his acceptance in April. No worries, we had already made the decision - not them. By mid-March a family should have just about all the letters - or email. Make sure to update your spreadsheets and keep the letters. Nothing is official until you get that letter or email.

*What is rolling admissions?*

Rolling admissions are exactly what they sound like. These are schools with no set deadline for applications. Instead the schools fill the class as they go. In theory, the school could be full by December 1 where the applications are cut off. In practice, the school is usually still looking at applications in May. Just as with regular decision, I urge students to get these applications done early. Whereas the school as a whole may not be filled, the program your student wants - nursing for example - may be full. In addition, just as with regular decision it is easier to argue for a marginal student early.

The one thing I use rolling decision for is a student that is really having problems. There are times I have used rolling decision schools as a last hope. To give a specific example, I was working with a young woman some years ago. Her numbers and activities were not bad, but the application was not wow. I advised her to apply at a variety of different levels of schools. She did not. Instead the student applied to all top notch schools. She was rejected by several and several others offered her financial aid packages that just were not tenable. By the time her parents decided to tell me what had happened, it was the middle of February. That is far too late for regular decision. As such, I had the young woman apply to several schools that were rolling admission. I am still convinced she would have received better results in the end had she put more variety in her original list.

This website is a good reference for schools that use rolling admissions.

http://blog.prepscholar.com/colleges-with-rolling-admissions

*Does the presentation matter?*

In today's electronic age everything is submitted digitally. 90% of all college applications will be done digitally. Every once in a while I will have a student submit an individual college application on paper. When this is done, and it is a rare occurrence today, ensure that everything is clean and crisp. In addition, for essays submitted manually try using a better quality paper with a thicker tooth. Do not go crazy with neon pink or designed paper. This just becomes distracting. A better quality paper can stick out, though.

*What if my student is undocumented?*

This is an increasingly difficult question to answer, and there is the possibility that by the time this book is published everything I say here is outdated. As I am typing this book, I am listening to reporters talk about President Trump's decision to cancel DACA. This will have a huge impact on college admissions. Not only does it affect admissions and financial aid, it also complicates issues like working on campus, loans, internships and travel to and from campus.

If you are facing this dilemma there are some rules to follow.

1) Be extremely careful who you confide in. There are mean spirited people who see opportunity in reporting your student. Be careful with school counselors and teachers. The

fewer that know the better. Once in school, your student should think twice about confiding to his or her roommate or even boyfriend or girlfriend. Many years ago I knew someone whose jilted girlfriend enjoyed getting him deported.

2) Public schools, even in state, are not usually an option. There are a few states - notably Washington and California - that have really made inroads in helping students. Very few states can claim this. Far more common are states like Arizona that put every obstacle in place for students missing certain paperwork. In state schools, even community college, can become prohibitively expensive. A much better choice is liberal arts private schools which do not use federal monies for financial aid. These schools have the option of fully funding a student despite his or her status. If a student inquires with a school, I have heard several different answers.

"We will do everything in our power to help a student that is fully qualified." Score! If you have the numbers, the student has possibilities.

"We will consider a student for admission, but not financial aid," or "Sure but the student will have to apply as an international student with the requisite visas." This means that the wealthy students can still go but not the poor students. For most students in this position, this is in reality a "no."

"We will never accept an *illegal*. You have broken the law! We don't want law breakers!" Unfortunately that is a direct quote from a school. Hang up the phone and cross them off your list.

3) A student must stand out and be extraordinary. If a student is missing paperwork, in order to compete with "citizen" students, your student *must* excel in every way. A family in this position is really asking for free money. Why does your student deserve it more than a citizen from Alaska or Georgia? Have your student go above and beyond. If a student is good enough

to gain admission to a top tier school like Harvard or Colby or Stanford, there is a really good chance the school can help a family that is in dire financial straits.

4) I do not usually recommend talking about status until after admissions. Once a student is admitted the game changes. Instead of trying to impress a school, the school is now trying to impress a student. It is far easier to find help for a student that the school has already said is wanted.

5) FAFSA. Every school is going to require a FAFSA for financial aid. If a family does not have papers, the family has not filed taxes. As such, a family can not file a FAFSA. Call the chief financial aid officer at every school being considered and ask for options. All decisions are on a case by case basis and what works for your student may not work for his friend.

6) Look into hiring a professional who has dealt with this before. Certain schools are more ... flexible. A family in this situation needs to know where to go. Again, just because a school let in Javier's son doesn't mean it will work with your daughter. Again, apply at multiple schools.

7) Remember, going to school and fixing your status is not the same thing. Barring a political change, there is the strong possibility that your son upon graduation will have a very serious problem getting a job. In addition, I have never known ICE (Immigration Control and Enforcement) to go onto a college campus. I have known ICE to pick up students driving to a nearby restaurant off campus. That being said, immigration may in the end deport your child or your child may choose to leave, but ICE can never take away his or her education or degree. A degree from an American university can often open up a lot of doors in other countries.

*What if my child is a citizen, but I am undocumented?*

In most cases this will not matter. Your student has all the rights and privileges as any other United States citizen. The biggest complication is going to be FAFSA as you are not filing taxes. Wait until your child is accepted and call the financial aid offices. Most will work with you. Any schools that refuse to work with your student despite your student being a citizen are schools that your student would not feel comfortable at. Again, this is another reason to cast a wide net when applying.

*What does senior year cost?*

Realistically I tell parents to be ready to spend a minimum of $500 in November and another $500 in April. More is needed in August for moving costs. So, what does this cover? In November I am looking at application fees and testing. These costs are pretty much it in November. I am really hoping that the student has the chance to visit at least the top choice school. Depending on the school, the visit might be an extra cost.

In April the fees are for sending the deposit, the final test score reports and any AP score reports. You will also, once the student is 18, need to update some vaccinations. Again, any travel to visit a school may not be covered by the school and would incur an extra cost.

In August a family is looking at the expenses of moving. If you live in . . . Texas and junior is moving to a school in Texas, then driving is probably the best way. You can load up the family car with the mini fridge and microwave. Throw the suitcase in the back and head down the road. If, however, junior is off to Vermont, driving from Texas may not be practical. A family of limited means could just put Junior on a plane and have him take a taxi or Uber to the school, but I still recommend at least one parent go to the school the first time. Your student will also need a lot of things that have been taken for granted at home. A short list, and many schools do a better job at giving a list, includes:

> clothing including a winter coat, hat and gloves (Sometimes it is better to buy these in the new city. San Diego does not understand cold and no one sells cold weather coats.)
>
> small appliances like a popcorn maker or microwave or mini fridge or rice cooker
>
> chargers and power strips, desk lamps and fans (see schools for restrictions)
>
> regular school supplies
>
> plastic bins and tubs for storage including for dirty laundry
>
> suit cases
>
> toiletries and cleaning supplies, don't forget the laundry soap

It all adds up. My recommendation is that in lieu of graduation / birthday / going away presents family and friends give gift cards to places like Target or Walmart where an aspiring student can get all the daily needs - and some junk food. Most of these items are better left at home. It is far easier to go shopping in Vermont than it is to try and fly everything from Texas.

*What if I am really broke?*

First speak to a high school counselor. It is entirely possible to get test waivers and even admission waivers for schools. Generally speaking, a high school counselor can give out two test fee waivers to a student who qualifies. Other tests need to be paid for out of pocket. School admissions waivers are on a case by case and school by school decision. If money is really an issue, call the admission's office and inquire. It is unrealistic to expect fee waivers for every test and every school. Do not use a fee waiver for the top choice school. This has the possibility of making a difference in admission. As to the deposits, speak to the school admission or business office. Some schools are willing to roll the amount - or a portion of the amount - into the first year's tuition or find a payment plan. Keep in mind, even if a student has a full scholarship the deposit is not usually included. Get every deal in writing.

*Ok. I have submitted all my essays, applications, test scores, and recommendations. Now what?*

Wait. First double check that everything has been submitted and received. If you are submitting everything online via Common App or Coalition App there are boxes that check off when everything is received. Once that favorite physics teacher has submitted her glowing letter of recommendation explaining how your son walks on water, the application portal will usually signify that the letter was submitted successfully. If you are physically mailing something in, it is not a bad idea to include a self-addressed and stamped postcard. The admission's office will simply drop this in the mail saying that everything was received.

A school will then provide an answer. Keep in mind, if a student has applied early decision or early action, an answer will be forthcoming around Christmas time - either just before or just after depending on the school. If a student has applied by November as I suggested, the first answers will probably come in about December to January with a few late stragglers in mid-March.

Possible answer 1: Yes! We want you! The crowd cheers. Grandparents go wild. Advance to "Go" and collect $200! Yes! This is one of the most exciting moments in life. Enjoy it. Celebrate it. Go out to dinner at your son or daughter's favorite restaurant (even consider taking your son or daughter with you this time). At this point the whole game changes. Instead of your student trying to convince a school, now the school is trying to convince a student. I do not recommend making any final decisions until all acceptance letters and financial aid packages are received. If a financial aid letter comes with the acceptance, do not stress over the amount. This is usually just an initial offer. Also, be sure to check email and junk mail. In the past schools would mail out large envelopes to accepted students. Many still do. My vote for absolute best admission's envelope goes to Hendrix. I was cleaning up black and orange confetti three weeks later. Some schools just email, though. Some elite schools have a very specific day and time when all decisions are released electronically. A teacher at a selective private school may have class interrupted one afternoon by a series of cheers and cries of despair as an entire class logs in at the same time to see acceptance or . . .

    Possible answer 2: No. Darkness and gloom descend across the land. The teenager hides in a room with curtains drawn listening to depressing music far too loudly. There really is no appeal or second chance with a "No." Cross the school off the list, take a deep breath and move forward. I advised ten applications. Your student may very well get one or two rejections. That is part of life. If all ten schools reject your student, something is seriously wrong and you have a very sincere problem. At this point, I would consider an in state school, community college, or a gap year. Figure out what was wrong so that the same mistakes are not made twice. I have never worked with a student that was rejected by everyone - though I had some come close. The scariest scenario I have had is a young man that ignored me and applied to eight "Ivy League" schools. Seven schools rejected him. I personally think God took pity on him for the eighth. By the numbers, all eight should have said no. If all schools are saying "no" the most likely culprits are: the student is aiming too high, test scores are really unacceptable, the list is too limited, or there is a huge red flag hiding in the personal statement or letters of recommendation. The biggest exception to a "no" is for early action and early decision. A "no" on E.A or E.D. still allows a student to reapply regular decision. Sometimes the school does this automatically. Sometimes a school wants to student to resubmit a separate application. Ask.

Possible answer 3: Wait list. This is by far the most confusing answer. It means the school might maybe want your student if the school has room. A school that is a solid school like Haverford or Tufts, but not top tier like Princeton or Stanford will have a cushion built in. I am using imaginary numbers in this example. Let's say a school has 300 spots in the freshman class. A school may accept 550 students and wait list another 150. A school knows that they are in competition with other schools for top students. A school like Princeton or Stanford is fairly confident that if a student is accepted, that student will attend. A school like Tufts or Haverford knows that a student will probably attend - unless admitted to Princeton or Stanford. As such, schools accept more students than needed.

One of the most important tasks in any admission's office is finding that magic number of acceptance letters that give a school the perfect sized freshman class, not too many or too few. Because this is not a perfect science, schools wait list. A wait listed student is a student that the school does want. In another academic year the student may have been accepted. This particular year, though, the school has too many good applicants - and your student just is not on top. If - and it is a big if - the school has more rejects than expected, your student might still be accepted. Some schools will not take a single student off the wait list. Some schools will take a dozen or so students. Every year is different. A wait list is essentially a school's insurance policy. As a whole I treat a wait list as a "no." Despite wait lists being negative, add your teen's name to any forms the wait listing schools send.

*What if my student really wants to attend a wait listed school?*

Any time a student is wait listed, I still advise a student to express an interest in the school. Sometimes there is a form to fill out and send in - do so. Sometimes a student needs to be proactive and send an email. If a student is really interested, make sure the school knows. Most important, tell the school what has changed on the resume. Sort of a, "What have you done for me lately?" scenario. Your student was wait listed for a reason. Show that the student is trying to do more. That could mean an updated ACT / SAT score. It could mean more community service hours logged. Another letter of recommendation. A new award or medal for an academic competition or sport's team. A new position as team captain or vice president of National Honor Society. Whatever you do, do not sit on the old application. Offer something else. Keep in contact with the school. Some schools having a ranking system. A school accepts 550 students. Your student is 563 (a number the school will never give you). Other schools will look at the whole list with new eyes. A student that has expressed a decided interest can come off the wait list before everyone else.

Two warnings about the wait list. A student will probably not be notified that he or she has come off the wait list until after May 1. This is after the deadline for a school decision. DO NOT WAIT! Send in the acceptance and deposit fees for the second choice school. If your student comes off the wait list a decision can be made in June to forego the initial deposit. If your student does not come off the wait list, he or she is still covered. Nothing is official until a school sends it in writing. I have known admission's offices to tell families that their son will come off the wait list shortly only to not have the move actually happen.

The second warning, and a question to ask in this situation, not all schools will still have financial aid monies for wait listed students. If a student comes off the wait list, will he still be considered for financial aid at the same rate as students accepted in the first round? In most cases, wait list still means "no."

*What is a gap year?*

Some students take a year off (notice I said one, not five or ten) between high school and college. This is not a terrible idea, especially when the university or college your son was really hoping for does not pay off. The key to a gap year is what did your son do with the year?

Not impressive

"I spent the year becoming a master at Modern Warfare 9. I am known on PlayStation as Masterkillemall."

"I worked at the mall."

"I sat at home and babysat my little cousin - for free."

"I waited for the next year to reapply."

"I bombed the ACT last year. I retook the test six times this year."

Better

"I took a year off for a church mission in Paraguay."

"I used the time to really immerse myself in Russian. I took some classes and joined a community group."

"I was finally able to pursue my martial arts with a national tour and achieved the honor of being offered a teaching position in my dojo."

"I was training for the Olympic team. By the way, how flexible are the professors to me missing a week for competing as a United States champion?"

"I devoted my time to gene therapy research. I was working with a professor at the local university. My name will be added as a research assistant to the published paper this spring."

A gap year is not always bad, but your student *must* show what he accomplished during the year. If a student is taking off the year because the application was not strong enough, what is he doing to make the application stronger this year? If your son said he needed the year to mature, then how can you prove he was successful? Keep in mind, letters of recommendation will be a year old. Grades and test scores will be a year old.

## Chapter 13: Show me the money!

Getting in is just the first step. The next step, and just as important for most families, is affording school. The biggest single reason I advise applying to at least ten schools is financial aid. If a student gets into all ten schools applied at, there is every possibility that the financial aid packages will range from owing $1000 a year to owing $56,000 a year. It is quite a spread and as tuition goes up the spread is getting bigger and bigger. A new trend that is increasingly popular is for a university to admit a marginal student but give no financial aid. The good news is that the game changes here. Whereas with admissions the student is hoping the university wants the student, now the tables turn. Once accepted a university has said, "Yes! I want you!" Now the question is, "Does the student still want the university?" Every school knows that the student applied to more than one school. The schools have imperfect information on what a student is paying at other schools. Now schools are trying to convince your student to commit to their particular school while paying the maximum the school thinks it can get from a family. The family, though, holds all the best cards.

*What should I pay?*

This for me is one of the most basic questions. I ask the same question when I look at buying a car. Just like buying a car, the answer varies. Three different Toyota dealerships in town may offer three different prices. The same is true with universities. Again, this is why one of the biggest pieces of advice I can give is to cast a wide net. The good news is that no one pays full price. There are two exceptions to this rule. Exception number one is a student who has no business of getting into a university of that caliber that can pay. The second exception is a foreign exchange student. The first group is basically buying their way in - yes, this is one way to go to top notch schools without the numbers. The foreign exchange students are usually not only exempt from merit and financial need scholarships, but these students often have to pay an extra fee. I only half-jokingly tell my students to hug all the students they meet from Japan and China and Saudi Arabia as these students are paying for you - and eight other kids in the class.

Costs for a university can be broken down into four categories. Category A: Tuition. Tuition is negotiable. This is covering the costs of the physical structure (usually already paid), remodeling, the costs of the professors, the costs of the staff, and the utilities. It does not take very many students in a class to make up this cost on a per student basis. Depending on the school, that one student from Yemen in class may be paying for everyone's tuition.

Category B: room and board. This is really difficult to get in full. There are some students who are so wanted by a university that the school pays all or some of this price. This is rare. No matter how one looks at the money, this will cost a university money. Even if the dorm is fully paid off and the roommate is covering the costs of utilities and staffing and grounds keepers in full, and that is a big *if*, your student is still eating in the cafeteria. Food alone is several thousands of dollars a year. As a parent, this would be paid even if the student goes to an in state university and lives at home.

Category C: fees. This is tricky. Most fees are non-negotiable. Some will not be covered by scholarships. Universities have been tacking on more and more fees over the years. There is a fee for the initial deposit, a fee for orientation, a fee for registration, a fee for the athletic fields, a fee for campus activities, a fee for a dorm cleaning deposit, a fee for the library, a fee for the use of computer labs, a fee for the exercise room (even if you won't use it), a health center fee, a fee for the pool, a fee for parking (in many cases this is the biggest fee), a fee for art supplies, a fee for the theater, a fee for being a student, a fee for converting oxygen to carbon dioxide. Ok. I am starting to exaggerate, but you get the point. Many universities I have worked with have claimed not to raise tuition, but the school does raise the fees. If tuition remains flat this year, but the school raises the fees by $500 per semester, a family will still pay more money! Fees have offered a school the ability to raise more money without looking like the school costs more. Many of these fees will be undisclosed until the first day of registration. I have asked schools every year what fees my students have to pay. It is extremely rare for a school not to overlook one or two fees. Other schools will add a fee as late as August. This is usually a price a student pays.

Category D: books. With books a student is pretty much on his or her own. As a general rule I tell families to plan on $500 a semester for books. Some areas of study like social sciences or literature may be a little less. Some areas of study like pre-med or engineering may be a lot more. This is one of the biggest money makers at a school. I taught for ten years as an adjunct professor at the Maricopa Community Colleges. The unique time I received a reprimand was when I told my class not to purchase a textbook the school had already decided to phase out. As such, professors will tell students to buy a whole shopping list of books that may or may not actually be used. To defray costs, students can often find cheaper books online. I often urge students to look for the previous edition of a book. If a student's chemistry book costs $140 for the 14th edition, a student might find the 13th edition for $2.50. In many cases the only information that changes is the cover art and one or two pages or charts. An increasing trend is for universities to have a flat fee on account with the bookstore or to make an exclusive deal with a publisher so that an exact book can not be found online. A few of the top end universities will give a student account credit that can be used in the bookstore, but as a whole a family should expect to pay for books.

To recap: I tell the families that I work with if a school gives scholarships covering full tuition, but the family still has to pay for room and board, fees and books then the family got a good deal. Income is a factor. We will talk about expected family contribution momentarily (EFC). To use really rough numbers, I aim to have the students below the poverty line pay less than $10,000 a year total. I aim to have middle class parents pay less than $20,000 a year total. I have found that for competitive students these costs have been fair. Obviously, I ask for more and work toward more, but this tends to be my litmus test.

*What is a full need university?*

A full need university is one that claims to cover all costs above the family's expected family contribution. These are really great schools to work with. A quick Internet search will garner a list of schools that claim to be full need. One example can be found at: http://blog.collegegreenlight.com/blog/colleges-that-meet-100-of-student-financial-need/.

There are three important notes about these schools. First, a family's expected family contribution is often much higher that a family might expect or believe to be reasonable. Second, the list of schools that try to be full need is always changing. Please check with whichever university you are considering before making a decision. Third, most of these schools are a lot more difficult to gain admissions to in the first place. A mediocre student will have a real challenge getting into these schools. All that aside, for a family whose resources are limited, this list of schools is a really good place to start. In most cases these schools will outbid all of their competition. This is especially true for lower income families, but as a general rule this is not as true for middle and upper income students.

*Ok. What is the Expected Family Contribution (EFC)?*

EFC is how much a college or university expects a student to pay. The number is generated by your government. This is the money that a school feels a family should have been able to save and / or afford each year. This is a really good starting point on how affordable a college or university will actually be. As with everything else, the number is not the exact same for everyone, it is not the exact same for each year, and it is not going to have the same effect on each university. Just because a family's EFC is $0 does not mean the family will actually pay $0. By the same token, a family who has an EFC of $23,000 may not actually pay $23,000 or may pay more. The EFC is a number generated by FAFSA - which I will talk about shortly - and is generated primarily from family income but also takes into account such things as savings, investments, size of family and number of people in college. Two nearly identical families may get two very different EFC numbers from FAFSA.

So, let's take this one step further. In the Obama years universities and colleges were required to add a cost calculator to their websites. The cost calculator works slightly differently for each university and some are a little harder to find or use than others. We are going to take six hypothetical students. Keep in mind I am using rough numbers and the results generated will change year to year. This model is simply meant as an example with data generated in 2017. My hypothetical students will all be from Tennessee - just to pick a random state. None will be married, have dependent children, have military service, be foster children, homeless or wards of the state. All are US citizens. All will come from a family of four. Parents will still be married and the student will be the older sibling. No savings or investments. No home equity. As much as possible I am going to try to keep all the numbers the same. The unique numbers I am going to change are the parents' income and test scores. I will run the numbers exactly for all six students for two universities each. One university will be a top tier school. The other university will be a very good school, though not necessarily top tier. All male students will be input with an ACT score of 24 and a GPA of 3.3, approximately the national average. All female students will be input with an ACT score of 33 and a GPA of 4.0, a perfect score on the ACT is 36. Keep in mind, the top tier university would probably not admit the male students with a score of 24. Please run these numbers yourself for the schools that your son or daughter are interested in. My sample groups:

    Albert and Agnes - EFC of $0, family income of $24,000 / year

    Mark and Margaret - EFC of $18,000, family income of $110,000 / year

    Thomas and Tiffany - EFC of $590,000, family income of $1,500,000 / year

    Top tier university = Amherst College

    Middle tier university = Juniata College

Amounts shown are the amount anticipated to be paid annually.

Albert at Amherst = $1,000

Mark at Amherst = $17,500

Thomas at Amherst = $72,000

Albert at Juniata = $13,349

Mark at Juniata = $27,000

Thomas at Juniata = $34,000

Agnes at Amherst = $1,000

Margaret at Amherst = $17,500

Tiffany at Amherst = $72,000

Agnes at Juniata = $9,860

Margaret at Juniata = $23,000

Tiffany at Juniata = $26,000

    A few things stand out. First, Amherst is a much better deal and does a better job at matching the EFC. Second, the girls (Agnes, Margaret and Tiffany) at Juniata are a decent (though not necessarily cheap) price. The boys (Albert) are getting to the point that the lower income families can not afford Juniata. Third, at Amherst test scores make no difference to financial aid. All aid at Amherst is need based, not merit based. At Juniata test scores seem to matter less than family income. That being said I can guarantee a few points. Students will probably not actually pay this amount. In most cases this is the worst case scenario. In addition, every college (and I have tried more than 100) will generate different numbers for the exact same inputs.

*How do I know what I will pay?*

    The glib answer is that parents never know for sure. Again - almost like a mantra - cast a wide net. There are some ways to take an educated guess. For this answer I prefer hard data, but the data is often misleading and there are a plethora of exceptions.

    For a wealthy family with no financial need, look up a school's merit-based scholarships. These are usually based on test scores and grades. For example, one of my favorite schools is St.

Mary's in San Antonio, TX. With a little time on the website this page on ACT scores in relation to merit based aid can be found https://www.stmarytx.edu/admission/financial-aid/scholarships/. So, let us pretend that your student received a 24 on the ACT with a 3.5 GPA. A wealthy family, on paper, would receive $15,000-17,000 in merit-based scholarships. If the student can raise his or her test scores to a 28 on the ACT with a 3.5 GPA, then that scholarship is $19,000 - 21,000 a year. In many cases this is about it for a student with no need. If you look up a school with a bigger name - Harvard - a family will note that there is no merit-based aid based on test scores. What does that mean? It means that for a family of means Harvard is pretty much full price. To be fair, both St. Mary's and Harvard will probably find a little more than I stated, but the stress here is on the word "little." There is a possibility, though, that a family without demonstrated financial need can get colleges in a bidding war with each school offering bigger and bigger discounts. The logic for the school is that a student with relatively decent numbers and no financial need has many choices. Why not offer a "discount" to attract the money? Even at a discount the student is paying more than the college spends per student. In this manner there are times that the wealthiest students can pay a very good discount price. Highly competitive universities will not usually get involved in this bidding war.

For a student that is completely broke with and EFC of $0 or "full demonstrated need" the whole equation changes. A school may be infinitely more affordable. So, for examples take two schools. The first is a decent liberal arts school in New York - Hofstra University. I first go to college board and look at the tab that say "paying" under Hofstra University (https://bigfuture.collegeboard.org/college-university-search/hofstra-university). Under this tab I see that as of this writing Hofstra charges about $65,758. Now go to "financial aid by the numbers." There are three specific numbers I want to point out here. First, the percentage of need met - 69%. Second, the percentage of loans - 33%. Third the percentage of students that had full need met - 22%. To break this down Hofstra does not give much money. If a family needs $10,000 Hofstra - on average - pays 69% or $6900 leaving the family to pay $3100. Keep in mind that of the $10,000 Hofstra will finance - on average - 35% in loans. So, Hofstra may finance 35% of $10,000 or $3500 as loans. In reality that family now owes $6600 (need met plus loans) a year on a demonstrated need of $10,000. Only 22% have full need met. Keep in mind, just because a school says need met does not mean free. For a family with an EFC of $0, this will be close to $0 but not necessarily $0. By the numbers Hofstra is going to be expensive. Of course, there is always the possibility that Hofstra is much more affordable than these numbers belie or that your student will be the exception. Nothing is concrete in financial aid numbers.

To look at our second example, Vanderbilt University in Tennessee, go back to the search on College Board and pull up Vanderbilt (https://bigfuture.collegeboard.org/college-university-search/vanderbilt-university). First note that Vanderbilt is slightly more expensive at $70,194, but in the scheme of things this is effectively the same price. Percentage of need met = 100%. Percentage of loans = 7%. Percentage of students that had full need met = 99%. On the surface Vanderbilt seems like it could be a really good deal. In theory a family with an EFC of $0 might only pay 7% in loans or just under $5,000 a year. In practice I can say that Vanderbilt will almost always be cheaper for a family of limited finances. The catch is that the student still has to gain admission. It is easier to get admitted to Hofstra than it is to get admitted to Vanderbilt.

Middle class families are where I see the most variability. It is a challenge to find a university that will be able to balance merit based and need based aid to find a number that is affordable. Please keep in mind that what is affordable in the eyes of a university financial aid office may not always be affordable in the eyes of a family staring at a diminishing bank account. Some general rules for middle class families on finding a school at the right price point.

Rule 1: be very careful of schools without merit-based aid. The real top tier, Ivy League, MIT, Stanford, and a handful of others will do everything possible to make the school affordable for middle class families. The next tier down is not often so generous. In many cases I have found that middle of the road liberal arts colleges with strong merit-based aid can cost less. These middle tier liberal arts colleges are usually much cheaper than the big state schools as well.

Rule 2: The higher a student's ACT / SAT scores are compared to the college averages the more affordable the school will become. So, if a school averages 22-26 on the ACT for its students and your son has a 32, you will get a significant financial aid package in most cases. If a school averages 22-26 on the ACT for its students and your son has a 25, you will get some money but the amount may not be terribly generous. If a school averages 22-26 in the ACT for its students and your son has a 21, he will probably be accepted, but he will not receive much money at all.

Rule 3: I prefer loan amounts less than 15%. The higher the percentage of students with full need met, the better the chance a middle class family can afford the school.

Rule 4: The more difficult admissions are for a school, the more affordable that school will be. This is a real blanket statement, but I have found the statement to be generally true. It makes sense when you think that the colleges with the most financial aid are the same schools with more applicants.

Rule 5: Play around with the net price calculator. If you can not find it immediately, put the term into a search bar and try. These numbers on the net price calculator are not solid and usually aim a little high, the net price calculators can give a family a good idea of where the price point will begin. With a little experimentation a family will notice that while all the input data are the same, the amounts per college vary widely. Also experiment with what one or two more points on an ACT will garner.

Rule 6: Do not be afraid to ask an admission's officer directly at the start of the application process, "Can this school be affordable for my son?" "How affordable?" I don't expect real numbers, but I do expect an honest discussion on available merit and need based aid. If a school gives a quick answer without even asking what test scores or GPA are being considered, that answer should raise some questions. I like to ask this after looking at the net price calculator. Most representatives will point a family at the calculator first. Then I follow up with, "How much closer can your school get me to numbers I can afford?" or "Are there other scholarships my son might be eligible for?"

Rule 7: For middle class families full ride scholarships and "special" scholarships can be essential. Most of the middle tier and some of the top tier universities have a handful of full ride scholarships or at least scholarships in a very significant amount. These scholarships can be a life saver. Start the research sophomore or junior year. Many of these scholarships require very specific criteria that may be met if a student starts early enough. Start looking at universities, what the top level of scholarship is worth and what requirements are necessary for that scholarship. One example of these scholarships can be found at Centre College (https://www.centre.edu/admission-aid/cost-aid/scholarships/). I usually pass on any school with just one full tuition scholarship. The competition is intense and there is always the chance that the president of the college has a nephew coming to the college that year. I prefer at least four possibilities. Because there is so much competition, I strongly urge families to apply to more than one scholarship and more than one school with such scholarships. The higher the test scores and the higher the GPA, the more competitive your student will be for these scholarships. A final note on these scholarships: don't share. This is a time to be selfish. A school will never (almost never to cover my bases) give these kinds of scholarships to two students from the same school in the same year and rarely to two students from the same school in consecutive years. Bragging to the mother of your son's best friend while waiting for karate practice to end may only result in one more applicant for the same scholarship.

*What do colleges and universities give money for?*

The short answer is financial need and merit-based aid. In terms of financial need the equation is simple. The more competitive schools give more money to students that need more money. This does not necessarily mean free as much as it should mean affordable. In a process I can not hope to explain, I have even had twins get different financial need information at the same school in the same year. Every school calculates these numbers differently and none will come to the exact same conclusions. Top tier schools often only give financial need on the theory - not incorrectly - that all of their students qualify for merit-based aid.

Merit-based aid is a multi-headed monster that is difficult to predict. The first, and in some cases the only, distinction is on test scores and GPA (grade point average). The higher the test scores and the better the grades, the more money is given to a student. In some cases, the amount is negligible. In other cases, the amount is rather significant even going up to full tuition and room and board. What I want to know is the cut off. What scores does my student need? Will one more point make a difference? Will a school super score (take the best English and the best math from different tests)? Though the November or December tests are the last chance for

ACT / SAT scores to be sent for admissions, a spring test might affect financial aid. Not all schools will update the scores. If one more point will make a difference, ask.

In addition to grades and tests, schools will give money for anything that the school values in a particular candidate. I have seen various measures and combinations used. Sometimes the factors stack. Sometimes the factors do not stack. I have seen merit-based awards for athletics, for art, for music, for forensics, for environmental awareness, for the student's ethnic group, for legacy status, for tribal identity, for community service, for geographic location, for religious affiliation, military or JROTC service, for last names and for membership in a particular group. Each school makes their individual decisions. A couple of things to keep in mind when evaluating a school's merit-based aid:

1) What are the award amounts?

2) Are there any awards that cover full costs of tuition or tuition and room and board?

3) If so, how many such awards are given and what are the requirements? (Generally, I tell students that if only one such award is offered, the student won't get the award. If only one award is offered there is always someone with better numbers, a better essay, or the direct number of the university president. I want multiple awards available - or the president's direct line.)

4) Do the awards stack?

5) If the student gets outside scholarships, do the awards stay the same or are they adjusted?

6) Are the awards renewable every year? On what criteria?

7) Is there a special interview or visit or portfolio or recording required for the merit-based awards? Are they any forms that need to be filled out?

8) Finally, just because your student is eligible for an award, does not mean a school will give it. For example, a student eligible for a merit-based award because she is Methodist may not receive it because the school forgot to note it or because the church did not forward a verification of membership yet. It is also possible that the school just runs out of money.

These are all questions to keep in mind even during the application process and good questions for your student to follow up with the admission's office. A university or college that decides the school really wants your student can make magic happen and money grow on trees. A university that is lukewarm about your student can be a tightfisted miser. A mediocre student that has kept in contact with the financial aid office and blown away the admission's office with an A+ interview may easily garner more aid that the star band student with straight A's. Both will lose to the all-state pitcher with a perfect SAT score. For a list of merit-based scholarships available at individual schools look at https://www.cappex.com/scholarships/ . Look toward to bottom at the box that says "Merit Aid Scholarships Offered by Colleges."

*Is financial aid negotiable?*

Absolutely! I will return to this point later, but the idea is crucial. The first offer a student receives from a university is just that, a *first* offer. Depending on what niche your student fits, what the demands of the university are, how big the universities endowments are, the impression of the admission's officer or financial aid office or special circumstances money is always available. How much your student will get is the question. Remember, every dollar that Susan is promised is one less dollar for Gregory. For this reason I urge, implore, beg, and cajole your student (not the parent) to speak often with his or her school admission's officer. View the admission's officer as an ally, a friend. Communicate! Explain how the University of OMG is really your first choice, but Dad just refuses to pay that much. If there are actually special circumstances (i.e. Dad was unemployed for three months last year or Mom's personal business took a downturn or a recent hurricane wiped out all family assets), ask for an appeal form. Be concrete and succinct.

The worst mistake a family can make is to take the first offer. Talk to the school. See what other options are available. Ask what else a student can do to stand out. There are two warnings with this. First, apply for outside scholarships and be proactive beyond the college itself. Financial aid offices get terribly tired of students expecting the financial office to do everything while the student makes no efforts. Second, be careful of telling too many schools that the particular school is the first choice. Schools will eventually catch onto the game.

*Do I need a FAFSA?*

Short answer: yes. FAFSA is from the federal government. It is a tool used by almost every university in the country. Most schools will not even consider a student for financial aid unless the family submits the FAFSA. More and more schools do not couch this form as a request but as a demand. If a family knows it will not receive any financial need and prefers to keep its financial records private, many schools become . . . difficult. I don't believe a school can force you to divulge the information, but I know of schools that say merit-based aid will not be processed without submitting a FAFSA.

For most families the FAFSA is a no-brainer. Mom or dad or the accountant submit the forms along with the taxes at the end of the year. Recently FAFSA started allowing families to submit approximations as early as October. This considerably speeds up the financial aid process. The school of course will require an updated form after the taxes are complete. A significant change can adjust a student's financial aid package.

A FAFSA looks at income, taxes, and savings. FAFSA also looks at a student's income and savings. FAFSA will look at how much equity is in a home, how large the retirement accounts are, and any investments including stocks and bonds. In short, a school wants to verify that if a family is asking for financial need, the need is actually present and not perceived. Keep in mind, it is extremely rare for a school to give a family everything that the expected family contribution is short.

I strongly feel that some universities abuse this system and try to milk a family. It is increasingly common for a financial aid officer to ask a family to take out a second loan on their home or refinance the primary house. Very often I have seen financial aid offices advise a family to liquidate savings, stocks, bonds and investments in order to pay for college. The lower income families have nothing to take. The upper income families already plan on not receiving need based aid. The families so callously fleeced tend to be middle class families. I am often frustrated talking to families that finally - after twenty years - are seeing income levels rise above subsistence to where the family can finally start to really save money only to have a university try to take all of it and base the entire sum on what income is this year, not the last twenty.

If a family knows this will be the situation, I urge the family to speak to a financial advisor, one who is licensed, at least two years before junior applies to college. I have urged many single parents not to get remarried during the son's senior year in high school. If a single mother starts dating again but does not marry, the income is based only on Mom's income and Dad's income. As soon as Mom remarries, a third (or fourth) income is added to the equation.

This does not have a huge impact with FAFSA but can be absolutely crippling with the CSS Profile.

*Ok. What is the CSS Profile?*

Not very long ago universities felt that too much money was slipping through the fold. The feeling was that FAFSA was allowing a creative financial advisor to hide some assets. As such the CSS Profile was created. If FAFSA is a spotlight on the family's finances, the CSS Profile is the invasive probe. The CSS Profile is designed to uncover every last penny that a family may have in an account or under the couch cushion. It is such a nasty form that for years I avoided using colleges and universities that require the form. I can no longer avoid it as the CSS Profile has become far too common place. I feel even more strongly that this is a tool to strip all financial assets that a middle class family has spent the last twenty years acquiring.

The majority of schools that are top tier schools and schools that offer full need use the CSS Profile. To some extent I know that the university uses the form to ensure that a family is not being tricky and asking for more that the family really does not deserve. If a university asks for the CSS Profile, a FAFSA will also need to be submitted. A few schools even require a third in-house financial aid form. Do check in the application process which forms will be required. I have even found schools that do not post that a CSS Profile is needed until around January. Whereas FAFSA is free to submit, the CSS Profile charges a fee for each school. The fee is not huge, but if all ten schools require it, prices can rise fairly quickly. For me, working with FAFSA and the CSS Profile are the most unpleasant parts of my work with students. Again, if a school requires a CSS profile, you will still need to complete the FAFSA. Buy aspirin before you begin and make everyone else leave the house. It will be a long afternoon full of storm and fury.

*What if my parents do not have legal residency?*

Both the FAFSA and CSS Profile will need access to tax forms - which you will not have. In this case, please contact the financial aid office directly. I do not recommend contacting financial aid until a student has actually been admitted as this information may have an impact on admissions. In addition, not every school will be willing to work with the family. This will be a trial and error process. Even schools that were willing to work with a family last year may be unwilling to do so this year.

*It is March. My daughter applied at ten schools and was accepted at nine. Now what?*

This is one of my favorite times of year. This is where the real game begins. Getting a student into a school is just Act I. Finding the money is the next part.

Step 1: Put all the costs on the chart side by side. Put the total tuition costs, room and board, and fees in one column. Notice, I did not include books or travel expenses. I don't include either as prices vary. As much as possible I want to compare apples to apples. By the same token, I will include room and board even for the in state school where a student will still live at home.

Step 2: Put all financial aid in the chart. Include grants and scholarships. Include any private scholarships that have already been awarded. Do not include loans or work study yet. I will talk about loans shortly. I do not want to include work study as the amounts vary and every school has different ideas of how work study will affect financial aid. Once you have the numbers, subtract total costs and total financial aid. This is what college will actually cost. Monthly payment plans typically divide the amount owed by ten equal payments. So, if after the math, Vanderbilt has a price tag of $13,500 a family could plan on $1350 a month. We will work on adjusting this shortly.

Step 3: Have your son or daughter start ranking the schools with you. This gets tricky as parents usually just see the bottom line. Students often want to make an emotional decision. Parents: remember this is not a final price, but the price should be in the ball park. If a school wants $26,500 a year, asking to pay only $7,000 is unrealistic. Students: before ranking the schools try listing the attributes that are most important to you individually. Look at things like the strength of the major, geographic location, small school or bigger school, travel abroad opportunities, distance from home, school's reputation, research opportunities, how close the beach is. Everyone's list will be different. Instead of telling Dad you really want to go to New School of Florida, try to figure out why. Go beyond the glossy brochures and the fantastic visit you had there. Go beyond the images of teenage girls on the beach. Use real data about what is important. Then rank.

I tell students that a few thousand dollars between a first choice school and a second choice school is negligible. In the scheme of things, if the first choice school only costs $2,000 more, the price is worth it. If the difference is $7-8,000 a year, the second choice starts to look quite good.

Step 4: Make a financial decision as a family about what a family can or can not actually afford. So, let me use a hypothetical situation. The numbers are not exact numbers but they are approximate numbers. For this example, let's pretend I have three students: Claude, Camille and

Chris. Claude is low income. Camille is middle income. Chris is flat out loaded. Once again, let me remind readers that this is a sample - not an absolute.

Camille has been accepted at 9 of 10 schools applied to. Her family has decided that Camille will take the first $5,500 a year in debt herself in Stafford loans. After that loan the family decided between Mom and Dad the family can afford $10,000. That comes out to $1,000 a month. It is really tight at that level, but if Mom puts off the new car she was hoping to get and Dad puts in a few more hours at work every week, this is the absolute limit the family can afford. After looking at the nine acceptance packages, Camille and her parents agree that five schools are reasonable. Her top choice school will cost $16,500 a year. Second choice comes in at $14,700 a year. Third choice only costs $8,500 a year. The fourth and fifth choices are both about $15,000.

Claude and his family have a much lower threshold. Claude's parents only make $24,000 a year. This is darn close to minimum wage. Like Camille, Claude decides that the first $5,500 will be his personal debt. Claude's family decides that they can afford another $300 a month for a total of $8,500 a year. To be fair, I have had low income (and even middle income families) tell me that $300 a month is too expensive and that the family can afford $0.

I have no patience for this. Your child is receiving a college education! It is completely unreasonable on the parent's part to say he or she will pay nothing. I have also seen divorced parents try to split the amounts in some really creative fashions. In the end, only the student loses that argument. I can tell you that from experience universities tend to dig their heels in when speaking with parents that are completely stubborn and keep insisting that their child should go for free. A family should be willing to meet part way. Keep in mind, if Claude is going away to school a family is no longer paying his food, his clothing, his toiletries or the $10 a week he bums from Dad to pay for Wendy's on a late Thursday afternoon. A family can save $200 a month just on food. Have you ever watched a teenager eat? Teens are worse than locusts.

For argument's sake let's say there are three schools on Claude's list under around $9,000 or less a year. Claude's top choice school will cost $2,300 a year. The second choice is $9,200 and the third choice is $3,000 a year. Obviously, Claude has made some good choices up to this point.

Chris does not even worry about FAFSA. His parents know that he will receive no need based aid. That being said, the parents don't want to pay more than necessary. All that Chris is receiving is merit-based aid. Chris's first choice school costs $32,000 a year. His second choice gave him a full ride (almost). His family would only pay $8,000 a year for room and board. The next three choices are all around $29,000 a year.

Step 5: Let's make a deal. Start calling or emailing schools. Let us use the examples again. Camille obviously wants her first choice school. Whereas the price is not bad, the third choice is a lot better. Camille should call her first choice school and say something like -

"Good afternoon. My name is Camille Wannabe. I was reviewing my financial aid packages last night. I really want to attend the University of OMG (her 1st choice), but my family is just not willing to pay that. Is there anything I can do? ...... Oh. Well my second choice school (I know it is really third) is only asking for $8,500 (don't lie about numbers - the school will see the numbers). While I really want to attend the University of OMG, my parents are pretty firm on the second choice school. So? ...... Oh, you want me to send the numbers for my second choice? Ok. Can my Mom fax them to you tomorrow? What is the number? To the attention of whom?"

This is a strategy I use quite a bit. It is not unlike shopping for a car and then pulling out a quote from the dealer down the street. Just as the car dealer will insist that the "other" car is not quite the same, after all floor mats were not included, colleges in the same fashion will insist the "other" college is just not the same. Just as with a car dealer, if the college meets your price the school will expect a family to then pay up. Negotiations are pretty much finished at that point.

Once Camille puts a real number out there a college or university will have three possible answers. Possibility 1 (the worst choice): no. This is the best we can offer. Translation: we like Camille, but we don't like her that much. We at the University of OMG are willing to lose her to another school. Some schools will even tell you at that point to go to the other school. Take the admission's counselor at his word if this is the case and go.

Possibility 2 (not my favorite): yes. I don't generally love this answer because I know that financial aid officers are not authorized to give much more money. In this case the line is moving somewhere around $500-$2,000. While not bad, I want more.

Possibility 3 (score!): I need to check with the dean of financial aid. Can I get back to you in a few days? While there is always the possibility that the dean just says no, there is a better chance that the dean will authorize an extra $4,000-$7,000 a year. Notice: I did not say an extra $20,000. That is just not realistic. $7,000 is about the most I have ever seen the needle move and $5,000 or less is the most common. If a family is hoping for $20,000, pray. That is the only way I know to get amounts that large.

If the University of OMG refuses to budge, and Camille thinks that number 2 school is about the same, rinse and repeat. Start the whole process over. The second choice now becomes the first choice. This happens more often than I would care to tell you. Every school makes these evaluations differently. Some schools just don't want your student as much as you would hope (crazy, I know). Other schools are sure that what they have offered is fair - and the school might be right. Other schools simply don't have the money. Not every school has the same endowments. Harvard and Yale could probably stop charging admission all together and do just fine. Most other schools are not quite that well off. Some schools in fact are in dire financial straits. As such, funds are often limited.

In the case of Claude, the fact that the first choice is also the cheapest is a bonus. The family can still ask for more, but at this amount I usually don't bother. This is more than fair (and I see these kinds of numbers for top notch students every year). I would advise Claude to take out the $2,300 in personal loans. I would then ask the family to send him $150 a month for allowance. In this way Claude does not need to work. $150 a month won't give Claude much of a social life, but he can buy toiletries and still have enough to split the occasional midnight pizza with his roommate.

In the case of Chris, it seems like this is going to be a case of money. Is the money worth the top choice school? The difference between the first and third choice school is negligible. I would advise the family that in the scheme of things $3,000 is not much. The real question is the first and second choice school. Is Chris's first choice worth $100,000? I might try to bribe Chris. Take the second choice and Dad throws in a car. If Chris says yes, he is willing to negotiate. If Chris still says no, well . . . the family needs to talk.

*How can I get more money?*

Let's assume that the price is still a little more than hoped for. First, if your student was working with a specific admission's counselor, coach, music director, or professor, have your student call that individual. Ask if that individual can help. Admission counselors have quite a lot of influence on this whole decision. The admission's officer can not sell every student, though. This is why it is imperative that your student keeps in touch with the admission's officer throughout this entire process.

One of my favorite conversations is in mid-April when an admission's officer calls me and asks, "How much will it take to get 'Camille' here?" I can tell you, though, these conversations will only happen once or twice a year. Some students are easier to sell - the student fills more boxes. Some students are simply more charismatic. Some schools have more resources. A deal for one student will not translate into the same deal for another student. I have generally found, though every admission's officer I know denies this, a single school will have few students with better than average deals. If Boston College gives a great deal to Camille at Central High School, it is much harder for Claude to get the same deal or better from Boston College. Please don't let your teen brag until everything is done. As Camille's parents, you really don't want Claude's parents to call Boston College with your numbers asking for the same deal.

Another option is to get creative with the financing. I always advise that as a first step the student takes the first $5,500 in federal loans. I advise this for multiple reasons. First and foremost, I want the student to have skin in the game. I have known students who love college so much that it takes seven or eight years to graduate. When one considers that scholarships generally only cover the first four years, that extended vacation can really add up. I don't want the student to feel that he or she is getting a free ride. This loan also creates a credit rating. I sweeten the deal by saying that if the teen finds more scholarships then those scholarships come off of what the teen owes. In the worst case scenario, the teen graduates $22,000 in debt or the price of a car, a small car. In addition, this is the limit the teen can take unassisted.

Another option is work study. Every school does work study differently. Some schools pay the student nothing and the money earned goes directly to what he or she owes. Some schools pay the student everything and if the student is foolish enough to run to the nearest shopping center, oh well. Some schools do half and half. Ask about how the school processes the earnings. Keep in mind, not every student is eligible for work study. Even a student who is eligible for work study may not get it. Work study also runs a gamut. A student could end up mowing the football field or doing dishes for three hundred classmates every night. I personally think the best choices for work study - and options usually reserved for upper classmen -

Library: get paid to study.

Computer lab: get paid to study.

Lab assistant: Get paid to play with machines (in engineering) or science projects (in chemistry) or mold samples (in biology). All give really good experience and often lead to research projects or really good letters of recommendation from a professor in the student's field.

Financial aid or admission's office: When the discussion for scholarship dollars comes up the next spring, it is really hard for a financial aid officer to short a student that is well known. It is much easier to short some anonymous student elsewhere on campus.

Another option for money is a real job. Work study usually pays minimum wage. The advantage is that no transportation is needed, and the campus jobs generally do a wonderful job working around a student's schedule. A real job off campus can pay quite a bit more, but the job is often not flexible. The best jobs I have found in terms of money are computers and waiting tables. Anything with computers is in high demand and tends to pay well. Even data entry can often be done remotely. Most computer jobs are more concerned about a student's ability and less concerned with a student's current degrees. Waiting tables, especially at a restaurant where the average bill is about $100 can really make a lot of money. A good waiter or waitress can make $50 an hour easy. The down side is that these jobs are extraordinarily competitive, don't like to hire anyone under 19, and want a good waiter to work every weekend and holiday which kind of kills a social life.

If a student can not balance work and school - and many students can not - then have the student work in the summer. If this is done, I would recommend taking the student's paychecks otherwise too many students spend everything earned. In a summer and the month of winter break a student can reasonably save $2,000. Depending on the job and the pay rate this amount might be more.

Beg relatives. Ask grandma and grandpa, uncles and aunts, cousins and older siblings to chip in. Grandma may not be able to give the teen $3000, but between Grandma, two favorite uncles, an older sister, a godfather and a stepmother it may be possible to get $3000 total. Force the teen to write hand written thank you notes to all concerned every year.

So, let's give another hypothetical example. The numbers are not one specific school, but the numbers do reflect schools I have worked with. Our student is Danielle. Danielle is a decent student. She played soccer for four years. In addition, she made the mock trial team her senior year and went to nationals. Her grades were good with a weighted GPA of 4.1 on a 4.0 scale. She took mostly honors classes with three AP classes junior and senior year combined. Her ACT was . . . disappointing. Her highest score in November was a 27. Unfortunately, Danielle is from a middle class family. On paper, the school says her family has plenty of money. Her parents' bank says that the family is barely making it. Her family does some hard math and figures that with Danielle's younger brother just two years behind her, a house payment, two car payments, a medical bill that came up last year for mom, two credit card payments, and a modest retirement plan all the family can afford - absolute ceiling - is $1000 a month.

Danielle's first choice school - the University of OMG - accepts her. It has a price tag of $65,000 a year! Now some numbers. Danielle's test scores and grades qualify her for a $20,000 presidential scholarship. There is no financial need. Ok. $45,000 left. (Have a good cry and get back to me.) This is still too much. Danielle calls her admission's counselor. She explains about how much she really wants to go to the University of OMG. She explains about how her parents have no real savings and that her brother will be in college in two years. She also explains that mom had a cyst that was removed last year and the family is still trying to make the payments.

The admission's counselor has heard all of this before, but he genuinely likes Danielle. Unlike so many of the students he worked with this year, Danielle was always enthusiastic and tuned in. Danielle always had good questions and most importantly visited the school twice. Danielle definitely has some real interest in the school and in his head the counselor really saw her on campus next fall. He tells her to write a letter explaining the financial problems. Danielle sends the letter the next day. The admission's counselor then takes a short walk down to financial aid to plead her case. Three torturous days later he is able to call Danielle's family back and tell them he found an extra $5,000. Dad is not as enthusiastic as hoped. Dad still sees a bill for $40,000 (before books). The admission's counselor recommends calling the soccer coach.

Danielle calls the coach the next day. The University of OMG is D3 and Danielle never really considered soccer in college. Mostly she played because all her friends were on the team. The coach explains that as a D3 school he does not have any money directly for athletics, but he will put a call into Danielle's coach in high school. The following week after the two coaches played phone tag the coach tells Danielle that while he is very happy to have her try out for the team, he just does not have more money for her.

Danielle is still $40,000 short. At that point she remembers that on the same page as the soccer information was something about a forensics team. The University of OMG, while it never really cared much about soccer, does pride itself on forensics. Danielle contacts the forensics coach via email. She explains that while she never did forensics in high school, she did participate in mock trial and many of the skills translate. After three weeks of more emails and some recorded film of Danielle in action (in her living room as nothing else was available), the coach not only offers her a spot on his forensics team but includes a $7,000 scholarship. She must maintain a 3.25 GPA in college, meet once a week and attend three annual competitions to keep the scholarship.

The same week Danielle gets another call from admissions. He has another $2,000 for her. He calls it a leadership scholarship. He doesn't say exactly why. Perhaps it was the soccer coach. Maybe he just felt bad for her and noticed that she was trying to make it work. Danielle now owes $31,000. She talks with her parents and agrees to take the first $5,500 herself in loans ($25,500). Danielle calls all four grandparents - another $1500 a year ($24,000). Danielle promises to get a job and save everything she makes this summer ($21,000).

This is still far too short. Danielle calls her admission's counselor again. He tells her that without better test scores that is the best he can do. Danielle asks what number she needed.

The presidential scholarship - which she received - was $20,000 a year. That was given to all students who had between a 24 and a 27 on the ACT. The Trustee's scholarship was $30,000 a year for an ACT of 28 or higher. Danielle's heart skips a beat. Her score in November was a 27. Her score in January was also 27, but in November her English score was highest. In January her math score was higher and English lower. Would the school super score - take the best English and the best math? The admission's counselor gets excited and asks her to send the scores immediately. The next day he informs her that the college did super score. Danielle only needs $11,000.

Danielle plans on work study - in admissions. That will give her an additional $3500 a year. If she puts everything towards her tuition, she now owes $7,500. Her parents gladly - and with relief - agree to pay $750 a month and kick in an extra $50 a month to Danielle for toiletries and laundry money. If Danielle wants more money she will need to find a way to balance her time and get a second job off campus, but this will work. Danielle happily calls the admission's counselor back with the news and sends the deposit the next day. The crowd goes wild.

*That all sounds good. What else can I do?*

Talk to churches (or temples or mosques or tabernacles), clubs, and jobs about scholarship funds.

Plan this out three years ahead and convince your boss to start a college scholarship fund - as a tax write off.

See what other clubs, sports, activities at the college offer scholarships.

Apply for outside scholarships a year out.

Look into taking money from investments or refinancing the house.

Sell the kid's car. Sell the Play Station and all the games. Sell the Pokémon cards.

Ask for a better option on the dorms. For example, a three person room instead of a two person room is often cheaper. Also check meal plans.

Take a second (or third job).

Take a Parent PLUS loan or get a loan from the bank.

Look into front loading the amount owed. For example, the first year may be too expensive. That does not mean that every year has to be. One of my favorites - though it is definitely not guaranteed - is working with resident life. Working for Resident Life as a resident assistant often pays room and board or at least a portion of it. That can be $10,000 - $12,000 a year! Other times there are departmental scholarships only available to non-Freshmen. Other times good academics can lead to higher scholarships. One of my favorite schools reevaluates grades after the first year. Students who do really well get more money - the student gets the money from students who did not do so well. Do well. Another school I use gives four full ride scholarships a year to students that had a phenomenal freshman year. The school does not advertise it, and the student must be nominated by the faculty. Always keep in mind that none of these are guarantees, though. It is entirely possible to bet on something like this only to end up with a huge debt.

Look at the next school on the list and try again.

*Can't my kid apply to private scholarships?*

I strongly encourage searching for private scholarships. Private scholarships generally do not provide too much money, but every dollar adds up. There are few problems with private scholarships. Problem 1: the scholarships are competitive. It is entirely possible to apply to twelve scholarships and receive nothing. I advise my students to forget about the $20,000 scholarships. Everyone applies for the big ticket scholarships. The big amounts will be awarded to the student with perfect grades, perfect test scores, perfect essays and perfect teeth who saved the whales while building a working satellite to track Iran's nuclear progress. I instead urge my students to apply for multiple $500 or $5000 scholarships. These lesser amounts are less competitive and more plentiful.

Problem 2: most scholarships are not awarded until late spring or summer. In most cases a student will not learn if the scholarship search was successful until after the student has committed to a college. How can a family make a good decision about a school if the family does not know how much college will actually cost? For this reason I generally do not advise families to see scholarship applications as money in the bank. Rather I see them as gravy - extra money on top of what is already received. One positive, though, is that most scholarships can be won junior year and banked. I strongly recommend this. Going into the financial aid process knowing that your son already has won $3000 in scholarships reduces some stress.

Problem 3: scholarships do not often renew. It is really common to get a scholarship for freshman year. Sophomore year a student has ... nothing. Most scholarships are for one year only. Be sure to know which scholarships expire and if a form needs to be submitted to renew. The good news is that most scholarships can be used by anyone in college. If the scholarship does not renew, apply for a different one or more than one sophomore year.

Problem 4: students are lazy. Many of my students simply do not want to put in the effort or time to get extra scholarships. I have tried to explain that most of the essays are similar. If a student applies to ten scholarships, she will probably only write three essays. I have tried to tell students that this disease of laziness not only afflicts them, but it also afflicts their competition making it easier to win the scholarships. I try to explain that if a student invests three or four hours to win $5000 in scholarships, the student will never be paid on that kind of hourly rate again. Students are still lazy.

Problem 5: many scholarships do not stack. Some universities, and this is more common with large public schools, will not give the students a credit for scholarships. If a student is awarded $15,000 in merit-based aid and then wins $5000 in scholarships, some schools reduce the merit-based aid to $10,000 leaving the student no better off. I have even seen schools reduce the package by $7000 on the theory that if a student found $5000, the student can find another $2000! I have had several students win and turn down scholarships because it was cheaper not to have the scholarship.

That being said I really encourage applying to private scholarships. Generally speaking this is money that can make a university much more affordable. Even $500 is $500 less out of Mom's pocket. Second, and probably more important, what does it say to a school financial aid office when a student will not even help themselves? I spoke with a very frustrated financial aid officer last year. He lamented after a really long day, "Why do all these kids expect me to keep finding money for them when they don't even look?" I did not have a good answer. If your student needs to ask for more money, please let the financial aid office know which scholarships your son or daughter is applying for. If nothing else, this will signal an effort on the student's part.

*Beware the scam!*

Senior year many students are bombarded with junk mail. In most cases the high school sells your address - even if you ask the school not to sell your information. Some of the mail will promise "secret scholarships." The mail will exclaim how every year thousands of dollars go unclaimed in scholarships. This is a scam. There is no such thing as a secret scholarship. Any money you give for a "personal list" is just lazy. All the service will do, if anything, is give a generic list that the service got using common and free scholarship searches. I have never found a secret list or any point to paying money for a list that can be found for free.

*Where can I find scholarships?*

A good place to start is www.fastweb.com. This is the website that most of the mailers who claim to have a "tailored list of scholarships just for your teen" use. It is free to access. When you first log on try typing different variables. The web site will search based on keyword criteria. For example: "Hispanic, left handed, volleyball, tall." Some other web sites to try (and these were still current at the time I wrote this but may be dead links when you read this):

www.supercollege.com

Www.brokescholar.com

Www.finaid.org

https://www.cappex.com/scholarships/

Www.ed.gov

Www.salliemae.com

http://www.imfirst.org/#! (For first generation college students)

Another good source is universities themselves. Many of the top big state universities list quite a few scholarships under their home financial aid page. These scholarships are not unique to the university. As many scholarships that work really well are local, try a local big state university's financial aid web page. For example, the university closest to me is Arizona State

University. ASU has done a wonderful job with listing private scholarships on their financial aid page at https://scholarships.asu.edu/scholarship-search.

Raise Me (https://www.raise.me/), a new scholarship application for the computer, offers a lot of promise. The program was begun several years ago in part by a generous grant from the Bill and Melinda Gates Foundation. The application allows students to create an account and follow several hundred colleges. The universities and colleges represented all have their own criteria, but for example a school might give very real money for a student taking an advanced placement class or doing exceptionally well in a math class or playing basketball or doing community service or passing an AP examination. Each participating school does this a little differently. I would recommend creating an account and playing around with the account. The cost to the student is maybe twenty minutes. The potential gain could be a full scholarship. See the following 2015 news story from CNN - http://money.cnn.com/2015/09/18/smallbusiness/raiseme-college-scholarship/. The unique caution I give my students is that not every college or university represented on Raise Me are colleges and universities I normally recommend. Please do the leg-work of investigating the graduation rates and the matriculation rates as well as the percentages of loans the school typically uses.

If your teen is truly desperate, he or she could try the public library. In addition to loaning movies and music, the public libraries have recently begun to lend things called books. Some of the best scholarships I have found are small unnoticed funds begun many years ago and largely forgotten. I have found a wealth of scholarships by looking through actual books as opposed to a computer search. I spent one afternoon searching for a young man who was white and middle class and interested in pursuing architecture. In about two hours I had found three or four pages (maybe 50 individual scholarships) of possible scholarships for him. Try starting around call number 378 or so. Please check the reference section first as so many of the best books are not available for check out. While you are in the library, speak with one of the librarians. Many of the public libraries have special sections for college searches and scholarships. Other libraries have public programs to help with admissions, FAFSA and financial aid. There are times I have found the public library to be far more helpful and useful than the local high school guidance counselor.

When it comes to private scholarships, start looking sophomore year and start applying junior year. I want students to know what scholarships he or she is eligible for while there is still time to follow through. If a student waits until senior year, he may find that perfect scholarship only to find out he is not actually eligible. One example is a scholarship for Trekkies. Star Trek fans rejoice. You, too, have a special place in the universe. http://sfi.org/scholarships/ The catch is that students have to have been a member of "Starfleet" - a relatively painless process - for at least a year before the application. Can you guess how many seniors who are devoted Star Trek fans wish that they had known that a year earlier?

I also want students to apply junior year in order to bank some of the earned scholarships. A student who has already earned $6,000 in scholarships before beginning her applications has a much stronger argument for financial aid. Most scholarship awards are given in June or July but the deadline for college notification is May 1. If a family really needs outside scholarships to make a particular school work, how can that decision be made unless the student applies a year earlier?

*Can a school reduce my package?*

I have never known a school to reduce what a student is receiving because the student asked for more money. I have known a lot of schools that reduce a student's aid package the next year. There are two reasons I see this. Some schools reduce (or add) to an aid package because of the student's progress.

Some years ago I was working with a young woman who really needed money for school. Her parents were just unable to pay anything. I called or emailed her top choice school at least five times trying to get her a little more money. After much pleading on my part and many promises on her part, the young woman was given a financial aid package where all she needed to do was take out a federally subsidized loan for just under $3,000. I was very pleased. Around Christmas time I learned that the financial aid office had cut about $25,000 from her aid package. The new amount made it impossible for her to return to school in the spring. It seems that the young woman had discovered boys and booze. Her grades suffered greatly and several incidents of public inebriation had reached the ears of the financial aid office as it was a rather small school. The result was that this young woman who had made so many promises was now applying for jobs at the local gas station. The following year I had a more difficult time arguing for more money at this particular school.

Yes, university students are pretty much treated like adults. The flip side is that students may have to deal with some adult like consequences for poor choices.

The other common reason that students lose financial aid is a funding strategy. Some schools will front load all the scholarships on freshman year and then reduce the aid year by year on the theory that it will be too hard for students to transfer. The only defense is ask around before committing to a college. Ask guidance counselors, teachers, and students currently attending the school. Look up comments online. Ask the student guide during the college tour.

I have noticed the front loading strategy is one of the major causes when schools have a low graduation rate. Too many students begin at a school where the school is no longer financially feasible the following year.

A college may also raise tuition, room and board or fees. When choosing a school, ask when the last time the school raised costs and how much the costs went up. Too often, just because the school costs more does not mean a student receives more. One young man I worked with received a "full ride" scholarship. The scholarship was renewed every year, but the young man paid over $7,000 senior year as costs had gone up, but his scholarship had not. This is another reason I counsel against families going all in on college costs or banking on a possible pay raise the next year. What a student is paying freshman year may actually be lower than what the student is paying senior year.

A popular new promotion for schools is a price guarantee or even tuition insurance. I have a dim view of the "insurance," but I love the price guarantee. This is a promise that the student in good standing will pay the same amount all four years even if costs rise. This might be a good question to ask of an admission's representative or during the college tour. If the promise is made, get the agreement in writing somewhere and keep the agreement on file for four years.

A final note on costs and scholarships: there is one last grade check in June of senior year after the final transcript has posted. If your student's grades suddenly got very . . . creative, a school has the choice of voiding all scholarships and even admission.

*Who should be contacting the school?*

Whenever possible I want the student to contact the school. This is true for initial inquiries, for admissions and even for financial aid. You want your son or daughter to start acting like a young adult. It is time to let the student learn. In addition, I know from experience that a school that is being contacted by a student tends to hold the student in higher esteem. Much more seems to be accomplished when speaking with a student. Schools have a more difficult time telling no to students than parents.

When negotiating for financial aid I still recommend that the student initiate the call, but I believe one of the parents should be present. I have personally worked with schools that use a student's inexperience and naiveté to mislead a student. From time to time a school will be reticent to have a parent or adult on the line. The school will cite FERPA which is a series of laws meant to protect a student's privacy. It may apply when the parent is making a call without a student, but FERPA laws are not really applicable when talking to a school about a student's financial aid and the student is present. If a school is still insisting about only the student being on the phone, a red flag should go up in your head.

In extreme cases I have asked students to put everything on speaker phone and have the parent listen in with a pad of paper and a pen to weigh in silently. In many situations where this is the route taken, the school takes liberties the school should not. I have had to follow up on these kinds of calls with a dean of admissions or provost more than once as there were issues that were . . . unethical.

A final warning about communication with a school. Nothing is final until it is received in writing. I always encourage families to ask an admission's or financial aid officer to send an email detailing the promises made at the end of conversation. If the school is unwilling to do so, the parent should follow up with an email that says something like:

"On Friday, February 20, I spoke with Samuel Adams. Mr. Adams told me that my son would be receiving an extra $7,500 in scholarships for financial need. I just wanted to verify that there were no misunderstandings. Please let me know if that amount is not correct. Thank you very much."

I provide this warning out of experience. A few years ago there was a young woman I was working with for a financial aid package. A university in Texas had assured me that she had won a full scholarship for four years due to her academic achievements and her submitted essays. Elated I asked if I could share the information with the young woman. The financial aid officer told me that I could, and that the young woman would be receiving notification in the mail within the next week. A week later she had still not received anything. I called the school back. The financial aid officer apologized and said he had been meaning to call me for some days. Evidently one of the administrators at the school had demanded that his nephew - a late applicant - should receive the award instead. The letter was never mailed, and I presume the nephew received the scholarship. Nothing is official until it is in writing.

*I don't feel comfortable making these calls with my student. Can a counselor or teacher make the call?*

This is rarely my first choice. The primary reason is that no matter how kind or helpful a counselor is, that counselor will not fight as hard for a student as you would. This is your student - and your money. In addition, schools are really hesitant to speak with a counselor or a teacher about finances. Many times, a university will simply not have the conversation with a counselor or teacher no matter how well meaning. If as a parent you feel there is no other way because of your communication skills or because you really don't know what to ask, then I recommend being in the room on speaker phone. At the bare minimum, talk to the counselor or teacher before the call and express what you are hoping to gain from the school. Don't trust that another person will be able to adequately convey what you need as a family.

*What should be done about financial aid when my student is a sophomore in college?*

Check what academic standing is required to keep the scholarships awarded. Almost every school will require a student to keep a specific GPA in order to keep the scholarships. Verify which aid is renewable and which expires. Ask if any forms need to be filled out in order to renew a scholarship. Private scholarships rarely renew. Make sure you are aware how much the next year will be short. If the amount is significant, apply again for outside scholarships.

Keep in mind, if a student begins to have problems academically, the college will not notify the parents. The first notification will be a new bill for an amount larger than expected. Every year before returning home for summer, the student should stop in the business office and ask for a printed statement of exactly what the account balance is and what the balance on any loans is. This information on a yearly basis can save a lot of headaches later.

*How much debt is too much?*

This question has a different answer for everyone. I begin by having my students take the first $5,500 a year themselves - Stafford Loans. After that it gets tricky. A low income family can not afford much more debt. Even $1,000 or $2,000 a year more in loans can really financially destroy a family that only makes $22,000 a year. A wealthy family should not need the loans. The real trick is middle class families.

I always multiply any debt each year by four. If a student will need an extra $15,000 in loans, the potential is for a debt of $60,000 upon graduation. There are ways to defray the debt by sophomore year, but I prefer to deal with worst case scenarios. When speaking of debt with families I try to put the debt in terms of car payments or house payments. For me, graduating with a $120,000 debt is insane. That is a house payment - with no house! Even a $50,000 or $60,000 debt seems extreme to me. Speak with a banker. Even if a family ends up using Parent PLUS loans, the local banker can give a good comparison and real numbers about how much this will cost.

Be careful with loans, especially bank loans. The original $5,500 that I speak of with students comes in two flavors: subsidized and unsubsidized. Subsidized loans are guaranteed by the government and do not accrue interest until six months after graduation. Unsubsidized loans start gaining interest from day one, though at this point no payments are necessary until graduation. Obviously, I want to pay off the unsubsidized loans first. Outside loans may require payments in September right after your child begins freshman year.

A family whose daughter plans to attend medical school or law school or finish an engineering, psychology or architecture degree needs to be especially careful about loans. A four year degree does nothing in these fields. All these fields require a higher degree. The career needs more education - and more money. I had a wonderful student, a daughter of Chinese immigrants, who majored in pre-med. She did well and scored above average on her MCATS. She could not, however, attend medical school. There were no scholarships that she could win and her family could not afford anything. Instead of medical school, the last I heard, she is working at a company designing prescription drugs. While not a bad profession, it is not the profession about which she had dreamed. When considering debt limits keep in mind that four years may not be adequate.

The final notes about loans are how hard the loans are to get rid of. As of this writing, student loans are exempt from bankruptcy. I spoke with someone once who took out massive loans for an elite university on the theory that she would just declare bankruptcy after graduation. She was horrified to learn that her student loans would remain. Another warning I give students regards marriage. I do everything I can to make sure that my students graduate in four years with little or no debt. Graduating debt free does little for a student's finances if he marries a girl with $94,000 in student loans.

*Is there any way to dispel my debt?*

There are several federal programs and a few state programs that allow a student debt to be defrayed or simply eliminated. The state of Oregon has recently promised affordable tuition to all community college students in Oregon and has been floating a plan allow students to pay with a percentage of future earnings. Other federal programs like Teach for America allow graduated students to work in difficult to fill positions for a period of years in exchange for ending some of the student debt. Many states offer some kind of program to help families with colleges. https://www.law.uh.edu/ihelg/documents/StatePrepaid.pdf

These plans come in two types: savings and prepaid college. I personally prefer the prepaid colleges. As university tuition has increased roughly 300% in the last ten years, I am not confident of my ability to ever save enough. The prepaid plans usually lock the current tuition rates and allow families to begin paying now. With either plan, please investigate all the rules. Specifically, what is your state offering, what is the interest rate, what guarantees are there, what is the solvency of the program, and can I use this money for a school in another state or must it be this state?

*What about the military?*

The military is rarely my first choice, but there are times when this is a viable option. I really treat this on a case by case basis. If a family chooses to pursue this, investigate the ROTC program. Many universities manage programs where a student will attend a university and do minimal service with the military until graduation. After graduation the student is obligated to serve a period of years in the military. In exchange, the military *may* pay a portion of the costs of university.

Keep in mind that the military service is required and that the student has little choice about where or what capacity he or she serves in. The promises of a recruiter have little impact on what country your son will wake up in. In addition, no matter how one looks at this angle, there are important forms to be filled out with the military. If the forms are not done or are filled out incorrectly, your student may receive nothing and still be required to serve. In my father's generation, the GI Bill covered pretty much 100% of college costs. That is not necessarily true today.

*What if my financial situation changes?*

Life happens. If the financial changes are positive such as your boss finally seeing how much you are really worth and doubling your salary, then expect the school to find out when FAFSA is submitted the next year. If the decrease in financial aid is substantial, appeal the decision.

If the financial changes are negative such as losing a small business, then contact the school's financial aid office immediately. Some schools will do nothing. Other schools will provide an adjustment at the year or the semester. Every once in a while, I find a school that will change financial aid packages mid-semester. In every scenario, expect the financial aid office to check on the academic progress of your student before any promises are made.

*I am white, middle class with few savings but no real disadvantages. What can my daughter do to actually afford school?*

This is the most difficult population with which I work. White and middle class seem to have all the disadvantages when it comes to affording college. Poor students and minority students regardless of income have distinct advantages. The wealthy, though they may not like paying, can afford it. I spoke to a gentleman last year who proudly told me that his children were self-sufficient. He *only* (emphasis added) gave $250,000 to each of his children for school. Anything over that was the child's responsibility. I don't know if he realizes what college actually costs, but $250,000 is more than enough.

Middle class parents, though, seemingly have few advantages and few assets. Most are in the position that while the bills are paid and the house is more than adequate, there is not exactly a huge savings account for college. Most middle class family's biggest savings are retirement, which I can not advise liquidating. By the same token, I don't like to advise refinancing a home that is nearly paid off. As of this writing, it is still illegal to sell organs to hospitals. So, what choice does a family have?

Step 1: Start early. I can do miracles with a student that begins preparing freshman or even early sophomore year. When a student comes to me senior year there is little that can affect an application. Everything is already done - or not done as the case may be.

Step 2: It is all in the tests. With a good test score (ACT or SAT), college can be affordable. A good test score will grant a sizeable merit-based package at many excellent schools. Even if the school says there is no financial need, a really solid test score (32 on an ACT or a 1420 on a "new" SAT) will qualify the student for a full ride scholarship at most universities. Keep in mind these scholarships are limited and everyone else is applying. Your daughter needs to stand out from the crowd in more ways than just tests. Enroll your student in test preparation courses, buy an ACT or SAT book and force her to devote an hour every other night from freshman year on to testing, test early and often. If all else fails, seek private tutors. While expensive, the payoff is more than worth it.

 Have her get the best grades from the hardest classes she can. Taking the easy way out or the easy teacher often has a price. Colleges want to see rigor and effort. Even one "C" can be caustic and a single "D" can be deadly. Make her study with you. Do not trust that she is getting the grades she should. By the time you find out what the real grades are, it could be too late. Be proactive in talking to counselors about class schedules and teachers about expectations and progress.

 Step 3: Don't let your daughter work in high school. I instead want her to get involved, do more community service, create programs, study for tests and get the grades. The discount on the really cool jeans can wait.

 Step 4: Start visiting universities on family vacations. Don't just go to Disney World. Also visit Stetson or Rollins or Eckerd. Don't just spend time with your sister in Chicago. Also visit the University of Chicago or Loyola - Chicago or Northwestern or rent a car and see Coe or Illinois Wesleyan or Lawrence or Earlham or Knox. Don't just enjoy the nation's capital. Make time to see Georgetown or George Washington or the Catholic University of America or go across the bay to see Loyola - Maryland or Goucher or (actually I could add about 50 schools in Maryland, Virginia and Pennsylvania alone!) I want your daughter to start imagining the schools and envisioning herself there. That will help give her the goals and the impetus to keep going when she can't do even one more SAT math problem. I also want the schools to see that she is interested. In that vein, she (not the parents) should make an effort to keep in contact with the admission's office. Expressed interest can really go far if it is sincere and consistent. There is nothing wrong with being interested in four or five schools.

Step 5: Start investigating schools. Pay special attention to costs. Look at the net price calculator, but also look at merit-based scholarships. Keep in mind that the really top notch schools like Princeton will not give merit-based aid, only need based aid. Many times it is more affordable for a middle class student to go to a college with a lesser reputation than the top tier schools. Try to find schools that have multiple full tuition scholarships. Look at the requirements. One of my favorite schools has an environmental scholarship for full tuition. Any middle class girl starting freshman year could knock that one out of the park and save the park in the process. See what other scholarships are available and in what amounts. If several schools you have an interest in have a forensics scholarship or debate scholarship that is sizeable, maybe it is time for your daughter to join the debate team. If your school doesn't have a debate team, even better. She can start one. If a targeted school really prides itself on crew, maybe it is time to learn how to row.

Step 6: Create and lead. Don't let your daughter be that pathetic girl that sits in a dark room wearing black and writing dark poetry by the light of a cell phone. Just as bad is the perky socialite that goes to all the right parties and dates all the right boys. None of that will get her money for school. Don't let her join eight different clubs. Instead pick two or three and have her excel. Don't just join, engineer a path to student leadership. And please notice I used the verb engineer. These opportunities do not happen by chance. If National Honor Society is her thing, then how does the group select officers? Is it a popular vote? Hit as many different groups as possible. Have her talk to everyone weeks before the election. Make cookies the night before a vote and have her pass the cookies out that morning in a little plastic bag that encourages a student to "Vote for (insert your daughter's name here)." If the officers are chosen by the sponsor, encourage your daughter to make that teacher her new best friend. Make sure your daughter takes that teacher's English or psychology class and asks lots of questions and stays after class for extra help.

Even better than joining clubs or sports is creating one. What is the need in the school? What is the need in the community? What can be created? Can she start a club with a national chapter like Sierra Club or Key Club? What are her hobbies? Can you turn that into a club? If she has no hobbies, let's go find one. Whatever your daughter chooses, do not just let her sit at home binge watching her favorite television shows while texting all of her friends night after night.

Step 7: Document. Just leading or creating is half way there. Now show what was actually accomplished. Okay, so you are president of the school "Glee Club." What does that mean? What did you do? How did you change the school or the community? Most important, how can you document it? If your daughter is involved in sports, win. If she is on the chess team, dominate. If she does community service, make sure that the service makes a difference. To paraphrase Shania Twain, having the coolest car or the best hair or passing out water at a local race does not impress me much. Rocket scientist works, though.

Step 8: Balance the college list. Your daughter has a better chance of getting more money at a school where she is over qualified. Maybe her numbers are good enough to get into Swarthmore. I am happy for her. It is possible that Knox will give her more money. Don't just apply for schools that are a stretch or at the limits of where the test scores can gain acceptance. Broaden your horizons and do look at state schools. In general I avoid big state universities. The two exceptions are for athletes and white, middle class families. Many times the state university can be competitive when other schools are not. Let me use Arizona as an example. Northern Arizona University currently has a scholarship called the "Lumberjack Scholarship." This will offer full tuition - not room and board - to students who have all A's and B's in high school core classes with a cumulative GPA of 3.5 or higher. One "C" and a student does not qualify. Out of state residents do not qualify. Many state universities have similar programs. Research the programs. Cast a wide net and apply to at least ten schools. Don't fixate on only one school. If a family's mantra is "Dartmouth or bust," you may bust.

Step 9: Communicate with the college admissions' officers senior year. Rather have your daughter communicate. Have her express interest and visit the school. Have your daughter explain how important that particular school is express what is and is not affordable. The key word: communicate. Please note, if you make $160,000 a year, you will never convince a school that you can not afford anything. On the other hand, if you have been making $64,000 and just got the great promotion, explain that to the school. Most schools understand that you can not save money for college with the earnings of just a single fiscal year.

Step 10: Speak with a financial advisor early. Ask not only about savings for a college plan, but how those savings would not necessarily show up on a FAFSA or CSS profile. Investigate what programs your state has for college. I like prepaid programs better than simply savings plans.

Step 11: Appeal all financial aid packages. Nothing is set in stone. Everything is negotiable. A school that wants your daughter will be willing to negotiate. Keep in mind, finding an extra $4-5,000 a year is entirely possible. An extra $32,000 is just not going to happen.

Step 12: Get creative with financing. Look at private scholarships. Ask grandparents, uncles and aunts. Look at personal loans. Ask your company several years early about starting a scholarship program for employees which you will volunteer to chair - as a tax write off for the company of course. Sell her car. Make her work in the summer after senior year. Look at further funding for sophomore year in college through additional private scholarships or school scholarships. Ask if your daughter would qualify for work study on campus or could get a job as a residence assistant. Have your daughter work while going to school.

*My son entered the university with an entire year's worth of AP credits. He is on track to graduate early. Should he?*

Keep in mind that once attending a university or college, the game starts over. In high school the goal is to attain that perfect college. In college the goal is graduate school and a job. Again, a student needs to stand out. When it comes to graduating college early there are two questions I look at. 1) How much is college really costing? 2) Will an extra year give the student a chance to stand out more?

If a student is receiving a financial aid package where he is not paying much at all every year, then why not stay another year? Most adults I know would love to go back and have one more year of college. One more year of a social life par excellence. One more year learning something new. One more year with few responsibilities. If college is costing a lot of money every year, then it may be worthwhile to leave early. Even a semester early can save a significant amount of money. Most students can arrange a schedule to graduate a semester early or even a year early. If early graduation is imperative, start looking at the class schedule as early as freshman year. Max out the credits possible. Take winter terms and summer classes. After three years these extra classes really add up. Pay attention to prerequisite classes and classes needed to graduate. Not every class is offered every year.

If a student has the flexibility, there are three options I recommend. In terms of costs, one of the best is to begin upper level classes that will translate to graduate school. Especially if your student is pursing medicine, law, psychology or engineering graduate school is essential. There is much less financial aid available for graduate school. If a student can shave off a year of graduate school by transferring upper level classes from an undergraduate school, a student can save a very large sum of money. Quality grades in these upper level classes, especially classes involving research, can also boost a graduate school application.

A second choice is to add another major or minor. Another major or minor can make a student more versatile and give a wider job pool. Another major or minor may help your student stand out from the pack for graduate school or job applications. Another degree can round out a resume very nicely. Common wisdom says to take something related. If a business major, add accounting. If a biology major, add chemistry. If a physics major, add math. This all makes sense. I also know that the offbeat major or interest (i.e. art history, music theory, sociology, psychology, East Asian studies, Russian) can really help an applicant look more well-rounded and stand out from peers. Pre-med students with a biology / chemistry degree are really quite common. A pre-med student with a biology / art history degree can really flesh out an applicant more than his competition.

A third choice is a semester overseas. While increasingly common at colleges and universities, a semester abroad still stands out. Having extra space in the degree requirements can open up a chance to study history in Japan, art history in Italy, romance languages in France, finance in England or environmental science in Iceland. As these programs are more and more popular, pricing has become much more reasonable. Most students would not have the option to live four months in China or Turkey until their retirement. Even if a future career includes a lot of travel, most careers allow professionals exciting views of the airports. Little time is given to actually enjoy a country or getting to know its people. In addition to an excellent talking point in an interview about learning the tango while doing a semester in Argentina or working with hydroponics in South Africa or perfecting Thai while working with elephants in Thailand, study abroad can show initiative, courage and self-discipline. All are positive attributes to future employers and graduate schools.

## Chapter 14: A Letter to Me

When I was going through the process of choosing a university, I did not have anyone to help me. While my parents sort of almost wanted me to attend a university, they took a hands off approach. My high school teachers were supportive, but I was never once steered in any given direction. That was the job of my guidance counselor. My guidance counselor in high school was completely disinterested and actually antagonistic. My peers were just as confused as I was. The vast majority of my class ended senior year and attended a local community college or made the short jump to a nearby big state university. While most of this book has been geared towards the parents, I have written this last part to the teen directly. I am not trying to rehash what the rest of the book says as much as I am trying to reflect what I wish I had been told as I approached attending a university.

Dear student,

Congratulations. You are about to embark on one of the most exciting - and scary - journeys of your life. Very little will affect you and whom you will become more than which university you choose to attend. Before we go any further, let me make one thing crystal clear. What happens next is entirely up to you. Not your parents. Not your teachers. Not your guidance counselors. Not your best friends. The choices are yours and yours alone. What you do or don't do, what paths you choose to follow or ignore, what you pursue with an ardent zeal and what you choose to leave undone will mark what options are available and ultimately where you go. In the end you alone need to live with the decisions. You alone are responsible. Do not trust that your favorite teacher or Dad will have everything covered. Do it yourself for yourself. That does not mean you should not seek advice or ask for help when you need it. It does mean that you must be proactive.

I personally have a great preference for small liberal arts colleges. I realize that the names of such schools do not resound nearly as clearly as other venerable institutions of higher learning. These schools have done the best for me and the best for my students. Probably the most familiar institution is the large state flagship school - the University of (fill in the name of your favorite state). These schools certainly get a lot of publicity. The schools attract a great number of students and promise low costs for in state students. The schools usually have sports teams that dominate local and national news. Everyone has a sister or a cousin that attended one of these schools, and it is usual for Mom to say, "Why can't you go to the university like your cousin? He seems to be doing fine." Many high schools have unique relationships with the big public schools where the teachers and counselors seem to really sell the school.

I have three objections to the big state schools. Keep in mind, these schools are not necessarily "bad." I just want better. My first objection is simply size. Big state schools are just that - big. The number of students number in the tens of thousands. While the school will advertise that it has small classes, in fact many of the introductory freshman classes will number in the hundreds. Such a setting makes it extraordinarily difficult for a student to be noticed or to get special attention. To the contrary I have memories of the football team sauntering in noticeably late to seize their accustomed seats in the back row where the team members pull their baseball caps down and proceed to check out. I want my students noticed. I don't want distractions or the unstated permission to check out. The small liberal arts schools will boast real class sizes of twenty. Often I have even seen classes of less than ten. Try escaping the professor's notice when there are only seven students in the seminar. Smaller schools create a smaller more familial environment and tend to offer a better education.

The second reason I love the smaller schools is costs. I know that the price tags displayed for these schools are often in excess of $60,000 a year and some are flirting with $80,000 a year. I also know this is sticker shock. In reality the costs of the school are far less than a big public school. The reason is simple math. The large public schools have far more students and far less money for scholarships. What money is available sees much diverted to athletics. The smaller schools have fewer students and more money. The result is that the smaller schools tend to be cheaper, even for middle class families. Many of the large public schools will put more financial aid money up-front freshman year and then gradually withdraw the money through successive years. This is a trick I rarely see among noted liberal arts colleges. The end result is that the small, liberal arts schools tend to be cheaper.

The third reason is opportunities. In a large public school, students find great difficulty in forming connections with professors. When internships, research opportunities or jobs are available, precious few trickle down past the graduate students to undergraduates. Every small liberal arts college with which I work will boast of the number of internships, jobs and research opportunities available to underclassmen. Leadership opportunities also abound. A student quite simply has a better chance of standing out which will in turn lead to better opportunities for graduate school and for jobs.

I have proved with more than twelve years' experience and hundreds of students that the small liberal arts school are not only more affordable but offer a better education and richer opportunities. I fully understand at eighteen a school that you have never heard of and a school that is far far away requires a leap of faith. I'm not asking that you simply take my word for this. Instead apply at ten schools. Pick one school that is a reach, your dream school. Pick one big in state university, and pick eight small liberal arts schools. Wait until March, start hammering out the financial aid packages and compare real numbers in April. I know that in an apples to apples (include tuition, room, meal plan, fees) comparison the big state schools have a hard time competing. After all the numbers are in front of you, compare. If the fear of the unknown is simply too much to overcome, at least you know the options.

Just as I am lukewarm towards big state schools, I am lukewarm to "Ivy League" schools and top tier schools like Stanford, Rice or MIT. Similarly, I have three reasons. First and foremost again is size. These schools tend to be larger. The schools are not as large as the University of (insert your favorite state), but they are still much larger than small liberal arts schools. While that does mean more class selection and more majors, it also means bigger class sizes and more students competing for the same internships, research opportunities and jobs.

The second reason is also financial. For a family that is truly broke, this level of school can be a real gift. Dartmouth and Brown and the rest all have such large endowments and are so generous with financial need that if a student can get accepted, she can afford the school. My concern is for middle class families. I will concede that this level of school will go really far in helping a student afford the school, but to be blunt a student with numbers competitive enough for Stanford or the University of Pennsylvania is also competitive enough for the full ride scholarships offered at many of the smaller liberal arts schools. The difference is paying a "fair" price (maybe $15-25,000 a year for a family making about $120,000 a year) or going free. In many cases the small liberal arts schools can out price the "Ivy Leagues" for the top tier students.

Finally there is a certain social background inherent at many of these schools. That is not to say a student will be ostracized, but I know many students who feel ostracized. For lower and middle income students there are constant and prevalent reminders that these schools are part of another economic world. Being in the shallow end of an economic pool can really grate on some students.

To be fair, there is certainly something to a name. A school like Harvard can absolutely open doors and will certainly help with contacts, networking and the first job. I am just not convinced that Harvard is for everyone. I firmly believe that a quality and challenging education can be garnered just as easily at a small liberal arts school that the average student has never heard of. Branding is important and a name carries weight. A big name school will help - with the first job. After the first job the name doesn't matter as much as what you have done in the first job. Shockingly, the unemployment numbers for Ivy League graduates are not that different from other institutions.

Assuming I have at least intrigued you enough to keep reading, there are a few factors that will help a student stand out as an excellent candidate for any institution. First, I truly hope this book finds its way to you early. I tell the students I work with that I can fix nearly anything sophomore year. After sophomore year challenges present themselves. The first step is grades. A student with grand aspirations must get the grades, and the grades must come from the most challenging classes possible. If as a student, you do not like a particular teacher or particular learning style or a particular subject - get over it! The grades show colleges you are ready for more difficult tasks. Poor grades speak poorly of your abilities as a student. If you really despise the teacher for AP United States history, okay skip that one class. Don't skip two. Colleges understand you will not like or be adored by every teacher. Part of high school is a test to see how well you as a student can work with difficult people.

Take the most challenging teacher you can. Every school has teachers that are easy and hard. Take the hard ones every time to push yourself and to better prepare yourself for the work load in the university. I have no patience with the pretty girl who says she is avoiding AP Biology because it is hard, but she wants to be a doctor. What do you think college biology is like? A more challenging teacher not only prepares you for college but prepares you better for the college entrance exams. By the same token, there is absolutely a difference between a teacher that will challenge you with difficult curriculum and a teacher that is a difficult person. Avoid the later.

The only factor more important than grades is test scores. Take the ACT or SAT early and take it often. STUDY FOR THE TEST! Nothing - nothing! - will affect how much college costs more than test scores. Studying one hour a day will pay off more than any job you could ever hold in high school. Do not take the tests blind. Figure out the timing and the content. Have a strategy for each section. Work on your weakest areas. If you struggle with math get help. I know you don't like asking for help. Suck it up! If you miss a question on grammar, do not just say, "Oh, I thought it was 'C' all along." Figure out why the answer was "C," and why you put a different answer. Remember these tests are written to trick you. A great test score can mean going to college for free. A good test score can mean saving tens of thousands of dollars. Some students need external incentives. Make a deal with your parents. "When I get accepted to college for less than $5,500 a year which I will take in loans myself, you owe me a car."

Get involved. What are you actually passionate about? What do you love? How can you prove it? Why would a college want it? I can sell almost anything (not video games or television or "nothing"). Find what makes you - you. Pursue your passions and demonstrate excellence. Convey those passions to the college. Sell yourself. Help the colleges see you and what makes you unique. Why would I want you and not Matt from Minnesota or Natasha from North Dakota or Owen from Oklahoma? Despite your name not being nearly so alliterative, why are you valuable to my campus? Begin with an organization early. Can't find an organization you like? Even better. Make one. Show growth, demonstrate leadership, be proactive and demonstrate what changes you specifically made.

Research colleges. Make a list of what actually matters to you as a student. What would cause you to choose college A over college B? Look up the web pages and get on the mailing lists. Don't wait until senior year. Visit colleges. Go to college fairs. Sharpen your resume and practice your interview skills. Display an avid interest in the school. Ask questions and get noticed. Keep in contact with the admissions' officers. Ask questions that put your own interests and intellect on display. Send thank you notes - real ones not email.

Pay gratuitous attention to the personal statement and the letters of recommendation. These matter. Everything else is pretty much a collection of numbers. How does 1510 really define you? What does 4.24 actually mean about your values? How does 23 of 321 show you will change the world? Take the time to tell a story. Introduce yourself in the best possible light.

Follow up and keep in contact with your favorite schools. Competitive colleges have hundreds of applicants. How can you stand out? How can you be remembered? (No, that idea is just weird . . . That one, too. Try something else.) Make sure your top 2-3 universities know that the particular school is at the top. Send emails, ask questions, visit the schools, text, tweet, and schedule an interview. Show a real interest in the school. Start picturing yourself at the school. Imagine yourself sipping hot chocolate outside on an alumni donated bench a beautiful October day when the leaves have changed to a vibrant explosion of color and the weather has just started to change. Now help the university picture the same moment with you. I guarantee that if you make an effort with three schools to show an interest and help the admission's office visualize you on their campus, the admission's representative for at least two of the schools will march down to financial aid innumerable times for more money - for you. The admission's representatives will move mountains to make her school the university you choose. Just let the school know that this is the right school for you.

I understand fully and completely how much time all of this takes. In the end you need to ask, "Where do I want to be in ten years?" Do you want to vacation at a local lake - or Loch Ness? Do you want to buy a new car every ten years - or every two? Do you want to live in a sensible ranch style house - or something a bit more opulent? Do you want to marry the girl who worked side by side with you in the copy room - or the girl whose father is CEO of Xerox? What does success mean for you? What are you willing to sacrifice for that success? How hard are you willing to work - or rather how smart are you willing to work?

A student does not need to be a hermit or perform an imitation of a Buddhist monk on the slopes of the Himalayas. A student that feels a need to attend every party and date every weekend and chat with friends every night and go to every social event should reevaluate the bank accounts carefully. There are students that are able to do just that: students of affluence who can buy their entry ticket to life. If you are not such a child of fortune, if you have ambitions and desire but precious little money, success will take more than just luck. Success will require sacrifice and effort. For such a student high school can be a social experience or the building blocks for a life of endless possibilities.

## Chapter 15: The Sage on the Mountain

I would never advise a family to take my word alone on college admissions. I have spent the last twelve years reading everything I can on college admissions. There is a lot of similarity in the literature and a few differences. Every author has his or her own tweaks and twists. I would encourage everyone to read more. I have included a list of other books I have read, consulted, and dog eared. This is by no means a comprehensive list, nor is it a tacit endorsement. This list is simply an encouragement to get multiple viewpoints. Your local public library will have many of these titles.

Finally, if you need more help look for a college admission's counselor with experience. If you so choose, the author can be contacted at wkiblerelves@gmail.com for a free initial consultation.

Andrews, Erinn *Best Book on Elite Admissions*

Antonoff, Steven R. *College Finder*

Arango, Peter *America's Best Kept College Secrets*

Asher, Donald *Cool Colleges*

Barron's College Division *Profiles of American Colleges*

Bedor, Deborah *Getting In By Standing Out*

Belasco, Andrew and Dave Bergman *The Enlightened College Applicant*

Bruni, Frank *Where You Go Is Not Who You Will Be*

Caine, Janice *College Road Trips*

Chany, Kalman *Paying For College Without Going Broke*

Chatterjee, Pria *Dirty Little Secrets Of Getting Into A Top College*

Christen, Carol *What Color is Your Parachute? For Teens*

Cohen, Katherine *How To Write A Killer College Application*

College Board *Book Of Majors*

College Board *Getting Financial Aid*

Dunbar, Don *What You Don't Know Can Keep You Out Of College*

Ellis, Kristina *Confessions Of A Scholarship Winner*

Eum, Jennifer *Forbes Guide To Paying For College*

Fergusen, Andrew *Crazy U: One Dad's Crash Course Into Getting His Kid Into College*

Fiske, Edward *Fiske Guide To Colleges*

Glastris, Paul and Jane Sweetland *The Other College Guide*

Goldman, Jordan *Students' Guide To Colleges*

Greene, Howard *Hidden Ivies*

Hammond, Bruce *Discounts and Deals At The Nation's Top 360 Colleges*

Henderson, C.W. *Open the Gates To The Ivy League: A Plan B for Getting Into The Top Colleges*

Hernandez, Michele A. *A Is For Admission*

Hernandez, Michele A. *Acing the College Application*

Hughes, Chuck *What It Really Takes To Get Into Ivy League And Other Highly Selective Colleges*

Jacobs, Lynn F. *Secrets Of Picking A College (And Getting In)*

Kaplan, Ben *Scholarship Scouting Report*

Kaplan, Greg *Earning Admission: Real Strategies For Getting Into Highly Selective Colleges*

Loveland, Elaina *Creative Colleges: Guide For Student Actors, Artists, Dancers, Musicians And Writers*

Mamlet, Robin *College Admission*

Marcus, David L. *Acceptance*

Mason, Michael James *How To Write A Winning College Application Essay*

Matthews, Arlene *Getting In Without Freaking Out*

Matthews, Jay *Harvard Schmarvard*

McWilliams, Susan *The Best Kind of College: An Insider's Guide to America's Small Liberal Arts Colleges*

Moyer, Mike *How To Make Colleges Want You*

Newport, Cal *How To Be A High School Superstar*

O'Shaughnessy, Lynn *The College Solution*

Paonita, Jocelyn *The Scholarship System*

Pope, Loren *Colleges That Change Lives*

Pope, Loren *Looking Beyond the Ivy League*

Princeton Review *Best 381 Colleges*

Sawyer, Ethan *College Essay Essentials*

Schritter, Tyson *Colleges Of Distinction*

Springer, Sally P. and Jon Reider *Admission Matters*

Staff of the Harvard Crimson *50 Successful Harvard Admission Essays*

Staff of the Harvard Crimson *How They Got Into Harvard*

Steinberg, Jacques *Gatekeepers*

Tanabe, Gen *50 Successful Stanford Application Essays*

Tanabe, Gen and Kelly *Get Free Cash For College*

Tanabe, Gen and Kelly *Get Into Any College*

Tanabe, Gen and Kelly *Ultimate Guide To America's Best Colleges*

Tanabe, Gen *Ultimate Scholarship Book*

Toor, Rachel *Admissions Confidental*

Toor, Rachel *Write Your Way In*

Upadhyay, Aayush *Behind the Ivy Curtain*

U.S. News and World Report *Best Colleges*

White, Kristin M. *Complete Guide To The Gap Year*

Willingham, John *Inside Honors*

Wissner-Gross, Elizabeth *What Colleges Don't Tell You*

Wissner-Gross, Elizabeth *What High Schools Don't Tell You*

Yale Daily News Staff *Insider's Guide To The Colleges*

## Appendix 1: Sample Four Year Plan

    I am including a sample four year plan with a focus on which classes a student should take. Any such plan is rife with pitfalls. The list is predicated upon the idea of a four year high school. Some high schools are only three years with freshman year offered at the middle school. Not every school offers the same classes. Not every district or state has the same requirements. So, for example, I have not included physical education. Some states require physical education to graduate. Other schools are on a block system or prohibit students from taking more than two Advanced Placement classes at once. Some schools have more spots available for classes and some schools fewer. If I mention a class that your current school does not offer, maybe a parent led initiative could get the class added. The list is biased toward AP classes. I have done so out of my own familiarity more than anything else. Remember: this is one possible sample, not a rule.

### Freshman Year

| | |
|---|---|
| Geometry H | *Explore the PSAT |
| English 1 H | *Begin joining clubs / sports / activities |
| Biology H | *Begin volunteer or community service |
| Health Education | *Begin documenting everything |
| Human Geography AP | |
| Spanish 1 | |

    *I begin with geometry, but if your student can begin with a higher level math, then by all means do so. The unique caveat is to make sure the school has sufficient higher levels of math. I do not want students to top out of the math classes at the end of sophomore year.

    *I love Biology AP but have found the class to be exceptionally difficult for a freshman student. I usually seek just an honor's biology as a freshman and then follow up with Biology AP senior year as an elective.

*Human Geography AP is a wonderful freshman level AP class. Not all AP classes are equal in ardor and difficulty. Human Geography is one of the easier and hence more accessible AP classes.

*Spanish 1 is just a filler for any foreign language. French, German, Japanese, Chinese, Navajo or any other offering will work well. I used to be cautious about sign language, but I have yet to find the university that does not accept sign language now. The only rule on language is to not mix and match. A year of French and a year of Spanish and a year of Japanese does not work.

*Investigate the possibility of taking a summer class between 8th grade and freshman year. I am only looking for classes for advancement. This can really be a bonus in regards to class rank.

*Read often and deeply. Find books at or above reading level. Read. Read. Read.

## Sophomore Year

| | |
|---|---|
| Advanced Algebra H | *Take the PSAT, Take the ACT in spring |
| English 2 H | *Continue with the sports / activities / clubs |
| Chemistry H (or AP) | *Continue with community service |
| World History AP | *Start researching and discussing colleges |
| Spanish 2 | *In the summer, take a road trip to nearby |
| Elective | schools (your B list) |

*The elective can be a class the school requires that is not somewhere else on this list. Given a choice, I would prefer an honor's or AP class as an elective. I would never discourage a student that really truly loves culinary arts or photography. If the class is just taking space, I would instead urge an academic class.

*Keep reading prolifically. Make sure you are reading at or above grade level.

## Junior Year

| | |
|---|---|
| Pre-Calculus H | *Take the PSAT and SAT in the fall. |
| English Language AP | *Seek leadership positions |
| Physics AP | *Retake whichever test was stronger |
| United States History AP | *Start making a list of colleges |
| Spanish Language AP | *Begin going to college fairs |
| Art History AP | *Do college visits and write 1st resume |

*This year is a heavy year for AP classes. It is intentional as these are the last scores and grades that will show up on the transcript for college applications. It is essential that junior year grades are stellar. Grades are a must this year. With luck a student will qualify for AP Scholar with Honors or AP Scholar with Distinction. See https://apscore.collegeboard.org/scores/ap-awards/ap-scholar-awards/ for details.

*In addition to grades, this is the year to start taking testing seriously. After the first semester a student will have an idea if the ACT and SAT scores are about the same. Retake whichever test was stronger several times in the second semester. PSAT counts this year.

*I personally really like art history. It is rare. Colleges really need a year of fine arts. Do not let counseling tell your student that business or shop or cooking will substitute for fine arts. Other really good fine arts classes are Music Theory AP and Studio Art AP. These classes really require a background in music and art respectively. Neither work well as a stand-alone.

*The previous clubs, sports and activities need to morph into leadership roles. Have your teen put himself or herself out there and shoot high. This will necessitate some serious time management.

*This summer needs to be active. I prefer competitive programs. Also, write the personal statement over the summer.

*READ!

<u>Senior Year</u>

| | |
|---|---|
| Calculus AP | *Finalize college lists. |
| English Literature AP | *Visit college fairs and colleges. |
| Biology AP or Chemistry AP | *Arrange interviews with colleges. |
| American Government AP | *Edit and perfect personal statement. |
| Micro or Macro Economics AP | *Demonstrate and document leadership |
| Spanish Literature AP | *Last retakes of tests in the fall |

*Grades are crucial this year as well. Notice that time management is still going to be an issue. Try to stack teachers so that your student does not have ALL of the most difficult teachers in the same year.

*Don't wait for interviews and college fairs and college visits to happen. Put everything on a calendar. Be proactive in seeking out the opportunities.

*Hopefully the service and activities have paid off with leadership roles. Document exactly what changes your teen made. Just being president of National Honor Society does not work well.

## Appendix 2: List of Universities and Colleges

I've composed a short list of some universities to look at. I tried to pick a fair number of choices with a wide regional variation. The majority are smaller liberal arts colleges that you have never heard of. The schools are not on this list if *I* haven't heard of the school. There are many that I left off because of incomplete information, low acceptance rates or low financial aid rates. I also left off schools that have misrepresented themselves, been overly tricky in financial aid, made racist or rude comments or otherwise have practiced deception of which I am personally aware. Other schools may have been omitted due to my own failings or oversights. I could easily triple this list.

I have three categories: "I Have a Dream" for schools under 25% acceptance rates. These are highly selective. "I Think I Can" are schools with acceptance rates between 26% and 50%. These schools are a challenge, but not usually an undue burden for the prepared student. "They Really Like Me" are schools with an acceptance rate over 50%. Any student who is well prepared should be able to garner acceptance at these schools. Use a mix of the three categories. An example of how I broke down the data:

Harvard (that's the name)                    MA (this is the state)
http://www.harvard.edu/ (website)
97% (percent returning sophomore year)       97% (percent graduating in 6 years)
economics, gov't, biology, engineering (this is the list of popular majors, more on this below)
6% (percent of applicants that get in)       32-36 (recommended ACT score*)
FN met: 100% (percentage of students whose full need was met – note: just because this is

100% doesn't mean it is free. Also, some schools don't report.)

\* For consistency I used ACT. ACT - SAT conversion charts can be found at https://www.studypoint.com/ed/sat-act-concordance/

\*\* a "TO" after the test score means the school is test optional and test scores may not be needed. Policies change yearly, so please check. Also, some schools are test optional only if an alternative is submitted. Other times schools will reduce your financial aid if you didn't submit test scores.

\*\*\* Data comes from College Board in 2017 https://www.collegeboard.org/

Majors: obviously this is a SHORT list. I've only included the majors that are notable or have large programs. I probably missed some. Some of the smaller majors won't be listed or fall under another category. For example: if you wanted to study Chicano History, you would look for that specific program in a related field (i.e. social studies or history or ethnic studies). Another option would be to look in one of the resources I've listed for specific schools that have this program. Most of the listed fields are rather large and include a number of smaller programs. A few last notes: law and medicine are masters and doctoral programs. A lot of schools have large biology programs (as in pre-med) or social science and political science programs (as in pre-law). There are a large number of schools specializing in economics and finance. For some of these schools, economics and finance is the B.A. and business is the M.A. (Bachelors – 4 years - = B.A. or B.S. / Masters – another 2 years - = M.A.) English often includes writing or journalism.

A legal disclaimer: this list is by no means comprehensive. Numbers are subject to change without notice. Program strengths may or may not reflect reality. This list is only meant to offer you a street map to guide you to possible choices. Once I've taken you this far, it is your responsibility to look it up yourself. I recommend the Internet (try Collegeboard and Zinch) but feel free to use osmosis or psychic powers. You are more foolish than I give you credit for if you put *your future* in someone else's hands completely. Always – **ALWAYS** – make the decision that is best for you. Unfortunately, some of you are really bad at knowing what you want. (I think it is hormones.) Beware of deadlines, though. Many of these colleges have deadlines the first of January. Some other schools have an early action or early decision deadline of mid-October. In general, it is better to submit earlier. If the deadline is Jan. 15, and you submit on Nov. 20 that shows an interest in the school and generally puts your application in a much smaller pile.

Without further ado – the "magic" list of dreams and happiness!

## I Have a Dream

**Amherst College**  MA
http://www.amherst.edu/
96%  93%
Social sciences, history, English, biology, math, physical science
14%  31-34
FN met: 100%

**Barnard College**  NY
http:// www.barnard.edu  dudettes only
96%  91%
Social sciences, psychology, English, fine arts, biology, ethnic studies, foreign language
17%  29-33
FN met: 99%

## Bates College                                                      ME
www.bates.edu
95%                                                                    88%
Social sciences, biology, psychology, English, history, fine arts, environmental science
23%                                                                    29-33 **(T.O.)**
FN met: 100%

## Bowdoin
http://www.bowdoin.edu/                                                ME
94%                                                                    94%
Social sciences, biology, foreign language, math, English, environmental science
15%                                                                    30-34 **(T.O.)**
FN met: 100%

## Brown                                                               RI
http://www.brown.edu/
98%                                                                    96%
Social studies, biology, math, fine arts, engineering
9%                                                                     31-34
FN met: 100%

## California Institute of Technology                                  CA
http://www.caltech.edu/
98%                                                                    93%
engineering, physical sciences, computers, math, biology
8%                                                                     34-36
FN met: 100%

## Carleton College                                                    MN
www.carleton.edu
96%                                                                    92%
Social sciences, physical sciences, biology, computer sciences, visual arts
23%                                                                    30-33
FN Met: 100%

## Carnegie Mellon University                                          PA
http://www.cmu.edu/
96%                                                                    90%
engineering, computers, fine arts, business, physical science, math
22%                                                                    30-34
FN met: 27%

## Colby College                                                       ME
www.colby.edu
93%                                                                    89%

Philosophy, social science, interdisciplinary studies, biology, English
19%  29-33 **(T.O)**
FN met: 100%

### College of the Ozarks MO
www.cofo.edu
75%  ?
Business, education, agriculture
15%  21-25
FN met: 32%

### Columbia University
http://www.columbia.edu/  NY
99%  96%
Social sciences, engineering, biology, English, foreign lang., fine arts, communications
6%  32-35
FN met: 100%

### Cooper Union  NY
http://www.cooper.edu/
95%  87%
Architecture, fine arts, engineering
13%  30-34
FN met: 100%

### Dartmouth University  NH
www.dartmouth.edu
98%  97%
Social sciences, biology, engineering, history, psychology
11%  30-34
FN met: 100%

### Franklin W. Olin College of Engineering  MA
http://www.olin.edu/
99%  86%
Engineering only
10%  32-35
FN met: 97%

### Georgetown University  D.C.
http://www.georgetown.edu/
96%  92%
international relations, social sciences, English, business, psychology
17%  30-34
FN met: 100%

**Grinnell College**  IA
http://www.grinnell.edu/
93%  86%
Social sciences, biology, foreign language, history, math, fine arts, English, philosophy
20%  30-33
FN met: 100%

**Harvard**
http://www.harvard.edu/  MA
97%  96%
Social sciences, biology, history, math, physical science, psychology, fine arts, theology
5%  32-35
FN met: 100%

**Harvey Mudd**  CA
http://www.hmc.edu/
98%  93%
computers, engineering, math, biology, physical sciences
13%  32-35
FN met: 100%

**Haverford**  PA
www.haverford.edu
97%  90%
Social science, biology, physical science, psychology, English, philosophy
21%  31-34
FN met: 100%

**Johns Hopkins**  MD
http://www.jhu.edu/
97%  94%
neuroscience, engineering, biomedical engineering, social science, music
12%  32-36
FN met: 99%

**Juilliard**  NY
www.juilliard.edu
94%  84%
Fine arts only
7%  **(T.O.)**
FN met: 21%

**Massachusetts Institute of Technology**  MA
http://web.mit.edu/

98%                                                                   93%
Engineering, physics, computers, math, biology
8%                                                                     33-36
FN met: 100%

**Middlebury College**                            VT
www.middlebury.edu
94%                                                          93%
Social sciences, biology, foreign language, visual and performing arts, English
16%                                                       30-33
FN Met: 100%

**Northwestern**                                    IL
http://www.northwestern.edu/
98%                                                        94%
Communications, social sciences, engineering, fine arts, psychology, biology, history
11%                                                      32-34
FN met: 100%

**Princeton University**                         NJ
http://www.princeton.edu/main/
98%                                                      97%
Social sciences, engineering, biology, English, psychology, history. physics
7%                                                      32-35
FN met: 100%

**Rice University**                                 TX
http://www.rice.edu/
96%                                                      93%
Engineering, social science, biology, nano technology, architecture, parks and rec.
15%                                                    32-35
FN met: 99%

**Stanford University**                          CA
http://www.stanford.edu/
98%                                                      94%
Social sciences, engineering, computers, biology, physical sciences, psychology
5%                                                    31-35
FN met: 90%

**Swarthmore**                                     PA
http://www.swarthmore.edu/
98%                                                      94%
Social science, biology, fine arts, foreign language, psychology, English, history
13%                                                   30-34

FN met: 100%

**Tufts University**     MA
www.tufts.edu
96%
    92%
Social sciences, engineering, biology, visual and performing arts, computers
14%
    31-34
FN Met: 99%

**University of Chicago**     IL
http://www.uchicago.edu/
99%
    94%
Social sciences, fine arts, biology, math, physical sciences, foreign language, English
8%
    32-35
FN met: 100%

**University of Notre Dame**     IN
http://www.nd.edu/
98%
    95%
engineering, theology, business, English, social science, finance, accounting, chemistry
19%
    32-36
FN met: 99%

**University of Pennsylvania**     PA
http://www.upenn.edu/
98%
    95%
Business, marketing, social science, engineering, biology
9%
    32-35
FN met: 100%

**Vanderbilt**     TN
http://www.vanderbilt.edu/
97%
    92%
social sciences, engineering, interdisciplinary studies, biology, math, education
11%
    32-35
FN met: 100%

**Washington and Lee**     VA
www.wlu.edu
95%
    92%
Business, social sciences, biology, foreign languages, communications, physical sciences
24%
    30-33
FN Met: 100%

**Williams College**     MA
www.williams.edu

97% 94%
Social sciences, English, history, physical sciences
18% 31-34
FN met: 100%

**Yale University** CT
http://www.yale.edu/
99% 98%
Social sciences, biology, history, ethnic studies, fine arts, psychology
6% 32-35
FN met: 100%

# I Think I Can, I Think I Can

**American University** DC
www.american.edu
88% 81%
Social sciences, business, communications
26% 26-31
FN met: 19%

**Babson College** MA
http://www.babson.edu/
95% 91%
Business/marketing only
25% 27-31
FN met: 53%

**Baylor University** TX
http://www.baylor.edu/
89% 74%
Business, biology, health professions, communications, education, fine arts
40% 26-30
FN met: 15%

**Bentley University** MA
www.bentley.edu
94% 89%
Business only
46% 26-30
FN met: 41%

**Berea College** KY

www.berea.edu
84%     63%
Fine arts, education, English, social sciences, biology, business, agriculture
33%     22-27
FN met: 100%

### Birmingham-Southern College     AL
www.bsc.edu
82%     68%
Business, fine arts, biology, education, English, social sciences, history
48%     23-29 **(T.O.)**
FN met: 34%

### Boston College     MA
http://bc.edu/
95%     94%
Business, social sciences, psychology, communications, biology, English
31%     30-33
FN met: 100%

### Boston University     MA
http://www.bu.edu
93%     87%
Business, social science, communications, health professions, biology, engineering
29%     26-32
FN met: 21%

### Brandeis University     MA
http://www.brandeis.edu/
93%     90%
Social sciences, biology, ethnic studies, psychology, business, sociology, fine arts
33%     29-33
FN met: 68%

### Bryn Mawr College     PA
http://www.brynmawr.edu/     dudettes only
94%     83%
social science, math, art history, English, physical science, biology, archaeology
40%     28-32 **(T.O.)**
FN met: 98%

### Case Western Reserve University     OH

www.case.edu
92% 82%
Engineering, biology, social sciences, business, psychology, health professions
35% 30-34
FN met: 61%

**Colgate University** NY
www.colgate.edu
94% 90%
Social Sciences, biology, history, foreign language, psychology, English
29% 30-33
FN met: 100%

**College of the Holy Cross** MA
http://www.holycross.edu/
96% 92%
Social sciences, psychology, foreign languages, English, history, math, fine arts
38% 28-31 **(T.O.)**
FN met: 100%

**Denison University** OH
www.denison.edu
89% 81%
Social science, biology, communication, psychology, fine arts, English, foreign lang.
44% 26-31 **(T.O.)**
FN met: 37%

**Dickinson College** PA
www.dickinson.edu
90% 84%
Social sciences, biology, ethnic studies, business, foreign languages, psychology, English
43% 28-31 **(T.O.)**
FN met: 85%

**Emory University**
http://www.emory.edu/ GA
94% 91%
Social sciences, business, biology, psychology
25% 30-33
FN met: 100%

**Fordham University** NY
http://www.fordham.edu/
91% 80%

Business, social sciences, communications, psychology, fine arts, English
45%                                                          27-31
FN met: 29%

### Franklin and Marshall College    PN
www.fandm.edu
91%
                                                             87%
Social sciences, business, biology, interdisciplinary, psychology
36%
                                                             28-31 **(T.O.)**
FN met: 100%

### George Washington University    D.C.
http://www.gwu.edu/
90%
                                                             84%
Social sciences, business, health professions, psychology, communications, engineering
40%                                                          27-32 **(T.O.)**
FN met: 47%

### Gettysburg College    PA
www.gettysburg.edu
90%
                                                             87%
Social sciences, biology, business, English, history, environmental science, psychology
43%                                                          26-30 **(T.O.)**
FN met: 88%

### Hamilton College    NY
www.hamilton.edu
94%
                                                             92%
Social sciences, foreign language, biology, math, physical science, psychology, fine arts
26%                                                          31-33 **(T.O.)**
FN met: 100%

### Kenyon College    OH
www.kenyon.edu/
92%
                                                             90%
Social sciences, English, fine arts, psychology, biology, foreign language, philosophy
27%                                                          29-33
FN met: 100%

### Lafayette College    PA
www.lafayette.edu
94%
                                                             89%

Social sciences, engineering, biology, psychology, visual and performing arts, English
28%      27-31
FN Met: 100%

**Lehigh University**      PA
http://www.lehigh.edu/
95%      89%
Business, engineering, social sciences, biology, architecture, engineering, environ. sci
26%      29-32
FN met: 82%

**Macalester College**      MN
http://www.macalester.edu/
93%      88%
Social science, foreign language, interdisciplinary studies, biology, English, math
37%      29-33
FN met: 100%

**Muhlenberg College**      PA
www.muhlenberg.edu
90%      84%
Business, visual and performing arts, biology, social sciences, communications
48%      26-30 **(T.O.)**
FN Met: 28%

**New York University**      NY
http://www.nyu.edu/
93%      85%
Fine arts, social sciences, business, health professions, communications, psychology
32%      29-33 **(T.O.)**
FN met: 6%

**Northeastern University**      MA
www.northeastern.edu
97%      86%
Business, engineering, health professions, social sciences, biology
29%      32-34
FN met: 37%

**Oberlin College**      OH
http://www.oberlin.edu/
89%      85%

Fine arts, social science, biology, environmental science, English, ethnic studies
21%                                                                28-32
FN met: 100%

### Occidental College                                             CA
http://www.oxy.edu/
91%                                                                81%
Social science, biology, fine arts, psychology, environmental science, English
46%                                                                28-31
FN met: 100%

### Pepperdine                                                     CA
www.pepperdine.edu
90%                                                                87%
Business, communications, social sciences, psychology, fine arts
37%                                                                26-31
FN met:  19%

### Reed College                                                   OR
www.reed.edu
87%                                                                78%
Social sciences, physical sciences, biology, psychology, foreign lang., English
31%                                                                29-33
FN met: 82%


### Rensselaer Polytechnic Institute                               NY
http://www.rpi.edu/
93%                                                                83%
Engineering, computers, biology, business, physical sciences, architecture
44%                                                                28-32
FN met:  21%

### Santa Clara University                                         CA
http://www.scu.edu/
96%                                                                87%
Business, social science, engineering, communications, psychology, biology
48%                                                                28-32
FN met: 31%

### Scripps College                                                CA
www.scrippscollege.edu                                             dudettes only
92%                                                                84%

Social studies, ethnic studies, biology, fine arts, psychology, communications
30%                                                                    28-32
FN met: 100%

**Sewanee: University of the South**         TN
www.sewanee.edu
88%                                                                    82%
Social science, English, biology, interdisciplinary studies, environmental science, history
44%                                                                  27-31 **(T.O.)**
FN met: 38%

**Skidmore College**                                NY
www.skidmore.edu
91%                                                                    89%
Business, visual and performing parts, social science, biology, psychology, English
29%                                                                  26-30 **(T.O.)**
FN met: 93%

**Smith College**                                    MA
www.smith.edu                                   dudettes only
94%                                                                    89%
Social sciences, biology, foreign language, psychology, visual and performing arts
37%                                                                  29-33 **(T.O.)**
FN met: 100%


**Soka University of America**                CA
www.soka.edu
94%                                                                    93%
Liberal arts only
38%                                                                  26-30
FN Met: 89%

**Southern Methodist University**           TX
www.smu.edu
91%                                                                    79%
business, social science, communication, engineering, visual and performing arts
49%                                                                  28-32
FN Met: 30%

**Southwestern University**                    TX
http://www.southwestern.edu/
85%                                                                   72%

Social sciences, biology, business, fine arts, communication, psychology, foreign lang.
45% 23-28
FN Met: 28%

### Texas Christian University    TX
www.tcu.edu
91% 77%
business, communications, health professions, social sciences, visual and performing arts
38% 25-30
FN Met: 28%

### Trinity College    CT
www.trincoll.edu
89% 84%
Social sciences, area and ethnic studies, biology, psychology, English
33% 29-31 **(T.O.)**
FN met: 100%

### Trinity University    TX
www.trinity.edu
89% 77%
Business, Social sciences, biology, communications, English, psychology
41% 27-31
FN met: 50%

### Union College    NY
www.union.edu
91% 86%
Social sciences, engineering, biology, psychology, physical science
37% 28-31 **(T.O.)**
FN met: 100%

### University of North Carolina, Chapel Hill    NC
http://www.unc.edu/
97% 91%
Social sciences, communications, psychology, biology, ethnic studies, business, parks
27% 27-32
FN met: 80%

### University of Richmond    VA
www.richmond.edu
93% 88%

Business, social sciences, biology, interdisciplinary studies, psychology
32%  29-32
FN Met: 83%

### University of Rochester  NY
http://www.rochester.edu/
96%  86%
Social sciences, biology, health professions, music, fine arts, engineering, math
38%  29-33 **(T.O.)**
FN met: 90%

### Villanova University  PA
www.villanova.edu
95%  90%
Business, engineering, health professions, social sciences, communications
44%  29-32
FN Met: 16%

### Wake Forest University  NC
www.wfu.edu
95%  88%
Social sciences, business, communications, psychology, parks and rec., biology
30%  28-32 **(T.O.)**
FN met: 100%

### Washington College  MD
www.washcoll.edu
86%  73%
Social sciences, business, biology, psychology, English, visual and performing arts
49%  23-28 **(T.O.)**
FN met: 32%

### Worcester Polytechnic Institute  MA
www.wpi.edu
95%  86%
Engineering, computer science
48%  28-32 **(T.O.)**
FN met: 44%

## They Like Me, They Really Like Me!

**Agnes Scott College** GA
www.agnesscott.edu dudettes only
84% 70%
Social sciences, psychology, biology, English, fine arts, foreign language, history
65% 24-30 **(T.O.)**
FN met: 25%

**Allegheny College** PN
www.allegheny.edu
83% 76%
Social science, biology, psychology, environmental science, English, physical science
68% 24-29 **(T.O.)**
FN met: 31%

**Austin College** TX
http://www.austincollege.edu/
83% 73%
Social sciences, psychology, business, history, biology, communications, English
53% 23-29 **(T.O.)**
FN met: 42%

**Bard College** NY
http://www.bard.edu/
86% 78%
Fine arts, social sciences, English, biology, foreign languages, psychology
56% **(TO)**
FN met: 26%

**Belmont University** TN
www.belmont.edu
83% 70%
visual and performing arts, health professions, business
87% 24-29
FN Met: 10%

**Beloit College** WI
www.beloit.edu
86% 73%
Social sciences, fine arts, foreign language, English, physical science, education, history
70% 24-30 **(T.O.)**
FN met: 17%

**Bennington College** VT
www.bennington.edu

80% 70%
Visual and performing arts, English, social sciences, biology, foreign language
60% 26-31
FN met: 14%

### Berry College GA
www.berry.edu
85% 66%
Biology, business, agriculture, psychology, social sciences, education, parks and rec.
62% 24-29
FN met: 29%

### California Lutheran University CA
www.callutheran.edu
85% 73%
Business, psychology, biology, communications, parks and recreation
64% 22-24
FN Met: 6%

### Carroll College MT
www.carroll.edu
79% 66%
Health professions, biology, business, education
71% 22-28
FN Met: 19%

### Catholic University of America DC
www.cua.edu
84% 70%
Business, social sciences, engineering, psychology, health professions, architecture
80% 23-29 **(T.O.)**
Fn met: 43%

### Centre College KY
www.centre.edu
93% 86%
Social sciences, biology, history, psychology, foreign lang., ethnic studies, English, math
74% 26-31
FN met: 32%

### Chapman University CA
http://www.chapman.edu/
89% 79%

Film and television, fine arts, business, communications, psychology, English
54%                                                                24-29
FN met: 9%

**Clarkson University**                                            NY
www.clarkson.edu
89%
                                                                   72%
Engineering, business
68%                                                                24-29
FN Met : 21%

**Coe College**                                                    IA
www.coe.edu
75%                                                                67%
Business, psychology, health professions, communications, biology, social sciences
50%                                                                22-28
FN met: 21%

**College of the Atlantic**                                        ME
www.coa.edu
84%                                                                64%
Human ecology only
65%                                                                26-30 **(T.O.)**
44%

**College of Wooster**                                             OH
http://www.wooster.edu/
87%                                                                76%
Social sciences, biology, physical sciences, English, history, psychology, math
58%                                                                24-30
FN met: 50%

**Cornell College**                                                IA
www.cornellcollege.edu
82%                                                                68%
Social sciences, biology, psychology, fine arts, education, English, interdisciplinary study
71%                                                                23-29 **(T.O.)**
FN met: 28%

**Cottey College**                                                 MO
www.cottey.edu
75%                                                                72%

Psychology, business, English, environmental science, social sciences
68%   21-26
FN met: 33%

**Earlham College**   IN
www.earlham.edu
80%   71%
Biology, social sciences, psychology, visual and performing arts, computer science
58%   25-31
FN met: 18%

**Fairfield University**   CT
www.fairfield.edu
89%   82%
Business, social sciences, health professions, communications, engineering
61%   25-28 **(T.O.)**
FN met: 32%

**Furman University**   SC
www.furman.edu
90%   84%
Social studies, business, fine arts, biology, health professions, physical sciences, history
68%   25-31 **(T.O.)**
FN met: 35%

**George Mason University**   VA
www.gmu.edu
88%   70%
Business, social sciences, English, psychology, computers, health professions, biology
81%   24-29 **(T.O.)**
FN met: 5%

**Gonzaga University**   WA
www.gonzaga.edu
92%   84%
Business, social science, engineering, biology, psychology, communications
67%   25-30
FN met: 25%

**Goucher College**   MD
http://www.goucher.edu/
79%   68%

Psychology, social sciences, fine arts, communications, foreign languages, business
79%                                                         21-28 **(T.O.)**
FN met: 23%

### Gustavus Adolphus College                               MN
www.gustavus.edu
89%                                                         80%
Business, social sciences, biology, psychology, education, parks and rec.
65%                                                         24-29 **(T.O.)**
FN met: 32%

### Hampshire College                                       MA
www.hampshire.edu
82%                                                         ?
Visual and performing arts, English, biology, social science
70%                                                         **(T.O.)**
FN Met:?

### Hobart and William Smith Colleges                       NY
www.hws.edu
85%                                                         77%
Social sciences, biology, environmental science, communications, architecture
55%                                                         26-30 **(T.O.)**
FN met: 68%

### Illinois Institute of Technology                        IL
www.iit.edu
engineering, architecture, computer science
92%                                                         ?
FN Met: 12%

### Illinois Wesleyan University                            IL
www.iwu.edu
93%                                                         78%
Business, social science, fine arts, biology, psychology, health professions, education
58%                                                         25-29
FN met: 4%

### Iowa State University                                   IA
www.iastate.edu
88%                                                         74%
Business, engineering, agriculture, veterinary science, biology, agriculture

87%  22-28
FN met: 34%

**Ithaca College**  NY
www.ithaca.edu
85%  75%
Communications, visual and performing arts, health professions, business, biology
72%  25-29 **(T.O.)**
FN met: 41%

**John Carroll University**  OH
www.jcu.edu
84%  77%
Business, social sciences, communications, psychology, biology
83%  22-27
FN Met: 27%

**Juniata College**  PA
http://www.juniata.edu/
84%  75%
Biology, business, environmental science, physical science, education, communication
75%  23-29 **(T.O)**
FN met: 25%

**Knox College**  IL
http://www.knox.edu/
87%  77%
Social sciences, English, education, biology, foreign languages, fine arts, physical science
65%  25-30 **(T.O.)**
FN Met: 26%

**Kalamazoo College**  MI
www.kzoo.edu
88%  81%
Social sciences, physical sciences, biology, psychology, foreign languages, English
66%  26-30 **(T.O.)**
FN Met: 41%

**Lake Forest College**  IL
http://www.lakeforest.edu/
83%  70%

Social sciences, Business, communication, psychology, biology, English, foreign lang.
57%                                                              24-29
FN met: 21%

**Lawrence University**                             WI
www.lawrence.edu
91%                                                              79%
Visual and performing arts, public administration, biology, foreign language, psychology
63%                                                              26-31 **(T.O.)**
FN met: 51%

**Lewis and Clark College**                         OR
http://www.lclark.edu/
85%                                                              79%
Social sciences, psychology, fine arts, biology, philosophy, math
55%                                                              27-31 **(T.O.)**
FN met: 54%

**Loyola University - Maryland**                    MD
http://www.loyno.edu/
87%                                                              81%
Business, communications, social sciences, health professions, psychology, biology
66%                                                              25-29 **(T.O.)**
FN met: 93%


**Marlboro College**                                VT
www.marlboro.edu
67%                                                              64%
Visual and performing arts, psychology, English, social studies
96%                                                              **(T.O)**
FN met : 100%

**Marquette University**                            WI
http://www.marquette.edu/
89%                                                              80%
Business, communications, engineering, biology, health professions, social sciences
84%                                                              24-29
FN Met: 27%

**McDaniel College**                                MD
www.mcdaniel.edu
75%                                                              67%

Social sciences, psychology, business, visual / performing arts, parks and recreation
78%                                                    21-28 **(T.O.)**
FN met: 25%

**Mercer University**                                  GA
www.mercer.edu
88%                                                    67%
Business, biology, engineering, social sciences, psychology, communications
69%                                                    26-29
FN met: 41%

**Mills College**                                      CA
www.mills.edu                                          dudettes only
78%                                                    66%
Social sciences, English, fine arts, biology, psychology
84%                                                    22-29 **(T.O.)**
FN met: 14%

**Millsaps College**                                   MS
www.millsaps.edu
81%                                                    72%
Business, biology, social sciences, psychology, fine arts, communication, English
59%                                                    23-28
FN met: 24%


**Mount Holyoke College**                              MA
http://www.mtholyoke.edu/                              dudettes only
91%                                                    8%
social sciences, biology, English, psychology, fine arts, foreign language, physical scien.
52%                                                    28-32 **(T.O.)**
FN met: 100%

**Mount Saint Mary's University**                      MD
www.msmary.edu
75%                                                    71%
Business, social sciences, biology, psychology, education
62%                                                    19-24
FN met: 24%

**New College of Florida**                             FL
http://www.ncf.edu
84%                                                    63%

Liberal arts
71%
FN met: 36%
26-31

### Ohio Wesleyan University
http://www.owu.edu/
81%
OH

67%

Biology, social sciences, business, psychology, fine arts, English, education, physical sc.
72%
22-28 **(T.O.)**
FN met: 21%

### Pacific Lutheran University
www.plu.edu
79%
WA

71%

Social science, business, health professions, biology, communications, education
77%
22-28
FN met: 23%

### Providence College
www.providence.edu
93%
RI

83%

Business, social studies, biology, health professions, psychology
55%
23-28 **(T.O.)**
FN Met: 26%

### Rhodes College
www.rhodes.edu
93%
TN

80%

Social sciences, biology, business, English, computer and information systems
54%
27-31
FN met: 42%

### Rochester Institute of Technology
www.rit.edu
87%
NY

66%

Engineering, computer science, visual arts, business
55%
26-31
FN met: 81%

### Rose-Hulman Institute of Technology
www.rose-hulman.edu
94%
IN

82%

Engineering, computer science
61%                                                             27-32
FN Met: 19%

### Saint Anselm College                                        NH
www.anselm.edu
85%                                                             72%
health professions, business, communications, political science
76%                                                             23-28
FN Met: 28%

### Saint Edward's University                                   TX
www.stedwards.edu
81%                                                             64%
Business, communications, psychology, English, visual / performing arts, biology
74%                                                             22-27
FN Met: 10%

### Saint John's College                                        MD
http://www.stjohnscollege.edu
79%                                                             76%
Great Books Program
53%                                                             27-33 **(T.O.)**
FN Met: 30%

### Saint Louis University                                      MO
www.slu.edu
92%                                                             77%
Health professions, business, engineering, biology
65%                                                             24-30
FN met: 23%

### Saint Mary's College of California                          CA
www.stmarys-ca.edu
86%                                                             73%
Business, communications, social sciences, liberal arts, psychology, parks and rec.
80%                                                             22-28
FN met: 0%

### Saint Mary's University, San Antonio                        TX
http://www.stmarytx.edu/
76%                                                             55%

Business, biology, psychology, security, parks and rec., communications
78%                                                                        19-25
FN met: 13%

### Saint Michael's College                                                VT
www.smcvt.edu
89%                                                                        79%
Business, social sciences, biology, psychology, communications, environmental science
77%                                                                        24-29 **(T.O.)**
FN met: 29%

### Saint Vincent College                                                  PA
www.stvincent.edu
83%                                                                        73%
Business, biology, education, social sciences, communication
66%                                                                        20-26
FN met: 28%

### Salve Regina University                                                RI
www.salve.edu
82%                                                                        68%
Business, education, health professions, biology, psychology
69%                                                                        22-26 **(T.O.)**
FN Met: 12%

### Samford                                                                AL
www.samford.edu
89%                                                                        73%
Business, health professions, communications, education, social sciences, fine arts
91%                                                                        23-29
FN met: 22%

### Sarah Lawrence College                                                 NY
http://www.sarahlawrence.edu/
89%                                                                        82%
Liberal arts only
50%                                                                        27-31 **(T.O.)**
FN met: 16%

### Seattle University                                                     WA
http://www.seattle.edu/
87%                                                                        75%

Business, health professions, engineering, social sciences
74%   25-30
FN met: 12%

### Seton Hall University — NJ
http://www.shu.edu/
85%   64%
Health professions, business, social sciences, communications, biology, security
79%   22-27
FN met: 22%

### Simmons College — MA (dudettes only)
www.simmons.edu
83%   74%
Health professions, communications, business
64%   24-29
FN met: 13%

### Simpson College — IA
www.simpson.edu
77%   63%
Business, social science, biology, education, mathematics
85%   21-27
FN Met: 23%

### Stetson University — FL
www.stetson.edu
79%   64%
Business, social sciences, visual and performing arts, psychology, music
66%   23-28
FN met: 19%

### Syracuse University — NY
http://www.syr.edu/
91%   82%
Business, communications, social sciences, fine arts, tv/radio/film, engineering
49%   25-29
FN met: 52%

### Temple University — PA
http://www.temple.edu/
90%   70%
Business, communications, fine arts, psychology, health professions, social sciences, bio.

52% 24-30 **(T.O.)**
FN met: 25%

**Thomas Aquinas College** CA
www.thomasaquinas.edu
94% 87%
Liberal arts only
75% 26-30
FN met: 100%

**Transylvania University** KY
www.transy.edu
86% 75%
Business, social sciences, biology, foreign languages, psychology, visual and perf. arts
95% 25-30 **(T.O.)**
FN met: 23%

**University of Dallas** TX
www.udallas.edu
83% 70%
Business, theology, biology, English, social sciences, history, psychology
80% 23-30
FN met: 25%

**University of Dayton** OH
www.udayton.edu
89% 75%
Business, engineering, education, communications, health professions
60% 24-29
FN met: 38%

**University of Denver** CO
www.du.edu
87% 79%
Business, social sciences, communications, psychology, biology
53% 26-31
FN met: 35%

**University of the Pacific** CA
www.pacific.edu
82% 68%

Business, engineering, biology, social sciences, education, music, pharmacology
66%                                                             23-30
FN met: 13%

**University of Puget Sound**                                    WA
http://www.ups.edu
86%                                                             80%
Social sciences, biology, business, psychology, fine arts, English, foreign lang.
79%                                                             26-30 **(T.O)**
FN met: 16%

**University of San Diego**                                      CA
www.sandiego.edu
87%                                                             77%
Business, social sciences, education, biology, communications
51%                                                             26-30
FN met: 13%

**University of San Francisco**                                  CA
http://www.usfca.edu/
86%                                                             72%
Social sciences, health professions, communications, psychology
71%                                                             23-28
FN met: 60%


**Ursinus College**                                              PA
http://www.ursinus.edu/
84%                                                             78%
Biology, social science, psychology, English, environmental science, parks and rec.
82%                                                             23-29 **(T.O.)**
FN met: 27%

**Valparaiso University**                                        IN
http://www.valpo.edu/
83%                                                             66%
Health professions, business, engineering, education, English, social sciences, biology
80%                                                             23-29
FN met: 61%

**Wabash College**                                               IN
www.wabash.edu                                                   dudes only
92%                                                             71%

Social sciences, biology, history, English, physical sciences, psychology, math
63%   23-28
FN met: 72%

**Wheaton College**   IL
www.wheaton.edu
95%   91%
Social sciences, business, English, theology, fine arts, education, biology, comm.
79%   27-32
FN met: 23%

**Wheaton College**   MA
www.wheatoncollege.edu
86%   79%
Social sciences, psychology, ethnic studies, fine arts, history, biology, philosophy
62%   24-30 **(T.O.)**
FN met: 48%

**Whitman College**   WA
www.whitman.edu
94%   88%
Social sciences, biology, physical sciences, psychology, English, fine arts, philosophy
51%   28-32 **(T.O.)**
FN met: 30%

**Whitworth University**   WA
www.whitworth.edu
85%   73%
Business, social studies, fine arts, communication, interdisciplinary study, physical scien.
89%   22-29
FN met: 14%

**Willamette University**   OR
www.willamette.edu
85%   78%
English, social sciences, biology, visual and performing arts, ethnic studies, music
78%   18-25 **(T.O.)**
FN met: 26%

**Wofford College**   SC
www.wofford.edu
87%   ?

Business, foreign language, biology, social sciences, English, physical sciences
70%  24-29
FN Met: 41%

**Xavier University**  OH
www.xavier.edu
87%  72%
Business, health professions, social sciences, biology, education
69%  23-28
FN met: 25%

Some more stand-alone schools devoted to music and the arts other than Juillard (in no particular order): Eastman School, New England Conservatory, Curtis Institute of Music, San Francisco Conservatory, Manhattan School of Music, Maryland Institute College of Art, and New School College of Performing Arts. Please note I intentionally left some really good schools off the list due to costs and affordability. Those I left on the list are still really expensive.

Last minute additions of two non-traditional universities:

**Deep Springs College** in Nevada for bright young men who just don't fit anywhere else.

**Webb Institute** in New York. You have only one choice – a dual major in naval engineering and maritime architecture. It is prestigious and the tuition is a bargain!

## Appendix 3: Extracurricular Activities to Stand Out

Below is a partial - a very partial list - of curriculum, courses, competitions, essays, tests, and summer programs available for teens. This list is not a comprehensive list by any stretch of the imagination, and I am not specifically endorsing any of the programs. Keep in mind, these programs come and go based on funding. In my research I found a host of programs, some going back to the 1960's, that are no longer funded. I have included the websites (current as of 2017) to facilitate your search as best as I can. Do your own research. All of the programs listed are national programs. There are many more that are more local. I would start with the local big state universities. All of the programs are designed with the idea a student could use the program on a resume. I have avoided programs that simply take anyone that can pay. Again, just participating is not the same as winning. In terms of the summer programs, some are very expensive. I made an effort only to include those programs for which scholarships or financial assistance is available. Available financial aid is not the same thing as guaranteed financial aid.

**Competitions and Curriculum**

*Academic Decathlon http://www.usad.org/

*Advanced Placement https://apcentral.collegeboard.org/

*American Legion Oratorical https://www.legion.org/oratorical

*Biology Olympiad https://www.cee.org/usa-biology-olympiad-usabo

*Boy Scouts http://www.scouting.org/

*Cambridge International Studies http://www.cambridgeinternational.org/

*Chemistry Olympiad https://www.acs.org/content/acs/en.html

*Chess http://www.uschess.org/content/blogsection/18/95/

*Computer Science Network Competitions https://www.cs2n.org/competitions

*eCybermission http://www.ecybermission.com/

*FIRST Robotics Competition https://www.firstinspires.org/

*Girl Scouts http://www.girlscouts.org/

*Google Science Fair https://www.googlesciencefair.com/en/

*Habitat for Humanity https://www.habitat.org/volunteer/near-you/youth_programs

*Harvard-MIT Mathematics Tournament https://www.hmmt.co/

*Hugh O'Brian Youth Leadership (HOBY) http://www.hoby.org/

*Imagine Cup https://imagine.microsoft.com/en-us

*Intel Science Talent Search https://student.societyforscience.org/intel-isef

*International Baccalaureate http://www.ibo.org/

*International Math Olympiad https://www.imo-official.org/

*International Model United Nations http://imuna.org/

*Japan Bowl http://www.japanbowl.org/

*John Lennon Song Writing Contest http://jlsc.com/

*Kid's Philosophy Slam http://www.philosophyslam.org/index.html

*Mandelbrot Mathematics Competition http://www.mandelbrot.org/

*Marshall Brennan Moot Court https://www.wcl.american.edu/impact/initiatives-programs/marshallbrennan/

*MIT Inspire http://getinspired.mit.edu/

*Mock Trial http://www.nationalmocktrial.org/

*National Academic Quiz Tournaments https://www.naqt.com/about-quiz-bowl.html

*National Economics Competition https://econchallenge.unl.edu/

*National French Contest http://www.frenchteachers.org/concours/

*National Geographic Bee https://www.nationalgeographic.org/bee

*National History Bee and Bowl http://www.historybowl.com/

*National Honor Society https://www.nhs.us/?SSO=true

*National Science Bowl https://science.energy.gov/wdts/nsb/

*National Science Olympiad https://www.soinc.org/

*National Underwater Robotics Competition http://robotics.mars.asu.edu/competitions/NURC

*North American Computational Linguistics Olympiad http://www.nacloweb.org/

*Odyssey of the Mind https://www.odysseyofthemind.com/p/

*Physics Bowl http://aapt.org/Programs/contests/index.cfm

*Regeneron Science Fair https://student.societyforscience.org/regeneron-sts

*Ross Program in Mathematics http://u.osu.edu/rossmath/

*Siemens Foundation Competition http://www.siemens-foundation.org/en/

*Sierra Club for Youth http://www.sierraclub.org/youth

*Special Olympics http://www.specialolympics.org/

*TEAMS: Tests of Engineering Aptitude, Math and Science http://teams.tsaweb.org/

*Think MIT http://think.mit.edu/

*United States Senate Youth Program https://ussenateyouth.org/

*We the People http://www.civiced.org/programs/wtp

*World Photography Organization Youth Competition

https://www.worldphoto.org/sony-world-photography-awards/2018/youth

*World Scholar's Cup http://www.demidec.com/newdemidec/worldscholarscup.aspx

*YMCA various locations

*Young Life  https://www.younglife.org/Pages/default.aspx

*Young Playwrights Festival (multiple cities and websites)

*Zero Robotics http://zerorobotics.mit.edu/

**Essays**

*Ayn Rand Essay Contest https://www.aynrand.org/students/essay-contests

*Gilder Lehrman Civil War Essay Contest https://www.gilderlehrman.org/programs-exhibitions/civil-war-essay-contest

*Horatio Alger Scholarships https://scholars.horatioalger.org/scholarships/

*Jane Austin Essay Contest http://www.jasna.org/programs/essay-contest/

*John F. Kennedy Profiles in Courage Essay Contest

https://www.jfklibrary.org/Education/Profile-in-Courage-Essay-Contest.aspx

*King Sejong Writing Competition

http://www.sejongculturalsociety.org/writing/current/essay.php

*National History Day https://www.nhd.org/

*National Peace Essay https://www.usip.org/public-education/students/AFSAEssayContest

*Reischauer Scholars Program

http://spice.fsi.stanford.edu/fellowships/reischauer_scholars_program

*Voice of Democracy https://www.vfw.org/VOD/

**Exams**

*American Mathematics Contest 12  https://www.maa.org/math-competitions/amc-1012

*National Merit Scholarship

http://www.nationalmerit.org/s/1758/interior.aspx?sid=1758&gid=2&pgid=424

*National Mythology Exam http://www.etclassics.org/pages/national-mythology-exam

*National Spanish Examinations https://www.nationalspanishexam.org/index.php/about-us/what-is-nse

**Summer Programs**

*American Legion Boy's State https://www.legion.org/boysnation/stateabout

*American Legion Girl's State https://www.alaforveterans.org/ALA Girls State/

*Brown University Pre-College Programs https://www.brown.edu/academics/pre college/

*Carleton Summer Programs https://apps.carleton.edu/summer/programs/

*Columbia University Three Week Immersion Program

https://sps.columbia.edu/highschool/3-week

*Concordia Language Village http://www.concordialanguagevillages.org/

*Cornell University Summer Sessions https://www.sce.cornell.edu/sc/

*Davidson Institute Think Summer http://www.davidsongifted.org/THINK-Summer

*Harvard Summer School

 https://www.summer.harvard.edu/high school programs/secondary-school-program

*Helios Scholars at T-Gen

https://www.tgen.org/education-outreach/helios-scholars-at-tgen.aspx#.Wdqy1siGOUk

*Johns Hopkins Center for Talented Youth http://cty.jhu.edu/

*LEDA Scholars  http://ledascholars.org/

*MITES https://oeop.mit.edu/programs/mites

*NASA Internship https://www.nasa.gov/centers/goddard/education/internships.html

*National Security Language Initiative for Youth https://exchanges.state.gov/us/program/nsliy

*Northwestern Equinox Program https://www.ctd.northwestern.edu/program/equinox

*Questbridge https://www.questbridge.org/

*Research Science Institute (RSI) https://www.cee.org/research-science-institute

*Secondary Student Training Program at the University of Iowa

https://www2.education.uiowa.edu/belinblank/students/classes.aspx?P=SSTP

*Stanford High School Summer College https://summercollege.stanford.edu/

*Summer Leaders Experience at West Point http://www.usma.edu/pne/SitePages/SLE.aspx

*Summer Science Program http://www.summerscience.org/

*Telluride Association Summer Program (TASP) https://www.tellurideassociation.org/our-programs/high-school-students/summer-program-juniors-tasp/

*Telluride Association Sophomore Summer (TASS)

https://www.tellurideassociation.org/our-programs/high-school-students/sophomore-seminar-tass/

*United States Naval Academy Summer Programs

https://www.usna.edu/Admissions/Programs/index.php

*University of Notre Dame Summer Scholars Programs

https://precollege.nd.edu/summer-scholars/

*Various Governor's Schools http://www.ncogs.us/programs-by-state.html

**Some other sources to consider further options.**

Berger, Sandra L. *Ultimate Guide for Summer Opportunities for Teens*

Brewer, Robert Lee *Poet's Market*

Brewer, Robert Lee *Writer's Market*

Karnes, Frances A. and Riley, Tracy L. *Competitions for Talented Kids*

Peterson's *Summer Programs for Kids and Teenagers*

Rivera, Noel *Artist's Market*

Rivera, Noel *Photographer's Market*

Schwebel, Sara *Yale Daily News Guide to Summer Programs*

Tallent-Runnels, Mary K. and Ann C. Candler-Lotven *Competitions for Gifted Students*

## Appendix 4: College Admission's Game

The following is a game I play with my students. There is no magic score or way to "win." Instead the game is designed to inform students about how ready the student actually is in terms of college admissions. In general, a score higher than "10" bodes well. A score in the negative numbers means that the student needs to rethink choices.

Start with a base of 0.

1) **Add one point if you expect to be valedictorian.**

    While fading in importance, class rank still counts. First is still best. 2nd and 3rd are excellent.

2) **Add one point if you expect to be in the top 3% of your class.**

    If valedictorian you now have two points.

3) **Add one point if you expect to be in the top 10% of your class.**

    Anything below 10% needs work. Below 25% and class rank becomes a liability.

4) **Subtract one point for every "d" of "f" on your transcript.**

    Even freshman year, these grades can kill an application.

5) **Add two points if you will take more than 3 AP classes.**

    IB, Cambridge, or dual credit classes also count.

6) **Subtract two points if you take the easiest classes you can.**

    This is subjective, but a student looking for an easy way out does not have the same skill sets and these choices tend to show up on a transcript. Results are also apparent on standardized tests.

7) **Subtract ten points if your unweighted GPA is under 2.5**

    At this level a community college might be the best choice. Rebuild the resume and transfer.

8) **Add two points if your weighted GPA is higher than 4.0**

    This is where I want students to be.

9) **Add one point if you are a dude.**

Thirty years ago most college applicants were male. That has changed. At many schools men now have an advantage. This is especially true when a school reaches that tipping point of around 60% female.

**10) Add one point if you are a female athlete.**

The inverse of #9, there are few female athletes. This gives women an advantage.

**11) Add one point for every club you are president of or team you are a captain of**

Show leadership. Anyone can say they join. Prove you lead.

**12) Add one point for two or more varsity sports**

Athletics though waning in importance still sells.

**13) Add two points for crew team**

Particularly for Ivy League schools, crew is a competitive and expensive sport that takes time to learn. A rare sport, there is a premium on talented students in crew.

**14) Add two points for four years of service with the same organization**

Colleges now value consistency. Quality over quantity.

**15) Add one point for at least 20 hours of community service a year.**

Service still counts. If your service is sincere, there are plenty of schools that offer scholarships for community service. Sometimes the organization itself will offer scholarships. At the minimum, these opportunities can yield some really powerful letters of recommendation.

**16) Add three points for creating an original organization of which you can document your accomplishments**

This is my personal preference. Don't join a program, create one! Then document what you did and how that impacted the community.

**17) Subtract one point for not being a member of NHS**

National Honor Society has become so prevalent that simply joining says little. Not joining can raise questions, though.

**18) Add five points for a perfect SAT or ACT score**

Five points is probably conservative here. A perfect score goes a long way for both admissions and money.

**19) Add three points if you score 27-34 on the ACT or 2100-2300 on the SAT (Old)**

**20) Subtract one point if you score 24-26 on the ACT or 1800 – 2100 on the SAT (Old)**

This is roughly national average.

**21) Subtract five points if you score less than a 24 on the ACT or less than 1800 on the SAT (Old)**

This is roughly below national average. It hurts.

**22) Add one point for a summer program or summer class**

Most schools I work with want to know how a student spent his or her time in the summer. Summer classes should be an advancement, not remedial.

**23) Add two points for an internship or published research project**

These are even better than an academic class. The more selective the better.

**24) Subtract two points for having free summers or summers full of family vacations**

Traveling to Disney or babysitting a cousin is usually seen as a wasted opportunity.

**25) Add one point for being 1st chair or section leader of an orchestra or band**

Again, leadership sells. Don't just play oboe: shine!

**26) Add one point for being member of state or national band or orchestra or choir**

Bigger is better.

**27) Add one point if you play the oboe or are top three violin player**

These are the most difficult seats to fill in a university orchestra or band.

**28) Add one point if you have participated in drama for at least two years.**

Drama shows dedication, builds interpersonal skills and can often lead to scholarships.

**29) Add two points for being member of winning academic team at state level**

I can always sell winning. There are times success here on a big scale can trump relatively poor test scores.

**30) Add one point for being member of winning academic team at regional level**

Regional isn't bad. State is better.

**31) Add three points if you published your own writing or own music**

Not impossible but extremely impressive. Any student can claim to be a good writer. Many can even entice a favorite English teacher to say such in a letter of recommendation. Not that many can get published. This shows tenacity and drive even more than talent.

**32) Add ten points if Daddy can write a check for $100,000 every year for four years**

Most universities will claim that money doesn't really matter in the admission's decision. The schools lie. Money talks. If you will not need financial aid, tell the school during the admission's process.

**33) Add four points if your mother / father attended the university of your choice AND have donated**

This is the alumni factor. It matters - especially at more prestigious schools. The second part, donating, is a key. Be sure parents start donating early if this is an angle. I would argue that consistency is more important than size.

**34) Subtract one point if you are nobody special and don't know anyone special**

Don't worry too much. This is most people.

**35) Subtract one point if you need financial aid**

Money talks. Despite schools claiming that the school is "need blind," most schools will peak under the blindfold.

**36) Add one point if you receive a college interview**

I love college interviews! Get as many as you can. Little can overcome a mediocre application more than a stellar interview.

**37) Subtract one point if you are bad at public speaking, interviewing or are generally shy**

I really wish high schools taught public speaking more. A poor public speaker is at a disadvantage not only with interviews but also with letters of recommendations and even just asking questions of a university.

**38) Subtract two points if your writing skills are poor or your grammar is in need of life support**

No matter who edits, poor writing and grammar tend to show up on an application.

**39) Subtract two points for every referral (other than being tardy) that you have received**

This is a reference to disciplinary action. If severe, I would recommend an accompanying letter explaining the circumstances. Anything involving drugs, gangs or firearms is a huge detriment.

**40) Subtract ten points if you have a criminal record that is not sealed**

Most teenage infractions are sealed. No one needs to know. If unsealed, the infraction will hurt. A lot.

**41) Subtract three points for a documented infraction involving drugs or alcohol**

Colleges are tired of dealing with these issues.

**42) Subtract five points for a documented incident involving a firearm**

No one wants the bad publicity or trauma guns can attract. Even an innocuous infraction will have consequences.

**43) Subtract five points for having references to suicide or anger issues on your social media**

One of a school's greatest fears is having a roommate walk in on a suicide. Easier to tell unstable students to keep looking for another school.

**44) Subtract two points for having pictures of you drunk or high on social media**

Similar to #40, colleges are tired of dealing with this issue.

45) **Subtract one point if you have ever received special education – for any reason**

A parent can argue that this is an unfair stigma. The parents are right. Special education will still hurt an application. There are times I urge families to treat issues outside of the purview of a high school for this reason.

46) **Subtract one point for a juvenile email address**

Don't be stupid. Just change it.

47) **Subtract two points if your essays are often wrinkled, torn or dirty**

If a student is often sloppy, little mistakes will show up on the application, on the essay and in the interview.

48) **Subtract one point if you procrastinate**

Not meeting deadlines is often a deal breaker. Procrastinators beware!

49) **Add two points if you know two teachers or community leaders that worship you**

A solid gold reference can be a real asset. Don't presume. Cultivate.

50) **Subtract three points if all of your teachers hate you**

If a student can not find at least some teachers to get along with, this can be a serious issue. The negativity shows up in the grades and in the references. A "good" reference may not always help. A bad reference can be a killer. Sometimes it is necessary to spread a little sunshine and dole out a little honey.

51) **Add one point if you can get a recommendation from a congressman or senator or governor**

Many elite schools see this often. It is not as impressive as it sounds, but it does carry weight. Absolutely imperative for a military academy.

52) **Add four points if you are 50% or higher Native American.**

Race matters less and less. The exception is Native American. Tribal membership is necessary.

53) **Add one point of you are minority.**

African American, Hispanic, disabled, Mormon, Jewish, Muslim - anything but WASP

54) **Subtract one point if you are white.**

I didn't say it was fair - just real. Depending on the school and on geography Asian may also hurt.

55) **Add two points if you are the first in your family to attend the university.**

Most schools I know document this. If this statement applies to your family, please highlight it.

56) **Add one point if you are a Latina going into engineering.**

A winning combination due to its rarity.

**57) Add one point if you are a Jewish woman going into the sciences.**

Another winner. No, I do not count medicine here.

**58) Subtract one point if both of your parents attended a university.**

As ironic as it is, this is a disadvantage for both admissions and financial aid.

**59) Add one point if you are involved at your church on a weekly basis.**

This can help in a lot of ways: community service, letters of reference, scholarships, or simply touching an admission's officer on a key note.

**60) Subtract one point if you are only involved in school activities**

Get out, get involved.

**61) Add one point if you have had to overcome a disability or death or terrible disease**

I hate playing the sad violin, but it does have its place.

**62) Subtract one point if you are majoring in pre-med, biology, pre-law, social sciences, political sciences, psychology or general business**

These majors are just far too common.

*Score.*

Made in the USA
Lexington, KY
28 August 2018